(Jean

s

GLOBAL PERSPECTIVES
ON
ADVERTISING SELF-REGULATION

GLOBAL PERSPECTIVES ON ADVERTISING SELF-REGULATION

Principles and Practices in Thirty-eight Countries

JEAN J. BODDEWYN

Foreword by Norman Vale

QUORUM BOOKS
Westport, Connecticut • London

Library of Congress Cataloging-in-Publication Data

Boddewyn, J. J. (Jean J.)
    Global perspectives on advertising self-regulation : principles
and practices in thirty-eight countries / Jean J. Boddewyn ; foreword by
Norman Vale.
      p.   cm.
    Includes index.
    ISBN 0-89930-723-X (alk. paper)
    1. Advertising—Self-regulation.   I. Title.
HF5834.B65   1992
338.4'76591—dc20   91-47662

British Library Cataloguing in Publication Data is available.

Library of Congress Catalog Card Number: 91-47662
ISBN: 0-89930-723-X

First published in 1992

Quorum Books, 88 Post Road West, Westport, CT 06881
An imprint of Greenwood Publishing Group, Inc.

Printed in the United States of America

∞™

The paper used in this book complies with the
Permanent Paper Standard issued by the National
Information Standards Organization (Z39.48-1984).

10 9 8 7 6 5 4 3 2 1

Copyright Acknowledgments

The publisher and author are grateful to the following for granting use of their material:

Gordon Borrie, "The Role of Advertising and the Need for Regulation," *Advertising in the 1990s: The Case for Advertising in the Single Market of the 1990s* (London: The Advertising Association, 1990). Courtesy of The Advertising Association (U.K.).

Roger Neill, "This House Believes That the European Parliament Should Not Control Advertising," speech given by Neill, IAA World President, at the House of Commons, London, October 22, 1990 (New York: International Advertising Association, 1990). Courtesy of the IAA.

International Chamber of Commerce, *International Code of Advertising Practice* (Paris: 1986). Copyright © 1986 by ICC Publishing S.A. All rights reserved. Reprinted with the permission of the ICC Publishing Corporation.

Canadian Code of Advertising Standards (Toronto: Canadian Advertising Foundation, April 1991). Courtesy of the Canadian Advertising Foundation.

Code Canadien des Normes de la Publicité (Montréal: Conseil des Normes de la Publicité, Avril 1991). Courtesy of Conseil des Normes de la Publicité.

Council of Better Business Bureaus, Inc., *National Advertising Division/National Advertising Review Board Procedures* (New York: 1991). Courtesy of the Council of Better Business Bureaus, Inc.

Mary-Jane Raphael, "NAD/NARB Process Explained," *Advertising Compliance Service* 9, no. 23 (December 4, 1989).

The British Code of Advertising Practice, 8th edition (London: Committee of Advertising Practice, December 1988). Courtesy of the Advertising Standards Authority.

Advertising Standards Authority (U.K.), "Looking Back—and Forward," *Case Report 191* (March 13, 1991). Courtesy of the Advertising Standards Authority.

Advertising Standards Authority (U.K.), "Review of 1988/89," *Case Report 175* (November 15, 1989). Courtesy of the Advertising Standards Authority.

Bureau de Vérification de la Publicité, "L'Autodiscipline en Europe," *BVP Echos*, no. 104, Mars 1989. Courtesy of the Bureau de Vérification de la Publicité.

European Advertising Standards Alliance, *Self-Regulation and Codes of Practice* (Brussels, Belgium: October 1991). Courtesy of European Advertising Standards Alliance (EASA).

To Michèle, Noëlle, and Marc Boddewyn

With love and pride

The assistance of Leah Bender, Ariella Bernstein, Florence Michelet, and the International Advertising Association in preparing this analysis is gratefully acknowledged.

Contents

Foreword

Advertising is an essential part of any real democracy, which is always based on freedom of choice. Democracy recognizes and respects the ability of each individual to assimilate information and to make well-informed choices.

Moreover, free and vibrant media are absolutely essential to democracy, to society, to open debate, to freedom of expression, and to freedom of consumer choice. And it is the revenue from advertising that enables these free and pluralistic media to exist or survive in most cases.

The disturbing reality is that, increasingly around the world, attempts are being made to impose regulations, restrictions, and even bans on advertising.

The IAA's core mission is to promote and defend the freedom of commercial speech and consumer choice. We see the encouragement and development of advertising self-regulation as the best means of preventing such unwarranted and unilaterally imposed restrictions. Indeed, written into the International Advertising Association's (IAA) bylaws is this objective: "To encourage adherence to codes of ethics and standards of practice, established both nationally and internationally, which are consistent with those established by the International Chamber of Commerce."

Since the 1970s, the IAA has published a number of studies and surveys by Professors Albert Stridsberg, James Neelankavil, and Jean Boddewyn. These have all played invaluable roles in fostering the knowledge and spread of advertising self-regulatory systems.

There is much that still needs to be done, and the IAA welcomes and commends this latest work by Professor Boddewyn. We are sure that it, too, will contribute to the further development and practice of self-regulation. This will enable advertising and informed consumer choice to play their full parts in driving the free-market system that has become the prime choice of an ever-increasing number of countries all over the world.

Norman Vale
Director-General
International Advertising Association

Acknowledgments

The moral and financial support of the International Advertising Association since 1977 was essential in preparing this book—particularly that of Sylvan M. Barnet, Jr., Mary Covington, Norman Vale, Richard Corner, and Ed Lucaire, together with their most able assistants, Amy Fleming and Ellen Corey.

Several MBA students at Baruch College helped conduct the various surveys mentioned in this book, as well as collect and update the country profiles—particularly Leah Bender, Ariella Bernstein, and Florence Michelet.

From Maurizio Fusi (Italy), Raymond Haas (France), Robert Oliver (Canada), Albert Stridsberg (United States), Sten Tengelin (Sweden), and Peter Thomson (United Kingdom) I learned much about the essence, inner workings, and external dimensions of advertising self-regulatory systems.

This book follows the format of J. P. Neelankavil and A. B. Stridsberg, *Advertising Self-Regulation: A Global Perspective* (New York: Hastings House and International Advertising Association, 1980), but it provides a thorough revision, expansion, and updating of its contents.

GLOBAL PERSPECTIVES
ON
ADVERTISING SELF-REGULATION

1

The Case for Advertising Self-Regulation

THE CASE FOR ADVERTISING

The market system is fast becoming the prime choice of an increasing number of countries all over the world. However, a vibrant market system depends not only on freedom of enterprise—the right to start a legal business—but also on the freedom of commercial speech for business people and on the freedom of consumers to receive information. These freedoms are inseparable, and they require that advertising be free of misplaced criticisms and unnecessary restrictions—as has been strongly expressed by the U.S. Supreme Court:

Advertising, however tasteless and excessive it sometimes may seem, is nonetheless dissemination of information as to who is producing and selling what products, for what reason and for what price. So long as we preserve a predominantly free-enterprise economy, the allocation of our resources in large measure will be made through numerous private economic decisions. It is a matter of public interest that these decisions . . . be intelligent and well informed. To this end, the free flow of commercial information is indispensable. (Virginia State Board of Pharmacy v. Virginia Citizens Consumer Council, Inc., 425 U.S. 1976, p. 765)

Yet, until the 1970s, the predominant view among economists and other social scientists was that advertising was bad or useless for the free-enterprise system. Various economists argued that the existence of adver-

tising proved that competition was imperfect because some firms could
advertise more than others. Besides, they assumed that advertising was
not necessary because people had perfect, total, instantaneous, and free
information about products—quite an unrealistic assumption indeed!

Of course, one could imagine an economic world where we would find
out about new products such as VCRs, smokeless cigarettes, and compact
discs from consumer reports, government publications, and the media at
large. This happens to some extent, as when we learn now about the
future availability of high-definition television sets. However, the bulk of
consumer information about old and new products comes from advertising and other forms of commercial communication, and public-opinion
surveys in many countries reveal that people do value them as sources of
information. Thus, a 1987 Ogilvy and Mather survey of 2,000 consumers
in six countries revealed high overall satisfaction in answer to the statement "Advertising is a good way to learn about new products":

Hong Kong	96%
Colombia	95%
West Germany	92%
United States	91%
Brazil	90%
United Kingdom	88%

In other words, there is not only a supply of advertising coming from
the business side, but also a demand for advertising because people lack
sufficient information. However, in the 1950s and 1960s, social scientists
like Vance Packard and John Kenneth Galbraith argued that advertising
had a sinister effect on people. There were "hidden persuaders" and
clever manipulators out there, who made people buy what they did not
need or want. Some people believed these social scientists, and the media
often propagated such negative views that amounted to cheap psychology.
In fact, according to recent psychological research, the central question
today is not "What does advertising do to people?" but "What do people
do with advertising?" Do people pay attention to it? Does it register? How
do people process it? What other sources of information and persuasion do
they use?

In this context, the freedom to impart and receive commercial communications is not limited to factual data about price and performance.
Regulators have the unfortunate tendency to concede that informative
advertising is needed, while urging that the use of feelings and lifestyle
imagery be banned from ads. In other words, they oppose what the
French advertising community considers to be advertising's most effective
weapon: *Faire rêver, faire sourire*—to make people dream and smile.

Indeed, "information" is any data or argument that truthfully puts forth the attractiveness of a product in the context of a consumer's own buying criteria: his or her personal history, immediate environment, current situation, and anything else that is relevant, whether factual or emotional.

As the most visible of all marketing activities, advertising is exposed to constant scrutiny by consumers, competitors, critics, and regulators. Each year, several hundred millions of different advertisements are printed, broadcast, displayed, and distributed around the world. A few of them are false, misleading, unfair, offensive, or socially irresponsible—or they are perceived as such.

Thus, reliable British data suggest that about 2 to 4 percent of ads might be open to challenge—which is not the same thing as establishing that further scrutiny and even litigation will support this initial impression. In the United States, the combined actions of the Federal Trade Commission, of the national advertising self-regulatory system—National Advertising Division/National Advertising Review Board (NAD/NARB)— and of the federal courts typically result in less than 300 adjudicated cases a year—a tiny fraction of the scores of millions of printed ads and commercials. The most developed and effective self-regulatory system in the world—the (British) Advertising Standards Authority—handles about 12,000 cases a year, based on its own monitoring of ads (about 150,000 of them a year) and on its active solicitation of complaints (many of them about the same ad). Only about 1,000 of these ads have had to be withdrawn or modified, out of millions of ads. In Australia, the United Kingdom, and the United States, a tiny minority of people (2 to 7 percent) think of advertising as problematic in general and in need of immediate attention and change, even though they often voice criticisms about its frequency, obtrusiveness, boring nature, or bad taste when asked to respond to prompted questions.

Still, something must be done about this tiny fraction of unacceptable advertisements, because they hamper the functioning of the market system, harm or insult consumers, and reduce the overall credibility of advertising because of a few "bad apples." This is where advertising self-regulation enters the picture as a complementary but essential and effective form of social control and redress.

WHAT IS SELF-REGULATION?

Advertising self-regulation fits into a variety of control and redress mechanisms available to competitors, consumers, concerned citizens, and watchdog organizations. What can they do when faced by improper print advertisements, television and radio commercials, posters, handbills and catalogs?

1. They can ignore the matter because the harm done is minor.
2. They can stop buying the product or service, or run counter-advertisements to set things straight.
3. They can contact the advertiser or medium and ask that such ads be stopped or corrected.
4. They can complain to a government agency and request that the appropriate regulations be enforced or that new ones be enacted.
5. They can sue the advertiser if they have suffered damages on account of the advertisement.
6. They can draw the attention of consumerist organizations and the media, and can ask them to publicize and otherwise pursue the matter.
7. They can approach an industry association and ask it to put pressure on the advertiser to have the ad withdrawn or modified—*in other words, they can rely on advertising self-regulation (ASR) to correct the situation.*

Thus, advertising self-regulation is one of several ways to eliminate bad advertisements, but also to ensure that good ones are produced. The following sections analyze its nature, relative advantages, current state of development, contributions, and limits, on the basis of various IAA surveys and of the growing literature on this very important societal institution.

All societies need *controls* to foster good business behavior and to discourage bad practices. In the case of advertising, there is general agreement that it ought to be truthful, not misleading, fair, in good taste, and socially responsible. Obtaining and maintaining such goals requires: (1) developing standards, (2) making them widely known and accepted, (3) advising advertisers before ads are released, (4) pre- and/or post-monitoring of compliance with the standards, (5) handling complaints from consumers, competitors, and other interested parties, and (6) penalizing bad behavior in violation of the standards, including publicizing wrongdoings and wrongdoers. These are complex tasks that can be achieved through a variety of complementary forms of societal controls, *and self-regulation is one of them.*

Under a *laissez-faire* system, the control of advertising behavior is left to competitors who run better ads and to consumers who refuse to patronize bad advertisers. Business' temptation to fool the clientele or abuse competitors is also tempered by *self-discipline* on the part of industry members, based on personal moral principles, on current notions of community standards and ethical business behavior, and on self-interest, since most advertisers fear a bad reputation, consumer retaliation, and further regulation. The laissez-faire and self-discipline approaches to advertising control must not be underestimated, but they have been challenged on the grounds that abuses are inevitable but will not always be redressed through the working of the market, a company's code of conduct or an individual's conscience.

With *statutory regulation*, advertising behavior is mandated or restricted by various governmental rules, and enforced through the use of legal penalties. This approach assumes that the public interest is best served through regulation because business cannot be trusted to self-discipline or self-regulate itself well, and because consumers and competitors lack the will or the means to challenge abuses by business.

Regulation's major advantages lie in its potentially universal reach and in the use of compulsion through judicial and administrative processes, as opposed to laissez-faire, self-discipline, and self-regulation, where only those who care enough apply standards of good advertising behavior. However, the regulatory approach has been criticized for being oppressive, ineffectual, confused, conflictual, costly, rigid, weakly enforced (recent budget-cutting is not helping here), amenable to capture by its targets, and the like. The recent deregulatory movement aimed at retrenching the State, applying cost-benefit analysis to regulation, and restoring greater scope to private initiatives rests on such philosophical and practical arguments.

Self-regulation refers to the voluntary control of business conduct and performance by business itself. It is control exercised by an advertiser's *peers*, including those in the agencies and media used. In the purest form of advertising self-regulation, industry assumes full responsibility for the six tasks outlined above, while "outsiders" such as independent members of the public, consumer representatives, and government officials are kept out of its functioning. However, hybrid forms involving outsiders are growing (see below). From the advertising industry's point of view, self-regulation provides a first line of defense against government controls, helps rectify problems within the industry, and serves as a vehicle for members of the advertising industry to fulfill their societal obligations.

THE PROS AND CONS OF SELF-REGULATION

Self-regulation is no panacea, but neither are government regulation and other forms of advertising control. Its major perceived advantages are as follows:

1. Self-regulation is usually faster and less expensive, as well as more flexible and up-to-date, than government regulation because industry knows better what the problems and their realistic solutions are. While antiquated statutory regulations tend to remain on the books, voluntary rules are subject to continuous market testing because they will be ignored if unrealistic. Should the industry lack information or expertise about certain matters (e.g., to what extent consumers are misled by particular advertisements), they can often be obtained by tapping experts or by commissioning research.

2. Self-regulation does not require that injury to a consumer or competitor be proven, as might be required by laws. Instead, it is in the industry's and the

public's interest that ads be true, not misleading and not offensive, so that proof of individual injury is not necessary. Besides, complainants can remain anonymous and free to pursue their case through other means (e.g., by publicizing their case through the media).

3. Self-regulation assists and complements statutory regulation, often going beyond the minimum prescribed by law. Thus, in Belgium, Canada, France, and the United States, the self-regulatory system applies legal standards—besides its own codes and guidelines—in adjudicating complaints. Furthermore, voluntary standards may more readily deal with matters that the law finds difficult to regulate (such as taste, opinion, and sexism). They might even be more stringent than regulation when the law itself does not forbid a particular practice (e.g., the broadcasting of hard-liquor commercials, which is prohibited by the U.S. distilled-spirits industry rather than by law). Self-regulation may also serve as a testing ground for rules to be ultimately incorporated into the law, once their effectiveness has been proven by industry practice (for example, direct-mail advertisers should always include a full mailing address rather than a mere postal-box number in their ads). In some cases, the judiciary system has little involvement in advertising matters, so that self-regulation largely substitutes for this legal void (e.g., in South Africa). Conversely, self-regulation allows government to focus on more important matters such as fraud and trade restraints, and on problems where solutions are clear-cut and consensus has emerged.

4. Self-regulation generates greater moral adhesion than the law because codes and guidelines are *voluntarily* developed and adopted by industry members who must obey not only the letter but also the *spirit* of self-imposed rules, and who are expected to abide by the decisions of their peers. The idea is to develop the feeling—and not only among those who formally subscribe to the voluntary standards—that the latter are really compulsory even though they are not. In this perspective, self-regulation represents a continuation or resurgence of an old type of norms familiar among the professions, namely, customs or mores.

5. The self-regulatory approach helps minimize the frictions between business and consumers as well as among business people, while statutory regulation tends to encourage such clashes by stressing compulsion, conflict (lawsuits), and penalization instead of persuasion, mediation, and negotiation.

6. Compared to self-regulation in other industries, advertising self-regulation benefits from one major element: *the intermediary position of the media.* The latter, in most countries where a self-regulatory system exists, usually agree to suspend the publication, distribution, or broadcasting of advertisements found to be deficient. Furthermore, most media have their own acceptance rules that provide additional screening of advertisements; and they react on their own to consumer and competitor complaints about what they publish, broadcast, or distribute. Only nonmedia advertisements (such as direct mailings) escape this further scrutiny, although there are self-regulatory direct-mail associations in quite a few countries, and post-office systems generally control the fraudulent use of the mails.

On the other hand, self-regulation has been criticized for the following shortcomings, some of which are more hypothetical than real:

1. Business competition and innovation are impaired because of self-serving restraints on the part of industry associations (e.g., some ASR bodies have opposed comparison advertising on account of industry opposition, among other reasons).

2. Self-regulation is a transparent device used by members of the industry (including the media) to subvert the adoption of more rigorous government standards by pretending that business will do the job when, in fact, voluntary standards might be set at minimal levels in order to avoid low membership or schism within the industry. Besides, voluntary enforcement may be lax.

3. Self-regulation may be hampered by antitrust and other laws (e.g., about freedom of association) that preclude *compulsory* membership, so that the worst offenders may stay out of the ASR system (the "free-rider" problem), and/or severe penalties such as fines, expulsion, and boycott may prove ineffective for lack of adequate reach.

4. It lacks effective judicial tools (such as the power to subpoena, and other discovery procedures used in courts), rules (such as those applying to evidence, due process, and adversary hearings), and penalties (restitution, corrective advertising, etc.), although ASR bodies tend to uphold a complaint when the advertiser cannot provide adequate substantiation for his claims.

5. There is too little financing, publicity (e.g., investigations and decisions are often kept secret, and offenders are not named), and promotion (e.g., consumer complaints are not actively solicited).

6. Its activities involve too few consumers and too many industry-selected representatives who may thus be "token" outsiders and meek participants in the self-regulatory process.

Whether valid or not, these criticisms suggest that industry self-regulation cannot *by itself* balance the relative bargaining powers of buyers and sellers. Instead, it must be considered as only one of several complementary means of achieving advertising control, although it is an essential one. Besides, the principles of *subsidiarity* (adopted by the European Community's [EC] Commission) promotes the notion that what can be successfully and adequately achieved at a lower level (for example, through industry self-regulation) should not require interference from a higher level such as government. As was aptly stated by the head of the British Office of Fair Trading, it is a matter of selecting "horses for courses," even though some advertisers will remain beyond the reach of both the law and self-regulation because they are irresponsible and elusive operators.

Figure 1 summarizes the respective strengths and weaknesses of regulation and self-regulation. It must be kept in mind, however, that these hypothesized advantages and disadvantages may not materialize, community standards and the marketplace also control the functioning of advertising, and the law, without self-regulation to complement it, is as weak as self-regulation is without the law to back it up.

Figure 1
Respective Strengths and Weaknesses of Advertising Regulation

ADVERTISING - CONTROL TASKS	REGULATION	SELF-REGULATION
Developing Standards	+ Greater sensitivity and faster response to emerging public concerns - Difficulty in elaborating standards in areas of taste, opinion, and public decency - Difficulty in amending standards	- Greater lag in responding to emerging concerns - Ability to develop and amend standards speedily in areas of taste, opinion, and public decency
Making Standards Widely Known and Accepted	+ Everybody is supposed to know the law - Compulsory nature of the law generates more hostility and evasion	- Difficulty in making the public aware of the industry's standards and consumer-redress mechanisms + Greater ability to make industry members respect both the letter and the spirit of voluntarily adhered to codes and guidelines
Advising Advertisers about Grey Areas before they Advertise	- This service is usually not provided by government	+ This service is increasingly being promoted and provided by industry -- sometimes for a fee and even on a mandatory basis
Monitoring Compliance	± Routinely done but often with limited resources	± Increasingly done by the industry although restricted by available financial resources
Handling Complaints	+ Impartial treatment is anticipated + Extensive capability to handle many complaints - Slower and more expensive - Cannot put the burden of proof on advertisers in criminal cases	- Treatment more likely to be perceived as partial - Limited capability to handle many complaints in some countries + Faster and chapter + Usually puts the burden of proof on the incriminated advertiser
Penalizing Bad Behavior, Including the Publicity of Wrongdoings and Wrongdoers	+ Can force compliance - Generates hostility, foot-dragging, appeals, etc. - Limited publicity of judgments unless picked up by the press	- Problems with noncompliers + The media will usually refuse to print or broadcast incriminated ads or commercials + More likely to obtain adherence to decisions based on voluntarily accepted standards + Greater publicity of wrongdoings and -- to a lesser extent -- of wrongdoers

NOTE: (+) refers to strengths, and (-) to weaknesses.

THE CURRENT STATE OF SELF-REGULATION

Advertising self-regulation usually starts when various advertising, industry and trade associations develop over the years a set of general principles and specific guidelines pertaining either to *all* advertising (excluding a few types, such as political advertising and personal classi-fied ads) or to *specific sectors* such as liquor and direct-mail advertising. In many countries, this is as far as self-regulation goes. Still, the develop-ment of standards is not necessarily an empty gesture or smokescreen, because it educates the industry, and it informs outsiders that major advertising practitioners care about good behavior. Growing public discontent, government prodding, the threat of new regulations, strong industry leadership, and the example and assistance of other countries with strong and effective self-regulatory systems are usually needed to move the industry past this initial stage toward the development of a *nationwide, all-industry and centralized system*—that is, one offering pre-advertising advice to practitioners, monitoring advertisements in various media, handling competitor and consumer complaints, penalizing bad behavior, and publicizing the system's availability and decisions. Some twenty national advertising self-regulatory systems around the world have reached that advanced stage by involving key associations of advertisers, agencies, media, and other supports. Another thirty countries have made definite progress, with some industry sectors better organized than others. However, about a hundred countries are still without an ASR system.

While deploring that self-regulation is insufficiently developed in much of the world, one must acknowledge that the same is generally true of gov-ernment regulation. Effective advertising control demands sizeable moral, personal, and financial resources, which are always in short supply. Otherwise, why would consumerists keep clamoring for more laws, larger enforcement budgets, and easier access to the judiciary redress system?

Over time, the scope of advertising self-regulation tends to move from settling competitor complaints within advertiser and agency associations, to handling consumer and general-public concerns through a national tri-partite (advertiser–agency–media) system. Its contributions vary in relation to the development of statutory regulation in a particular coun-try—ranging from self-regulatory systems that fill in for weak consumer-protection legislation (such as in Brazil and the Philippines) to those that work in parallel with well-developed legal systems, as in Australia, Canada, France, Japan, the United Kingdom, and the United States. In the latter case, self-regulatory systems have had to handle progressively more complex complaints and issues.

The sanctions typically applied by self-regulatory bodies include deny-ing access to most media (this is the most frequent sanction), publicizing

the names of recalcitrant advertisers (occasionally), denouncing the
advertisers to the authorities (rarely), expelling them from the relevant
associations (rarely), and suing to protect the interests of the advertising
profession (exceptionally). These sanctions apply to all or most advertisers, since the latter do not have to be members or supporters of a self-
regulatory body in order to be affected by its decisions, when the media
cooperate with that body and deny access to recalcitrant members and
nonmembers alike.

WHY SELF-REGULATION WORKS

Advertising self-regulation, in whatever form, will never fully satisfy
consumerists and regulators. They simply refuse to believe that private
interests can be turned into promoters of the public interest. Besides, consumerists and regulators have a vested interest in protecting their turf and
livelihood, irrespective of their true appreciation of self-regulation, so
that they have to be overtly critical in order to be perceived as doing their
jobs properly.

A good part of the skepticism expressed toward self-regulation centers
on the "free-rider" problem; namely, that not all members of an industry
will accept and apply voluntary standards and bear their share of the
costs. So, why do most advertisers, advertising agencies, and the media
join industry associations and accept industry standards?

Various explanations center on political objectives (e.g., obtaining legitimacy and checking the spread of government regulation), economic advantages (e.g., the information and advisory services provided by associations), and solidarity goals (e.g., feeling of unity, and confirmation of
societal worth and of personal self-respect). Of course, some people
remain impervious to these appeals and benefits, but there will always be
deviants under any control system, whether mandatory or voluntary.

Therefore, the problem is really about the extent to which advertising
self-regulation can *minimize* the problem of the "free rider." In this
respect, some of the most impressive performances among self-regulatory
systems are found in advertising on account of two factors. First, *advertising is inherently visible as well as recognizable*, because all business ads
include a brand or company name. Hence, its failings are readily detect-
able and traceable, compared to other improper practices and professional misdeeds that often remain hidden from public view (e.g., price
collusion). As such, competitors, consumers and their associations,
citizens at large, and law enforcers can more readily identify and react to
advertising's shortcomings. While critics point out cases of subtle mislead-
ingness, unfairness, and even "hidden persuasion" that might escape the

average person, it remains that there are enough expert watchdogs who can easily uncover such cases. Consequently, the pressure on advertising practitioners and the media to maintain and apply high standards is particularly strong because it is broadly diffused and sustained.

The second factor that favors advertising self-regulation is that about 90 percent of advertisements rely on the print and broadcast media or on postal services. Thus, there is always a screening mechanism between the advertiser and the public. This unique situation of depending on an intermediary (a "medium," in other words) provides a check on advertising practices through both the media's standards for the acceptance of advertisements and the media's tendency to abide by the decisions of advertising self-regulatory bodies. For example, Italian agencies and media have a clause in their contracts that requires acceptance of the self-regulatory code by advertisers.

Critics point out that this screening process is imperfect; and industry itself deplores the practices of advertisers and media that overlook self-regulatory standards and decisions, either out of ignorance or defiance. Still, while each screening mechanism may be imperfect, the cumulative effect is substantial. Besides, defrauders and recalcitrants can be denounced to the authorities who face the same problem of disciplining marginal and elusive operators.

Proof that advertising self-regulation works can be found in the following facts: (1) many members of the public have accepted to participate in the functioning of national ASR systems, (2) public-opinion polls in several countries (e.g., France and the United Kingdom) show that the awareness and acceptance of advertising self-regulation have increased, and (3) the overall image of advertising has improved in several nations where advertising self-regulation is well developed (e.g., France and the United Kingdom). These facts reveal that the industry's self-interest does not fundamentally impair the ability of advertising self-regulation to contribute to good behavior in advertising, and that it is increasingly accepted as a complementary and effective form of advertising control.

OUTSIDE INVOLVEMENT IN ADVERTISING SELF-REGULATION

Nonindustry members are always involved in advertising self-regulation to the extent that consumer complaints, government prodding, legal developments, and social-science research as well as criticisms in the media and scholarly publications have helped shape the development and application of self-regulatory standards.

Furthermore, most complaint-handling systems include one or more of the following features: an independent chairperson, independent members of the public, experts, and even representatives of consumer organizations. Such "outsiders" constitute a majority in Ireland, Italy, Singapore, and the United Kingdom; and they are well represented in Australia, Brazil, Canada, and the Netherlands. In these countries, industry has concluded that such outsiders are essential to impart expertise, legitimacy, and credibility to the application of industry standards. In many other countries, however, the consumer movement is too hostile, disorganized, or divided to provide effective outside members (e.g., in Belgium, France, and the Philippines).

In any case, advertising self-regulation has to retain a strong "inside" and "behind-the-scene" core. The gist of the problem lies in maintaining what has been called "user-friendly, practitioner-based regulation." While many voluntary systems have come, in varying degrees, to integrate nonindustry members in the *application* of ASR standards, the *development* of such standards must remain primarily an industry prerogative because it is a necessary condition for moral adhesion to such standards. While society, the marketplace, and government also impose standards, the voluntary and self-assumed nature of self-regulatory standards makes the difference. Outside experts, government agencies, and consumerist organizations are often consulted, but the resulting standards must be of the industry's own making—otherwise, they are no longer "voluntary" but become "negotiated" or "imposed" rules (as in the case of the World Health Organization's breastmilk-substitutes code) that tend to elicit lower moral adhesion on the part of the industry, irrespective of their appropriateness, which is sometimes questionable (see the EASA document in the Appendix section).

Besides, while there are open-and-shut cases of clear-cut and even bad-faith violations of legal and industry standards, there are also many borderline cases of truth, accuracy, and fairness, as well as subjective matters of taste, decency, and opinion. These require fine interpretations of the norms, and they justify approaching the advertiser directly but discreetly. They might also require using "friendly persuasion" rather than a heavy "enforcement" approach at the advising and complaint-handling stages because, in order to be accepted, self-regulation has to rely on peer pressure and media cooperation, without any heavy-handedness. Therefore, advertising self-regulation must remain fundamentally "private" in order to be effective, even if such privateness can limit its external credibility.

This situation militates against giving true parity to nonindustry members in self-regulatory bodies. In some fundamental sense, the industry has to remain in control of the voluntary approach, however hybrid the self-regulatory system might have become. Similarly, some of its deliberations have to remain secret because the industry itself is divided or needs time to develop consensus about new standards. (It should be observed that consumer organizations do not invite business to participate in their deliberations either.)

HOW GOVERNMENTS WORK WITH SELF-REGULATION

Statutory regulation and voluntary self-regulation are complementary approaches to advertising control, rather than mutually exclusive ones. Therefore, the role of government in acknowledging and fostering advertising self-regulation is crucial, yet delicate. The government's goal is clear, namely, to put to public purposes the type of social responsibility that associations can generate and embody. Many governments have come to realize the limits of their resources and effective reach, and to accept the contributions of self-regulation. Besides, the passage or threat of regulation is often effective in precipitating the development of self-regulatory systems.

The best public-policy solutions lie somewhere between mandating, capturing, or overloading a self-regulatory system, and ignoring or opposing it, thereby diminishing the effectiveness and legitimacy of self-regulation. The United Kingdom, Canada, and Australia offer illustrations of this first problem. While exemplary in terms of fruitful business–government cooperation, the British and Canadian experiences point to the potential danger of asking ASR systems to assume more and more tasks, which can become as burdensome as regulation, and can weaken voluntary adherence to industry norms. In the same vein, where governments demand the right to approve industry norms or to have outside consumerist groups participate in their revision, as has been the case in Australia, such an approach threatens the voluntary nature of self-regulation. Belgium illustrates the second problem because its government tends to ignore the role of its well-developed ASR system.

One would expect self-regulatory systems to limit themselves to devising and implementing standards that complement the law. In fact, there is considerable overlap between legal and industry standards. This overlap assumes several forms, ranging from the application by self-regulatory bodies of legal norms (such as in Belgium, France, and the United States) to the partial duplication of legal standards in self-regulatory codes, as in the British Code of Advertising Practice. For that matter, the International Chamber of Commerce's (ICC) International Code of Advertising Practice—the bible of advertising self-regulation—starts by stating that "All advertisements should be legal."

The overlap between the law and self-regulation is necessary to the extent that a good part of the law reflects generally accepted community standards against false, misleading, and unfair advertising. The role of advertising self-regulation is, then, to help practitioners internalize such standards and to generate moral adhesion to them.

DOES SELF-REGULATION DO ENOUGH?

The dominant criticisms of advertising self-regulation have been that (1) relatively few cases are handled by self-regulatory bodies in proportion to the true extent of advertising failures, (2) relatively little publicity is given to ASR standards, processes, and decisions in most countries, (3) many decisions come "too late," after the infringing advertisement has been discontinued, and (4) penalties are relatively mild, except for denial of access to the major media.

Before addressing these criticisms, one must acknowledge that legal approaches suffer from the same ills, as is evidenced by the constant demands made by consumerist advocates in many countries to strengthen legal redress systems. Furthermore, all advertising control systems face the reality that many advertising breaches are relatively trivial in terms of the harm done, so that they do not warrant the huge expenditures necessary to achieve speed, to handle high caseloads, to mete out severe punishment and to provide great publicity. In this perspective, all advertising control systems are only token responses.

With this in mind, the above criticisms are valid only to the extent that one conceives of self-regulation mainly as a *consumer-redress* mechanism. However, they must be tempered if one understands that the main purpose of advertising self-regulation is *to help advertising practitioners internalize high advertising standards*—something that can be done even on the basis of a few significant cases, of late decisions, and of apparently mild penalties. In this perspective, advertising self-regulation is much more concerned with *improving* advertising behavior on an industry-wide basis than with satisfying individual complainants, even though these two goals are obviously compatible and related.

This purpose of advertising self-regulation—namely, to improve advertising behavior both in the industry's and the public's interest—is bound to be misinterpreted as a token public-relations gesture designed to placate critics and to fend off the threat of regulation. Yet, in view of its private nature, this is the true purpose that distinguishes self-regulation from other forms of social control. It is a form of "soft law" precisely because it has only "asking power" rather than subpoena power in dealing with offenders, and it relies almost entirely on peer pressure, on media cooperation, and on publicity, rather than on harsh judicial penalties.

The advertising industry values complaints to the extent that they represent some sort of a random sample of what bothers consumers and competitors. The industry also prefers to be the first line of recourse (together with complaints directly addressed to advertisers or the media) for complainants—in lieu of suits, denunciations to the authorities, and exposés in consumerist publications and programs. However, too many complaints not only overburden underfinanced ASR systems but also trivialize the complaining process by generating cases that fall outside of their self-assigned mission. Moreover, many cases of misbehavior reflect the careless control of advertising copy by advertisers and agencies rather than the advertiser's intention to mislead. The really "bad apples" are best left to government agencies as courts of last resort. For that matter, governments also handle only a minuscule fraction of advertising complaints, so that all control systems really cover only "the tips of icebergs and the bottoms of barrels."

In this perspective, advertising self-regulation generally promotes *higher* standards—which is not the same as the *highest* standards, to be sure. This is essentially an educational and consciousness-raising task, although one backed by fairly effective sanctions (such as publicizing the names of wrongdoers in some cases, and recommending to the media to deny access in most cases). Besides, advertising self-regulation is more concerned with future behavior than with past errors—a distinction connected with how "fast" self-regulation should be. If redress and discipline were its main goals, great speed would be essential; but *deliberate speed* is sufficient for educational and consciousness-raising purposes. Still, the U.K. and U.S. systems have recently accelerated their handling of complaints, while the South African Advertising Standards Authority has the right, when it considers the complaint to be sufficiently serious, to suspend an advertisement until the complaint has been resolved.

Self-regulatory systems are reluctant to handle cases revolving around good taste, decency, and social responsibility, but so are most governmental agencies, because community standards about such issues are either only surfacing (e.g., in the case of sexism) or are too heterogeneous (as with the advertising of contraceptives).

As has often been remarked, advertising is and can only be "a mirror of society." This remark applies equally to its self-regulation. Therefore, taking public positions about controversial issues such as tobacco advertising is an exercise that self-regulatory bodies generally leave to capstone advertising and industry organizations (e.g., the U.K. Advertising Association and the American Advertising Federation). When they do handle such controversial issues as advertising to children, and cigarette and feminine-hygiene advertising, they limit themselves generally to imposing stricter standards of truth and accuracy rather than to addressing the core issue of the social suitability of such advertising. Settling questions concerning the usefulness of advertising, its volume, and its correspondence with societal values is outside the role of these ASR bodies in any case.

Therefore, advertising self-regulation is neither a panacea nor a substitute for other forms of advertising control. Its scope is limited, its reach is incomplete, and its methods are only partially effective. Even to realize its complementary potential, there has to be a collective interest in self-regulation, and industry associations must have sufficient resources to develop and implement a self-regulatory system. In addition, the issues at stake must not be too divisive. Still, although advertising self-regulation cannot cope effectively with every market failure, one can endorse Daniel Oliver, former chairman of the U.S. Federal Trade Commission, who observed: "The marketplace doesn't have to work perfectly to work better than government. It is our job, before we regulate commercial advertising, to weigh the promise of the marketplace against the promise of regulation." In other words, there are "regulatory failures" as well as "market failures"; and advertising self-regulation does not have to work perfectly or even better than other mechanisms to be accepted as a natural, complementary, and often effective form of societal control over advertising behavior.

INTERNATIONAL ADVERTISING SELF-REGULATION

Advertising self-regulation has proved to be compatible with all sorts of economic systems, including the current and former centrally planned economies of the People's Republic of China, Hungary, and Yugoslavia. In addition, it is functioning well in such developing countries as Brazil, India, and the Philippines. Even where self-regulatory bodies are absent and the relevant laws are embryonic, advertising has benefited from various international initiatives.

Since the mid-1930s, the International Chamber of Commerce (ICC) has played a key role in coordinating efforts to establish common grounds upon which national systems of marketing self-regulation should be based. It has outlined specific principles through its International Code of Advertising Practice—first introduced in 1937 and revised most recently in 1986 (see Appendix 3)—and it has encouraged business to set up national mechanisms for their application.

While this and other ICC codes are designed primarily as instruments of self-discipline and self-regulation, they are also intended for use by the courts as reference documents against the background of law. In fact, the ICC International Code of Advertising Practice has been used by the courts in Belgium, Denmark, France, Germany, and Norway; and it is integrated into Sweden's legal concepts relating to its consumer-ombudsman system. It is particularly in the legal vacuums found in many less-developed countries that the ICC codes have proven useful by providing basic rules about good advertising behavior.

The ICC has always left the questions of ASR structure and functioning to the appropriate bodies in each country; and it has confined itself to recommending voluntary or mixed bodies to handle marketing and advertising self-regulation, to urging cooperation between business and consumer organizations, and to fostering participation by both in the law-making process, as far as consumer protection and industry competition are concerned.

At the international level, the ICC's International Council on Marketing Practice has assumed the responsibility for working with international bodies involved in the control of advertising and marketing—such as the Council of Europe, the European Community, the Organization for Economic Cooperation and Development, and the United Nations. It also handles international complaints on a very limited basis when national self-regulatory systems do not exist or cannot cope with them because the complaints emanate from other countries.

Outside of the ICC, several advertising bodies have worked toward sharing information about regulatory and self-regulatory developments—for instance, the European Advertising Tripartite, and the World Federation of Advertisers. Besides, a few national self-regulatory bodies—notably, the U.K. Advertising Standards Authority—have helped other countries (e.g., India) develop more effective self-regulation. Several industry groups have also developed international standards and even started to handle complaints, for example, in the pharmaceutical and direct-mail fields.

In mid-1991, the European Advertising Standards Alliance (EASA) was created to bring together all those organizations in Europe—particularly, those from European Community states—which operate self-regulatory codes of advertising practice. One of the stated aims of the Alliance is to promote a system whereby complaints received against advertisements appearing in foreign media can be speedily and effectively dealt with by reference to the relevant self-regulatory body in the country of origin of the advertisement (see Appendix 12).

The EASA is developing a convergence of the principles of self-regulation in Europe, a European Code of Advertising Practice for Advertising, the referral of complaints against advertisements appearing in foreign media, and the general defense and promotion of advertising self-regulation in the face of a growing number of proposed directives emanating from the EC Commission, that ignore or downplay the role played by national ASR bodies.

THE IAA'S ROLE IN PROMOTING ADVERTISING SELF-REGULATION

The International Advertising Association has defined its core mission as promoting, defending, and sustaining the freedom of commercial speech and consumer choice; and it sees the encouragement and development of advertising self-regulation as a prerequisite to this mission. Thus, under "Aims and Objectives," Paragraph 1.4 of the IAA bylaws reads: "To encourage adherence to codes of ethics and standards of practice, established both nationally and internationally, which are consistent with those established by the International Chamber of Commerce."

In recent years, increased communication about self-regulation has been spearheaded by the International Advertising Association through its research reports, publications, policy statements, biennial world congresses, and the activities of its national chapters. These efforts have resulted in the formation of at least four new ASR bodies in Brazil, Hungary, India, and the United Arab Emirates. The IAA has also helped other countries such as Egypt, Pakistan, Turkey, and Venezuela set up industry associations. It works closely with advertising and media associations all over the world and also with governments, as in Argentina and P.R. China. At the international level, the IAA has taken a leadership role in working with global organizations such as the United Nations in order to advance the cause of advertising self-regulation. It strongly supports the work of sister organizations within a particular region, such as the European Advertising Tripartite, and the European Advertising Standards Alliance, which also foster the development of self-regulation.

The IAA is indeed most interested in seeing that the advanced ASR systems already operating around the world be emulated in more countries. It continues to spread the gospel of self-regulation through further studies such as this one, through resolutions and position papers, through the work of its brain trusts, and through its unique worldwide tripartite network of IAA chapters that work with national advertising associations.

SOURCES AND SUGGESTED READINGS

Advertising Association (U.K.). *The Systems of Control of Advertising Standards; Report to the Advertising Association by the [Clucas] Committee of Inquiry.* London, May 1987.

Advertising Association (U.K.). *Advertising in the 1990s: The Case for Advertising in the Single [EC] Market of the 1990s.* London, 1990.

Baudot, B. S. *International Advertising Handbook.* Lexington, Mass.: Lexington Books, 1989.

Best, Arthur. "Controlling False Advertising: A Comparative Study of Public Regulation, Industry Self-Policing and Private Litigation." *Georgia Law Review* 20 (Fall 1985): 1-72.

Boddewyn, J. J. "Advertising Self-Regulation: Private Government and Agent of Public Policy." *Journal of Public Policy and Marketing* 4 (1985): 129-141.

_____. *Advertising Self-Regulation: 16 Advanced Systems.* New York: International Advertising Association, 1986.

_____. *Advertising Self-Regulation and Outside Participation: A Multinational [12-Country] Comparison.* Westport, Conn.: Quorum Books, 1988.

————. "Advertising Self-Regulation: True Purpose and Limits." *Journal of Advertising* 18, no. 2 (1989): 19-27.

Borrie, Gordon. "Horses for Courses: Efficient Enforcement and Self-Regulation." *Annual Report of the Director General of Fair Trading*. London: HMSO, 1982, pp. 9-12.

Burleton, Eric. "The Self-Regulation of Advertising in Europe." *[International] Journal of Advertising* 1, no. 4 (1982): 333-344.

Circus, Philip. "Industry Self-Regulation: Reflections on Its Growth and Present Role." *International Journal of Advertising* 7 (1988): 307-321.

Coronel, Mary. *Self-Regulatory Systems and Codes in Europe*. Brussels, Belgium: European Advertising Tripartite, January 1992.

Darvall, L. W. "Self-Regulation of Advertising and the Consumer Interest." *Australian Business Law Review* 8, no. 5 (October 1980): 309-320.

European Advertising Standards Alliance. *Self-Regulation and Codes of Practice*. Brussels, Belgium, October 1991.

European Advertising Tripartite. *Self-Regulation and Codes of Practice: A Discussion Paper* [also in French and German]. Brussels, 1983.

European Consumer Law Group. "Non-Legislative Means of Consumer Protection." *Journal of Consumer Policy* 6, no. 2 (1983): 209-224.

Garvin, D. A. "Can Industry Self-Regulation Work?" *California Management Review* 25, no. 4 (Summer 1983): 37-52.

Hondius, E. H. "Non-legislative Means of Consumer Protection: The Dutch Experience." *Journal of Consumer Policy* 7 (1984): 137-156.

International Chamber of Commerce. *Marketing, Discipline for Freedom*. Paris, 1978.

International Chamber of Commerce. "Law and Self-Regulation: A Study Comparing Government Regulation and Self-Regulation as Means of Consumer Protection." Paris: ICC Commission on Marketing, Advertising and Distribution, March 1984.

Jones, T. T., and J. F. Pickering. *Self-Regulation in Advertising: A Review*. London: Advertising Association, 1985.

LaBarbera, P. A. "Analyzing and Advancing the State of the Art of Advertising Self-Regulation." *Journal of Advertising* 9, no. 4 (1980): 27-38.

Levin, H. J. "The Limits of Self-Regulation." *Columbia Law Review* 57, no. 4 (April 1967): 603-644.

Miracle, G. E., and T. R. Nevett. *Voluntary Regulation of Advertising: A Comparative Analysis of the United Kingdom and the United States*. Lexington, Mass.: Heath/Lexington Books, 1987.

Moyer, M. S., and J. C. Banks. "Industry Self-Regulation: Some Lessons from the Canadian Advertising Industry." In *Problems in Canadian Marketing*, ed. D. N. Thompson. Chicago, Ill.: American Marketing Association, 1977, pp. 185-202.

National Advertising Review Board. *Advertising Self-Regulation and Its Interaction with Consumers*. New York, 1979.

Neelankavil, J. P., and A. B. Stridsberg. *Advertising Self-Regulation: A Global Perspective*. New York: Hastings House and IAA, 1980.

Oliver, Daniel. "Who Should Regulate Advertising, and Why?" *International Journal of Advertising* 7, no. 1 (1988): 1-9.

Rijkens, Rein, and G. E. Miracle. *European Regulation of Advertising*. Amsterdam and New York: North-Holland, 1986.

Rogers, Martha. "Advertising Self-Regulation in the 1980's: A Review." In *Current Issues and Research in Advertising*, ed. J. H. Leigh and C. R. Martin, vol. 13, no. 1-2. Ann Arbor, Mich.: Division of Research, School of Business Administration, University of Michigan, 1991, pp. 369-392.

Stridsberg, A. B. *Effective Advertising Self-Regulation*. New York: International Advertising Association, 1974.

Thomson, Peter. "Advertising Control: Advertisements in Media Other Than Television and Radio." In *Advertising Association Handbook*, ed. J. J. Bullmore and M. J. Waterson. London: Holt, Rinehart and Winston, 1983, pp. 327-351.

_____. Self-Regulation: Some Observations." London: Advertising Standards Authority, 1983.

Wyckman, R. G. "Industry and Government Advertising Regulation: An Analysis of Relative Efficiency and Effectiveness." *Canadian Journal of Administrative Sciences* 4, no. 1 (March 1987): 31-51.

Zanot, E. J. "The National Advertising Review Board, 1971-1976." *Journalism Monographs* 59 (February 1979): 1-46.

_____. "Unseen but Effective Advertising Regulation: The Clearance Process." *Journal of Advertising* 14, no. 4 (1985): 44ff.

2

IAA Survey Findings

The International Advertising Association (IAA) has conducted four surveys of advertising self-regulatory (ASR) bodies. The first one was prepared by Albert Stridsberg in 1974 on the basis of secondary information and personal interviews.[1] The second one, by James P. Neelankavil and Albert B. Stridsberg in 1979-80, was mainly based on secondary data collected from ASR bodies around the world.[2] Its country profiles were updated in 1989-92, and are included in this report.

In 1986 Jean J. Boddewyn conducted a mail survey that focused on sixteen countries with a well-developed ASR system:

Australia	Japan
Belgium	Netherlands
Brazil	Philippines
Canada	Singapore
France	South Africa
F.R. Germany	Spain
Ireland	United Kingdom
Italy	United States

Only Argentina, Austria, India, and Switzerland may have been over-looked as countries with an advanced self-regulatory system, but no detailed answers could be obtained from those countries.[3] The highlights of that 1986 survey are given below.

In 1988-89, Jean J. Boddewyn surveyed a larger number of countries, with the assistance of Leah Bender, Ariella Bernstein, and the IAA staff. They mailed each a long questionnaire, similar to the one used in the 1986 survey, and requested an updating of the country profiles collected by James Neelankavil in 1980. The response rate was uneven. Some of the thirty-seven responding countries completed either the long questionnaire or the country profile, but not both. Hence, the 1988-89 research findings are not fully comparable with those of 1986, since the former covered more countries, some of which do not have a fully developed ASR system.

The following section highlights the findings from thirty-one of these thirty-seven responding countries. The country profiles in Chapter 3 cover thirty-eight nations from which an updated version was obtained in 1990-91, with the assistance of Ariella Bernstein and Florence Michelet.

In both the 1986 and 1988-89 IAA surveys, "advanced ASR systems" and "centralized self-regulatory ASR bodies" refer to those units where, in most cases, advertisers together with advertising agencies, the media, and supports (e.g., printers and filmers) have formed a capstone, nationwide, all-products, and most-media organization that applies a code and/or guidelines—sometimes, with the participation of "outsiders," that is, independent members of the public, consumerists, government representatives, and/or experts. Other countries, however, have a less developed ASR system where only certain parts of the advertising industry or particular industries (e.g., alcohol, pharmaceuticals and tobacco) have issued rules and apply them, without the benefit of a capstone ASR body.

HIGHLIGHTS OF THE 1986 IAA SURVEY

Most advertising self-regulatory systems were born in the 1970s, a reflection of the rise of consumerism as a major issue and force during that decade, and the concurrent development of consumer-protection regulations in many countries.

Seven (out of sixteen) ASR systems had *officially* adopted the International Chamber of Commerce's (ICC) International Code of Advertising Practice. In the others, ICC principles and guidelines were usually incorporated in some form in ASR rules.

Nine ASR systems had their own full-fledged code. Others relied on general principles, on guidelines about some specific products (e.g., alcoholic beverages), targets (e.g., children), and practices (e.g., testimonials), and/or on their own previous decisions. Nine ASR systems also applied national laws in addition to their own rules.

Eleven ASR systems require that advertisers have adequate substantiation *prior* to the release of an advertisement. (The ICC Code only states that "advertisers should be ready to produce evidence without delay to the self-disciplinary bodies.")

While all sixteen ASR systems accept complaints from customers, competitors, government agencies, and members of the public, only six of them regularly monitored ads and commercials on their own: Brazil, France, Italy, Spain, the United Kingdom, and the United States. In other words, most systems defined their role as an intermediary between advertiser and complainant rather than as a watchdog for the industry. However, eleven ASR systems accepted anonymous complaints and assumed them on their own, if valid.

ASR systems varied in terms of accepting complaints about personal, help-wanted, opinion/controversy/advocacy, and nonprofit ads. Nine of them handled ads in all media, while the others excluded such media as radio and television, which were often handled by separate bodies (usually governmental ones).

All systems, except Germany's, handled complaints about false and misleading ads. However, unlike the German system, about half of them shied away from cases of "unfairness" and of "taste, decency and opinion."

Complaints were typically settled within one to two months—more quickly in Germany and Ireland, more slowly in Japan and the United States. An appeal system was available in ten of the sixteen countries, and it often included nonindustry members.

More inquiries and complaints came from consumers and their associations than from competing firms (except in Spain and the United States). On the other hand, disputes between competitors were more often resolved within professional associations. Ads coming from abroad were seldom handled, but most ASR systems expected to scrutinize more of them in the future.

The caseloads of ASR systems differed considerably. Some, such as France, Japan, South Africa, and the United Kingdom, handled thousands of inquiries from consumers and competitors. Regarding actionable complaints, the number of cases settled ranged from a handful in Spain, to 24 in Japan, and to over 3,000 in the United Kingdom. These huge differences reflected varying policies: some ASR bodies actively solicit complaints and monitor ads while others do not; some single out important cases while others handle all valid complaints; some handle national ads but not local ones; and some deal with all media while others handle only some of them.

When an ad was found to be in violation of the rules, the advertiser was always asked to withdraw or modify it. If the advertiser did not comply, fourteen ASR systems asked the media to stop printing or showing the ad—a practice restricted by antitrust law in Germany and the United States. Various amounts of publicity were given to the ASR body's decisions and to the advertiser's compliance, but the names of noncomplying offenders were seldom publicized. Strong penalties such as expulsion, fining, and denunciation to the authorities were rarely used.

Most ASR systems provided free preliminary advice to advertisers and agencies. However, prescreening was not required, except in Canada (for TV commercials targeted at children and at women for feminine-hygiene products), the Philippines (for all commercials), and the United Kingdom (for cigarette ads and new slimming products).

Only five ASR systems (in Belgium, France, Ireland, Japan, and the United Kingdom) had recently surveyed the public in terms of familiarity with self-regulation and of satisfaction with its performance. From one-fifth to one-third of the people surveyed in these five countries were aware of the existence of an ASR system.

Press releases and publicity campaigns were the most common means used to publicize ASR systems. Also widely used were industry conferences and academic lectures, as well as regular contacts with government bodies.

Outsiders were often informally consulted when self-regulatory guidelines and rules were developed and amended. In Australia, Canada, Italy, the Netherlands, Singapore, and the United Kingdom, consumer representatives and independent members of the public played significant roles in resolving complaints.

Permanent ASR staffs were generally small, ranging from one person in Germany to fourteen in Japan, fifteen in the United States, and fifty-four in the United Kingdom. Secretariats tended to make routine decisions and to prepare difficult ones for higher-level panels. Only in France and the United States did the staff make all the decisions (except at the appeal level in the United States).

Regarding the limits of self-regulation—what it can and cannot do by itself, and why—the following comments were obtained from the sixteen countries:

- ten thought that industry is willing to spend some money and resources on self-regulation but not too much;
- nine countries felt that self-regulation needs to be backed up by regulation in order to deal with uncooperative advertisers;
- eight responded that self-regulation can only assist personal self-discipline on the part of advertisers, agencies, and media; and
- past a certain point, in two countries self-regulation was felt to be as burdensome as regulation.

HIGHLIGHTS OF THE 1988-89 IAA SURVEY

As mentioned before, the 1988-89 findings are not completely comparable with the 1986 ones because of different country coverage, and because the later survey also included countries without a well-developed, centralized ASR system. Still, they provide more recent information, as well as complementary data. The highlights here focus on only thirty-one of the responding countries.

Nineteen of these thirty-one nations had a centralized advertising self-regulatory body (the United Kingdom and the United States are not included among these nineteen nations, for lack of response to the survey). Twelve countries had some other form of advertising self-regulation, which fell short of a centralized system. All of the 19 centralized advertising self-regulatory bodies had advertiser, agency, and media representation. However, their membership composition varied from country to country. In some nations, only these three main groups constituted the self-regulatory body. In other countries, peripheral members of the advertising industry (e.g., marketing-research firms, and sign and display manufacturers) as well as government and consumer representatives, experts, and/or independent members of the public were also part of that body.

Seven of these countries had officially adopted the ICC International Code of Advertising Practice. Of the other twelve, the Netherlands, South Africa, and Trinidad & Tobago had national codes based on it.

All nineteen countries with a centralized advertising self-regulatory body followed some standards. Eleven applied general principles and guidelines; sixteen developed and followed more detailed national codes; and fourteen relied on industry codes or guidelines about specific products (e.g., tobacco, alcohol, and pharmaceuticals), services (e.g., direct mail) and/or targets (e.g., advertising to children).

Radio, newspaper, and magazine media were covered by all nineteen centralized self-regulatory systems. Television advertising was covered in sixteen countries, but not in Indonesia, France, or Spain. Outdoor advertising was included in eighteen countries, cinema advertising in sixteen countries, and direct-mail advertising in twelve countries.

Almost all centralized advertising self-regulatory bodies promoted and publicized their self-regulatory systems (seventeen countries); twelve provided information and preadvertising advice; twelve monitored ads to ensure that they conformed to the norms; ten prescreened ads and commercials; eleven were involved in lobbying government bodies, and four conducted research on advertising issues.

All nineteen centralized advertising self-regulatory bodies investigated complaints registered by consumers; seventeen handled complaints from competitors; thirteen investigated complaints as a result of their own internal monitoring; and six dealt with complaints registered by government departments, authorities and agencies.

Food products and mail-order sales tied as the product/service categories that generated the most complaints. Other categories receiving the highest rankings in some countries included household goods, employment advertising, automobile products, pharmaceuticals, cosmetics, non-alcoholic beverages, credit and investment, and holiday/travel.

Complaints concerning misleading/deceptive ads were ranked first as the advertising malpractice generating the most complaints. Other issues to receive first rankings included matters of opinion/taste/decency, inaccurate price claims, inaccurate comparisons, unfair competitive practices, and matters of religion, as well as ethnic and sex discrimination.

Thirteen of the centralized advertising self-regulatory systems included participation by outsiders (consumer or government representatives, independent members of the public, representatives from other industries, and/or experts) in the complaint-handling process. Independent experts participated most frequently (in eleven of the thirteen countries). Only Ireland included government representatives in the complaint-handling process. Outsiders never participated directly in the development of standards, but they were involved in the handling of complaints. Nine countries with a centralized self-regulatory body had an appeal process.

Twelve survey responses came from countries with no centralized advertising self-regulatory body. Self-regulation in these countries was undertaken by key advertiser, agency, and/or media associations, by separate industry associations, or by a government-sponsored authority involving industry representatives (for example, the consumer-ombud system in Sweden).

Consumer groups were most concerned with whether to limit or ban the advertising of particular products or services. Industry was most concerned about an increase in government regulation directed at specific product categories (e.g., cigarettes, alcohol and pharmaceuticals). A majority of the respondents thought lack of financial resources most affected the development of self-regulation. The least frequently cited cause was lack of effective leadership.

The country profiles in Chapter 3 provide more detailed information about the composition of ASR bodies, their functioning, and the issues they currently face. The names of those who checked or revised them are listed at the end of each country profile.

NOTES

1. A. B. Stridsberg, *Effective Advertising Self-Regulation* (New York: International Advertising Association, 1974).

2. J. P. Neelankavil and A. B. Stridsberg, *Advertising Self-Regulation: A Global Perspective* (New York: Hastings House and International Advertising Association, 1980).

3. J. J. Boddewyn, *Advertising Self-Regulation: 16 Advanced Systems* (New York: International Advertising Association, 1986).

3

Country Profiles

AUSTRALIA

Organizing for Industry Regulation

The Australian advertising industry has a long history of self-regulation. In recent years, external pressures have been mounting, but the industry still has a powerful voice in regulatory matters.

Its strength lies in the fact that all arms of the industry cooperate in the self-regulatory process. Agencies, advertisers, and media uniformly accept the discipline of a single series of codes of advertising practice, and join together in the councils responsible for ensuring that these codes adequately reflect community standards—a situation that leads to a high degree of compliance not only with the letter of the codes but also with their spirit.

Three representative bodies are jointly responsible for maintaining the industry self-regulation system: the Media Council of Australia, the Advertising Federation of Australia, and the Australian Association of National Advertisers.

The Media Council of Australia. The MCA speaks for all major media in Australia—press, magazines, outdoor, television, radio, and cinema. Members of the MCA are required to observe the requirements of the codes and of the regulatory systems. Thus, virtually all media in Australia are bound to comply.

The MCA has the legal carriage of the advertising codes, and it operates the advertising-agency accreditation system that gives the codes their "teeth." The industry councils that maintain the codes are administered by the MCA. Members of these councils are representative of media, agencies, and advertisers, but they also include "public members" nominated by the federal government to speak for specialized interests such as health, youth, ethnic affairs, consumer affairs, and women.

> Media Council of Australia (MCA)
> 186 Blues Point Road
> North Sydney, NSW 2060

The Advertising Federation of Australia. The AFA is the national association of Australian advertising agencies. Its members collectively account for about 90 percent of the dollars spent through agencies in Australia. To the discussion and negotiation of regulatory affairs, the AFA brings the viewpoint of the people who create, direct, and place most main-media advertising in Australia. It has a strong independent role in all issues relating to the advertising business.

> Advertising Federation of Australia (AFA)
> 140 Arthur Street
> North Sydney, NSW 2060

The Australian Association of National Advertisers. The AANA speaks for major advertiser companies in Australia, and it has taken an active interest in the evolution of the advertising codes and standards. Individual AANA members provide specialist input in several areas.

> Australian Association of National Advertisers (AANA)
> Level 11, Stockland House
> 181 Castlereagh Street
> Sydney, NSW 2000

The Codes and the System

The five codes of advertising practice supported by the industry are as follows:

- Advertising Code of Ethics
- Therapeutic Goods Advertising Code
- Cigarette Advertising Code

- Alcoholic Beverages Advertising Code
- Slimming Advertising Code

Print, radio, and outdoor advertisements for the four product-category codes are subject to mandatory prepublication approval by the clearance authorities maintained by the media organizations. All but a few limited-use advertisements for television are precleared by the Commercials Acceptance Division of the Federation of Australian Commercial Television Stations.

The MCA, AFA, and AANA are charter members of, and jointly support, the judicial authority of the Industry's regulatory system, the Advertising Standards Council (ASC). Modeled on the British Advertising Standards Authority, the ASC is chaired by a former judge of the Supreme Court. Its constitution mandates that it have a majority of nonindustry members. These include a former deputy prime minister of Australia.

Functioning of Self-Regulation

The ASC hears complaints from any source, against advertisements in any medium. An adverse ruling against an advertisement means that the advertisement does not appear again in any publication of a member of the Media Council of Australia. An advertising agency responsible for an advertisement ruled by the ASC to be in breach of the advertising codes or the law may be further penalized by loss of commission by the Australian Media Accreditation Authority, an administrative arm of the MCA.

The system also includes a Joint Committee for Disparaging Copy, a MCA-supervised council drawn from senior representatives of agencies, media, and advertisers. It provides fast and cost-efficient resolution of disputes between advertisers, using criteria of unfair disparagement of identified competitors.

The advertising codes and the system as a whole have been "authorized" by the federal Trade Practices Commission as being of public benefit. However, the industry has been assailed in recent years by consumerist and single-issue groups (notably anti-smoking and anti-alcohol organizations) seeking representation within the industry's councils. But in a landmark decision, the highest fair-trading authority, the Trade Practices Tribunal, ruled that the system does operate in the public interest and, in passing, accepted the industry's view that direct representation of specific (outside) organizations could be "disruptive and harmful."

Research indicates that, so far as the community at large is concerned, the disciplines of advertising in Australia are working well. The industry intends that this will continue.

The Consumer Movement

There are about fifty significant consumer organizations in Australia. The oldest and largest is the Australian Consumers Association (ACA), which tests products and makes the results available to 180,000 member-subscribers through *Choice*, its monthly magazine. Only a few hundred people are, in fact, voting members of ACA. In 1974, these consumer groups joined in a loose confederation called the Australian Federation of Consumer Organizations (AFCO). The federal government provides about $100,000 a year to help AFCO prepare submissions to official inquiries, and so on.

Since the Australian system is a largely self-regulatory one, consumer groups have no official role in an organizational sense. However, consumer groups do make themselves heard through their energetic lodging of complaints; and they have been strong critics of many aspects of the self-regulation system, with the overall objective of intruding into the system in order to pursue a range of single-issue objectives.

Government Involvement

Each advertisement or commercial is carefully scrutinized by individual publishers, radio stations, and television stations before being printed or aired. These procedures ensure that the advertisement or commercial complies with government laws and regulations as well as with the advertising codes.

The most significant federal legislation is the Trade Practices Act, with an overriding prohibition on misleading advertising. Television and radio advertising is governed by the Broadcasting Act, or more specifically by regulations imposed and enforced under the act by the Australian Broadcasting Tribunal. These include restrictions on the use of overseas-made television commercials in Australia, on alcohol advertising, and on advertising to children.

Health claims in food advertising are proscribed by the Australian Food Standards, which have national effect and prohibit, among others, any kind of therapeutic claim and "advice of a medical nature." Additionally, each of Australia's states has numerous acts and regulations bearing on advertising, particularly retail advertising.

Advertising remains low on the list of genuine community concerns in Australia. Research reveals no strong feelings about any issue involving advertising, and certainly no great antipathy—the industry disciplines are working well. Nevertheless, advertising freedoms are increasingly threatened by the imperatives of bureaucracies, at both state and federal levels, pursuing private agendas in such areas as health, consumer affairs, and the environment. Persuading policymakers of the realities of these issues is the industry's greatest challenge.

Trend

While self-regulation and trade-practices legislation have mainly dealt with the contents of advertising, the function of advertising has increasingly been receiving attention on all fronts in relation to its effects on prices, alcohol and drug abuse, road safety, children's education, the portrayal of women, and so on. These areas are the subject of continuous inquiries and public hearings by the Prices Justification Tribunal, Industries Assistance Commission, and Broadcasting Tribunal as well as by various standing committees of the Senate and departments of local government.

Insofar as content is concerned, an increasing number of complaints have begun to focus on the socio-cultural aspects of various product categories. This, in turn, has raised concerns about the principle of freedom of commercial speech.

Information for this section was supplied by David Jackson, deputy director of the Advertising Federation of Australia.

AUSTRIA

Organizing for Self-Regulation

A single, centralized body for the administration of advertising self-regulation exists in Austria:

Oesterreichischer Werberat
(Austrian Advertising Council)
Wiedner Hauptstrasse 63
1045 Vienna

This council was organized in June 1971 through the initiative of the Federation of Austrian Industrialists. Statutes were drawn up, following discussions among the key industrial federation, advertising-agency representatives, and government representatives (namely, the Federal Economic Chamber, the Federal Corporation of Economic Advertising, and the Mininstry of Trade and Industry). The body was modeled on the lines of the Austrian Press Council.

Participants in the Advertising Council include representatives of important companies with major advertising programs, the managing directors of recognized advertising agencies, a representative of the Austrian Press Council, and representatives of Austrian radio and television. Advisers to the council include the president of the joint advertising council of the

Federation of Austrian Industrialists and of the Association of Brand Manufacturers, the chairman of the Federal Corporation of Economic Advertising, and a representative of the Institute of Publicity and Advertising of Vienna's Commercial University.

Besides the above council, there are two more industry associations that bring the advertising sectors together:

> Gemeinsamer Werbeausschuss der Vereinigung Oesterreichischer
>   Industrieller und des Oesterreichischen Verbandes der
>   Markenartikelindustrie
> (Advertisers Association)
> Schwarzenbergplatz 4
> 1031 Vienna
>
> Fachverband Werbung und Marktkommunikation
> (Association for Advertising and Marketing Communication/
>   Advertising Agencies)
> Wiedner Hauptstrasse 63
> 1045 Vienna

There are no radio or television associations because all radio and television stations are owned by the state.

Functioning of Self-Regulation

The Austrian Advertising Council meets as a committee, deliberating on the basis of hearings and arriving at decisions by a two-thirds majority. Decisions are based on the Code of Advertising Practice of the International Chamber of Commerce, together with supplemental guidelines and recommendations developed by the Association for Advertising and Marketing Communication in cooperation with the Ministry of Economic Affairs.

Council members, while representing various industrial sectors, are expected to act independently according to their conscience, and they are not committed to any instruction.

The sessions of the council are held at specified dates at least every two months, or are specially scheduled at the request of three members. Complaints can be introduced by outside parties or on the basis of investigations initiated by the council itself. Both the hearings and the minutes of meetings are private and are treated as confidential. Parties to any inquiry are invited to be present at the discussions but not during the final decision-making process. The council may also invite testimony from qualified people suggested by these parties or from independent experts from the advertising field.

If the council finds the advertising objectionable, it seeks to have it withdrawn or modified. Appeals are possible. The results of the hearings are announced to all participating advertising enterprises, advertising media and clients, and to their associations. The council may publicize its decisions. In 1990, the council received fewer than ten complaints, suggesting that the system is insufficiently known or that legal procedures are preferred.

The Consumer Movement

The principal consumer group in Austria, the Association for Consumer Information, is sponsored and financed by the government. The Association for Consumer Information, jointly financed from the budget of the Federal Economic Chamber and that of the Federal Ministry of Trade and Industry, sets out advisory guidelines for advertisers, dealing with specific matters such as advertising to children, health-product ads, the emotional content of ads, and so on.

In addition to issuing guidelines, the association has plans to carry out comparative testing and evaluating of products, but there is still some disagreement about this role. The Association for Consumer Information and the Advertising Council have worked together on the Association's guidelines, and the council has applied them in practical instances.

A second consumer group actively concerned with the role of advertising is the Chamber of Workers. This body has taken the position that advertising increases the cost of products to consumers and, hence, is contrary to the best interests of all workers.

Government Involvement

The Austrian government not only has played an active role in the formation of the Advertising Council but also maintains an advisory presence in its deliberations.

A legal ban on the advertising of alcoholic beverages and tobacco products was blocked by the intervention of the Advertising Council and of an industrial federation. However, the Austrian State Tobacco monopoly voluntarily terminated its advertising on television.

Since the broadcast media in Austria are state-owned and controlled, responsibility for further government restrictions on advertising can be transferred from the central government to the director-general of the Austrian radio and television company. According to statutes now in force, the director-general is responsible for the whole complex of advertising on broadcast programming.

The following practices have recently been prohibited on television and radio:

- advertising for tobacco and liquor;
- advertising for the services of lawyers, doctors, and accountants;
- advertising conflicting with national policy and public morals;
- misleading advertising.

Trend

Since the Advertising Council has been able to ensure concerted action among representatives of the advertising industry, the consumer movement, and the government, unnecessary public controversy has been avoided. Periodically, consumers have called for stronger action, but it has been possible to deal with such requests successfully as they arose.

No further government restriction on advertising is currently foreseen, although additional limitations could result from the transfer of restrictions on advertising related to public health from the responsible government bodies to the director-general of the radio and television company. At this time, there are no major problems regarding advertising self-regulation in Austria.

Information for this section was supplied by Mag. Herbert Bachmaier, general secretary of Fachverband Werbung.

BELGIUM

Organizing for Self-Regulation

In the early 1960s, some industries in Belgium set up their own specialized bodies to regulate their product fields. A good example of this kind of regulation was the Comité de la Publicité pour les Médicaments (drug advertising). In 1967, however, a body was set up under the name of Commission du Code to regulate most advertising in Belgium. In 1974 the commission's name was changed to Jury d'Ethique Publicitaire (Advertising Ethics Jury), and its authority was extended to act promptly in cases of advertising considered illegal or unfair. The activities of the various industry self-regulatory bodies were brought under the control of this body.

Jury d'Ethique Publicitaire/Jury voor Eerlijke Praktijken (JEP)
18-24 Rue des Colonies, Box 9
1000 Brussels

The JEP's seventeen members are appointed by the Advertising Council and drawn from industry: four from advertisers, three from agencies, and ten from the media, plus the president of the JEP, who is an independent person.

Functioning of Self-Regulation

The JEP meets every two weeks to deal with questions and complaints in light of existing laws and regulations and of specialized product- and practice-related codes of fair practice in advertising, most of which are based on the ICC's International Code of Advertising Practice.

The jury may intervene in three different ways:

- when an advertiser, agent, or a medium calls for advice prior to publication;
- when a person, business concern, or institution introduces a complaint; and
- when a member of the JEP or its secretary wants to have an advertisement considered.

There is no systematic monitoring of advertisements, but sensitive subjects receive occasional attention. Prepublication advice has increased in recent years. The competence of the Jury is restricted to commercial advertising, and cases are examined from the consumer's point of view, with the exception of disputes between competitors.

When the advertisement is considered not to be truthful, honest, decent, or legal, or it lacks a sense of social responsibility, the advertiser is recommended to change it or to stop it. In case of refusal, the JEP may recommend to the involved media to respect its advice and stop the advertising. The JEP publishes an annual report with a summary of activities and a list of the cases resolved. It is funded by levies on media spending.

The Consumer Movement

There are more than a dozen active consumer associations. One of them publishes periodicals, and a majority of them maintain contacts with the press, broadcasters, and other mass media. While cognizant of the existence of the JEP, they do not lodge complaints about objectionable advertising with it, preferring to voice their criticisms in their own publications. These consumer groups in general favor a greater degree of regulation.

Of the fourteen Belgian consumer associations, the most important are as follows:

- Socialist and Christian Democratic Trade Unions
- Test-Achat—Test Aankoop (product testing)

- Fédération des Coopératives Socialistes
- Ligue des Familles Nombreuses (large-families association)
- Bond der Grote Gezinnen (large-families association)

These associations are helped by the Centre de Recherche et d'Information des Organisations de Consommateurs (CRIOC), a consumer research and information body subsidized by the Ministry of Economic Affairs. They influence advertising regulation and other consumer interests through their participation in the official Conseil de la Consommation (Consumers Council), which groups representatives of consumers, industry, agriculture, commerce, and public services.

Government Involvement

The Belgian law on trade practices (which has just been revised, effective February 29, 1992) sets forth general principles to govern advertising. The law conforms with the basic elements of the ICC Code, except in regard to comparison advertising, which is, for all practical purposes, forbidden in Belgium.

Certain restrictions or preclearance requirements are imposed on advertising for stock shares. In addition, the advertising of pharmaceuticals and tobacco is very restricted, and the advertising of foodstuffs is particularly regulated. The laws governing competitive marketing methods (labeling, packaging, coupons, lotteries, price cutting, etc.) are numerous.

The relationships between the government (principally the Ministry of Economic Affairs and the Ministry of Public Health) and the self-regulatory bodies are good. In principle, the activities of these ministries embrace advertising questions as well as marketing methods.

Trend

Public opinion favors more government regulation, in part owing to consumerist pressures. Within the government, the tendency remains to strengthen regulation by product/service category or for specific items. The advertising industry considers present regulations adequate, and it is working to handle the consumer-protection function via self-regulation.

The JEP's positive action is well known and recognized by professionals, as well as by public opinion and the government. The JEP is working closely with various professional federations in order to elaborate or strengthen advertising standards in their sector.

Information for this section was supplied by Jean-Claude Dastot, director of the Conseil de la Publicité (Advertising Council).

BRAZIL

Organizing for Self-Regulation

Self-regulation had long been an aspiration of the advertising industry and of advertising professionals in Brazil. In April 1978, a new self-regulatory code, titled the Codigo Brasileiro de Auto-Regulamentacao Publicitaria (Brazilian Code of Advertising Self-Regulation), was approved by the Brazilian Association of Advertising Agencies (ABAP) at the Third Brazilian Advertising Congress held in São Paulo. At the same time, ABAP also formed an Inter-Associative Commission of Brazilian Advertising, composed of advertisers, agencies, and media, plus members of the Confederation of Commerce and the Confederation of Industry. Since May 1980, however, this commission has been reorganized into the National Council for Advertising Self-Regulation (CONAR), the body responsible for applying the Code and reviewing complaints.

> Conselho Nacional de Auto-Regulamentacao Publicitaria (CONAR)
> 1140 Rua Bahia
> 01244 São Paulo

To avoid earlier problems connected with a lack of public exposure and of inputs from various sectors, the new code received, from its very inception, the widest possible publicity so that every member of the advertising community would be fully informed of its contents. Comments of every kind and from every quarter, including those by industry leaders, government officials, and consumer advocates, were invited. In this way, the authors of the code hoped to achieve liaison with all possible interested parties and to create a real exchange of ideas and a sense of participation.

Functioning of Self-Regulation

CONAR is made up of representatives from all sectors of the advertising industry, including the following organizations as well as 12 consumer representatives and 194 individual members:

- Associacao Brasileira de Anunciantes (ABA) (Brazilian Advertisers Association)
- Associacao Brasileira de Agencias de Propaganda (ABAP) (Brazilian Advertising Agencies Association)
- Associacao Brasileira de Emissoras de Radio e Televisao (ABERT) (Brazilian Radio and Television Association)
- Associacao Nacional de Jornais (ANJ) (National Newspapers Association)

- Associacao Nacional de Editores de Revistas (ANER) (National Magazine Publishers Association)
- Central de Outdoor (Outdoor Advertising Association)

CONAR has a two-tiered structure. The Higher Council (Conselho Superior) consists of advertisers, advertising agencies, and media representatives. This Higher Council has twenty-one members representing the six founding bodies and the prior past-president: three from the Advertising Agencies Association; three from the Brazilian Advertisers Association; six from the Brazilian Radio and Television Association; three from the National Magazine Publishers Association; three from the National Newspapers Association, and two from the Outdoor Advertising Association.

The Higher Council is vested with both executive and normative functions. As to the first, it appoints an eight-member directorate: a president (also chairman of the board of CONAR), a vice-president, a secretary, a second secretary, a treasurer, two directors, and a full-time executive director. As to its normative functions, the Higher Council can improve and amend the Code, and approve the Ethics Council's bylaws. It also elects the five Ethics Chambers' presidents (two in São Paulo, and one in Rio de Janeiro, Brasilia, and Porto Alegre) and it may propose changes to the bylaws, convoke the General Assembly, and answer queries about advertising ethics for its members and for the government.

The Ethics Council (Conselho de Etica), which consists of 117 advertising professionals (advertisers, agencies, and media) as well as 20 consumer representatives and an executive director, is responsible for reviewing complaints. Complaints can be introduced to the Ethics Council by consumers, governmental authorities, competing advertisers, and the Ethics Council itself as a result of its own monitoring.

If an advertisement is found to be unacceptable, the Ethics Council may recommend that the ad be withdrawn or modified, or it might just issue a warning to the advertiser. Decisions of the Ethics Council are communicated to all interested parties and the media. Advertisers may appeal the decisions of the Ethics Council. There are two appeal bodies on the Ethics Council. The first is the Special Appeals Chamber. It examines the ordinary appeals lodged against first-level decisions. It is convoked whenever necessary. Its president may be any Superior or Ethics Council member, especially designated by CONAR's president. The reporter-counselor must not have any prior knowledge of the case.

If the Special Appeals Chamber's decision is not unanimous, it may be presented as an extraordinary appeal to the Ethics Council Plenarium (all of its members), headed by CONAR's president. Also, the public disclosure of recommendations that were not followed by practitioners is decided by the Plenarium so that the names of advertisers, agencies, or media may be publicized.

The number of complaints handled in recent years is as follows:

	1987	1988	1989	1990
Number	145	142	173	197
Ad Modifications or Withdrawals	70	94	51	79
Public Announcements	1	4	–	2

CONAR's success is demonstrated by two facts: (1) there is no longer any government advertising censorship in Brazil and (2) consumer groups as well as government authorities send complaints to CONAR and request its opinions.

The Consumer Movement

Consumer activist groups are numerous and extremely well organized. The three main consumer groups are as follows:

- Departamento Nacional de Proteçâo e Defesa do Consumidor (DNPDC) (National Department of Consumer Protection and Defense, a unit within the Justice Ministry)
- Grupo Executive de Proteçâo ao Consumidor (PROCON) (Consumer Protection Group within the State Secretariat for Industry and Commerce)
- Instituto Brasileiro do Consumidor (IDEC) (Brazilian Institute for Consumers' Defense, a private institution)

These consumer groups succeeded in having a law passed that characterizes untruthful advertisements as a crime (Law 8078/90—Consumers Defense Code). They continue the fight to ban all advertising for tobacco products, alcoholic beverages, agricultural insecticides, and any kind of drugs (the New Constitution of October 1988 only imposes warnings on the advertisements for these products).

Government Involvement

The major laws and restrictions affecting advertising in Brazil today are (1) the Health Protection Law, which prohibits the advertising of drugs that can solely be purchased with a prescription, (2) laws requiring that cosmetic products, insecticides, and foods be registered with the Health Ministry, (3) laws about tobacco advertisements (warnings were imposed), and (4) the Consumers' Defense Code.

The Consumers' Defense Code (Law 8078/90) was approved by the National Congress on September 11, 1990, and became effective on March

11, 1991. This law characterizes untruthful or abusive advertisements as a crime. The code is designed to protect consumers against false or exaggerated advertisements, faulty products and services, poor usage instructions, and unclear contracts. If found guilty of harming or misleading a consumer, a marketer or advertising executive can be fined up to $500,000 or given a prison sentence of up to five years. Furthermore, a judge can rule to close a business or to prohibit the manufacture and sale of a particular product. This code also allows a judge to place the burden of proof on the defendant, instead of requiring the complainant to prove damage; and the defendant may be required to pay all legal costs.

Trend

Advertising self-regulation in Brazil is now recognized by all advertising professionals, as well as by the government. It has recently become better known by the public, after several institutional campaigns. The new directorate, elected in July 1990, is in the process of updating the CONAR Code and of reconsidering advertising's relations to Brazilian society.

Information for this section was supplied by Edney G. Narchi, executive director of CONAR.

CANADA

Organizing for Self-Regulation

Self-regulatory activity in Canada is centrally coordinated via a multi-tiered structure originally under the sponsorship of the Association of Canadian Advertisers and the agencies' Institute of Canadian Advertising. Sponsorship has been broadened to include media and advertising-supplier participation and, at the operational level, public representation, including nominees from the national Consumers' Association. The capstone administrative bodies for advertising self-regulation are as follows:

Canadian Advertising Foundation (CAF)
350 Bloor Street East, Suite 402
Toronto, Ontario M4W 1H5

La Fondation Canadienne de la Publicité
4823 Sherbrooke Street West, Suite 130
Montréal, Québec H3Z 1G7

The Canadian Advertising Foundation was formed in 1957 and reconstituted in 1966. Its objective is to establish a single, responsible voice that can speak for the entire advertising industry to government, educators, and the public. The CAF is a voluntary organization, and it administers and publicizes the industry codes, handles liaison with the Canadian governmental authorities, works with educators, funds research, and works to broaden public awareness of the advertising function.

Participating organizations and industry associations include the following:

- Advertising and Sales Executive Club of Montréal
- Association of Canadian Advertisers
- Association of Medical Advertising Agencies
- Association of Quebec Advertising Agencies
- Better Business Bureau of Canada
- Brewers Association of Canada
- Canadian Association of Broadcasters
- Canadian Broadcasting Corporation
- Canadian Business Press
- Canadian Cable Television Association
- Canadian Community Newspapers Association
- Canadian Cosmetic, Toiletry and Fragrance Association
- Canadian Daily Newspaper Publishers Association
- Canadian Direct Marketing Association
- Canadian Magazine Publishers Association
- Canadian National Yellow Pages Association
- Direct Sellers Association
- Grocery Products Manufacturers of Canada
- Institute of Canadian Advertising
- Le Publicité Club de Montréal
- Magazines Canada
- Non-Prescription Drug Manufacturers of Canada
- Ontario Funeral Service Association
- Outdoor Advertising Association of Canada
- Pharmaceutical Advertising Advisory Board
- Retail Council of Canada
- Society of Ontario Advertising Agencies
- Telecaster Committee of Canada

- Trans Ad Limited
- Trans-Canada Advertising Agency Network
- Welcome Wagon Ltd.

The CAF oversees and finances three separate divisions (two English and one French) charged with two distinct responsibilities. The Advocacy Division, in Toronto, addresses the social and economic issues related to advertising in the English language. Two self-regulatory mechanisms, the Advertising Standards Council (ASC, made up of volunteers and assisted by the CAF staff) plus the Standards Division in Toronto and the Conseil des Normes de la Publicité in Montréal, administer standards and codes of ethics.

> Le Conseil des Normes de la Publicité (CNP)
> (Advertising Norms Council)
> 4823 Sherbrooke Street West, Suite 130
> Montréal, Québec H3Z 1G7

The Fondation Canadienne de la Publicité, sharing the office of the CNP, handles fund-raising and the administration of the Guidelines on Sex-role Stereotyping in Québec Province. These two mandates used to be the responsibility of the Confédération Générale de la Publicité from 1982 to 1987. When necessary, the executive director of the CNP wears a second hat and acts on behalf of the CAF's Advocacy Division, addressing social and economic issues in the French language.

The ASC and CNP self-regulatory councils are made up of two-thirds industry professionals and one-third public representatives, a specified ratio of the English-language Council being nominees of the Consumers' Association of Canada, and representatives of other special interest groups.

The permanent staff of the CAF's Standards Division deals with complaints, performs consultative functions, seeks voluntary corrective action where deemed necessary, proposes and prepares cases for review at ASC council level, and carries out a public-communications program. Also, the Advertising Standards Council is supplemented by six regional councils located in Halifax, Winnipeg, Regina, Calgary, Edmonton and Vancouver. These regional councils are totally voluntary groups, but the same ratio of industry and public representatives participate, along with a similar representation nominated by the Consumers' Association of Canada and special interest groups.

The permanent staffs of the two councils provide continuing liaison with federal and provincial administrations, the Better Business Bureau of Canada and its local operations, and consumer-oriented associations. The Advocacy Division carries out active programs of educational liaison and ensures contact with the education and youth sectors, while the public relations and advertising staff communicate CAF activity to the public.

The norms applied by the Advertising Standards Council/Conseil des Normes de la Publicité are found mainly in the Canadian Code of Advertising Standards. Its relatively short fifteen clauses are loosely based on the ICC's International Code of Advertising Practice. However, the Standards Division, the Advertising Standards Council, and the Conseil des Normes de la Publicité also apply eight additional codes issued by particular industries (e.g., horticulture, ethical and over-the-counter drugs, and cosmetics) or in cooperation with the government and pressure groups (concerning, for example, advertising to children, feminine-hygiene products, comparative advertising, and environmental guidelines). The Advocacy Division and the Fondation Canadienne de la Publicité (via the CNP, acting on behalf of the Advocacy Division in the French language) handle the guidelines on sex-role stereotyping in advertising.

Functioning of Self-Regulation

The CAF's Advertising Standards Council and the Conseil des Normes de la Publicité serve as CAF's self-regulatory arms, and they handle complaints in their own language. These may be introduced by the public, governmental bodies, trade bodies, competing advertisers, and other sources.

Complaints must be submitted in writing and signed; the complainant must supply a copy of the advertisement or indicate where it can be located or observed, and he or she must also provide a definite statement of the challenge addressed to it.

While the bulk of such complaints are initiated by consumers, a growing number stem from competitors and trade organizations. This latter development seems to relate to the growth of comparison advertising that names competitive brands. Except in trade disputes, the identity of complainants is treated as confidential.

If the complaint has merit under the Canadian Code of Advertising Standards, the advertiser must substantiate any claim or statement that has been challenged. Each council's staff investigates all reasonable complaints and seeks voluntary corrective action on code infractions. If correction is not forthcoming, the matter is moved to the full council for decision. If the ruling sustains infringement of the code, the advertiser is informed and expected to cooperate. If the advertiser refuses to do so, the council enforces its decision by informing the media. Most of the latter have agreed not to carry advertising that, in the opinion of either council, violates the code.

In the instance of trade disputes between competitors, there is a special procedure involving examination of supporting data and of allegations by a special Advertising Review Panel, which renders a preliminary decision. This decision may be appealed. New procedures were introduced in summer 1991.

While generally no more than 15 percent of English-language complaints are sustained as Code infractions, every complaint receives a reply, and all parties directly concerned receive a detailed statement of reasons for the council's decision. The Conseil des Normes de la Publicité usually sustains a higher percentage of complaints received.

The Consumer Movement

Several local and regional consumer interest groups are active in Canada, and the oldest Canadian consumer group is the Consumers' Association of Canada. In addition, special-interest groups have taken positions with regard to advertising in particular product categories and industries, and to the portrayal of various groups in society.

Many of these special-interest groups, with government funding and encouragement, are proposing changes in the following areas: the portrayal of women, disabled persons, ethnic groups, and aged people, as well as environmental claims in advertising.

Government Involvement

In June 1988, the Canadian Senate passed drastic anti-smoking legislation that includes a ban on all forms of tobacco advertising. The law, which went into effect in stages after January 1, 1989, bans not only broadcast advertising of tobacco products, which the tobacco industry voluntarily agreed to end over a decade ago, but also newspaper and magazine ads as well as all billboard and other outdoor advertising after 1991. In addition, this legislation banned the use of tobacco brand names in connection with cultural and sporting events, as well as point-of-sale advertising and promotional techniques. This ban, however, was declared unconstitutional in July 1991, but an appeal is pending.

It is important to mention the vast differences in codes administered in the two Canadian cultures—French and English. These two groups do not share the same problems. For example, advertising to children below the age of thirteen has been banned in the province of Québec, so that the self-regulation of ads directed at children applies only to the other nine provinces. In those English provinces, the advertising of feminine-hygiene products and multi-culturalism are sensitive matters, but are less of an issue in the French part of the country, which was originally much more concerned about sex-stereotyping and pornography in advertising than was English Canada.

Trend

Currently, the Canadian Advertising Foundation, through its Advertising Standards Council and the Conseil des Normes de la Publicité, continues to provide well-respected and credible handling of complaints in the general areas of the Canadian Code of Advertising Standards as well as preclearance and complaint-handling under the Broadcast Code for Advertising Directed to Children, the Television Code of Standards for the Advertising of Feminine Sanitary Protection Products, and the Advertising Code of Standards for Cosmetics, Toiletries and Fragrances. In other areas, the Canadian Advertising Foundation, through its Advocacy Division and the Fondation Canadienne de la Publicité, administers guidelines on sex-role stereotyping. To date, these guidelines have been successful in holding off the specter of greater government regulation. Advertiser responsiveness to concerns regarding the portrayal of ethnic groups appears, at the moment, to have quieted calls for government regulation and even for formal self-regulation in this particular area.

In the areas of the disabled and the aged, the Canadian Advertising Foundation is keeping a watchdog view. While some have called for more controls from government and through self-regulation, no specific moves have been made by either the government or the industry.

Information for this section was supplied by Susan Burke, vice-president of the Canadian Advertising Foundation, and by Niquette Delage, executive director of Le Conseil des Normes de la Publicité and director for Québec Affairs of La Fondation Canadienne de la Publicité.

CHILE

Organizing for Self-Regulation

The central body for the self-regulation of advertising in Chile is as follows:

Consejo Nacional de Autorregulacion Publicitaria (CONAR)
(National Council for Advertising Self-Regulation)
San Sebastian 2812—Of. 608
Las Condes, Santiago

CONAR includes representatives from various branches of the advertising industry. The Association of Advertising Agencies (ACHAP) and the Advertisers Association (ANDA) each supply three representatives. In addition, Network TV 11 (Corporacion de TV de la Universidad de

Chile), Network TV 7, and the Radio Association (ARCHI) are represented by one person each. One expert lawyer serves as secretary.

In April 1986, a self-regulatory code, Codigo Chileno de Ethica Publicitaria was sanctioned by the Asociacion Chilena de Agencias de Publicidad (ACHAP) and the Asociacion Nacional de Avisadores (ANDA). This code, which is modeled after the ICC's International Code of Advertising Practice, established CONAR as the nationwide body responsible for applying the code.

Some of the main functions of CONAR include: (1) promoting and publicizing the self-regulatory system, (2) monitoring and prescreening advertisements to ensure that they conform with the provisions of the code, and (3) adjudicating complaints.

Functioning of Self-Regulation

Any advertiser, agency, media, individual, or CONAR itself can complain about advertising that is found to contravene the Chilean Code of Advertising Ethics. The CONAR board analyzes the complaint. If the complaint is accepted, the involved parties are immediately informed and they are given five to fifteen days to answer it. Occasionally, the campaign is stopped while a decision is being made. After the investigation, CONAR issues its verdict by a majority of votes, and informs the interested parties.

In case of a violation of the Chilean Code of Advertising Ethics, CONAR can request a change in the advertisement or campaign, request that it be withdrawn, make a private admonition, or make a public admonition. It can also recommend that the media refuse the advertisement.

The volume of complaints is extremely low. In 1987, forty-one complaints were received. The largest number of cases involved complaints about inaccurate product or service comparisons. In general, the cases were found to be violations of the Code of Advertising Ethics. In only one case was CONAR's decision not executed, but the Chilean Association of Advertising Agencies (ACHAP) punished the agency that did not comply.

The Consumer Movement

At present, there are no major consumer groups in Chile.

Government Involvement

In Chile, only one medium, Television Nacional, is government-owned. The only law that deals with advertising is the National Television Council Act, which treats ethical aspects and regulates advertising targeted to children, the advertising of alcoholic beverages, and the warnings applied to cigarette advertising.

Trend

The Advertising Self-Regulation Council has become stronger and is being acknowledged by advertisers, media, and agencies. More authority regarding ethics-related complaints is needed, however.

Information for this section was supplied by Henry G. Northcote, general manager, and Marta Barba of Northcote Asociados and Ogilvy & Mather; Ernesto Labatut, president of the Consejo Nacional de Autoregulacion Publicitaria; and J. P. Fahes, vice-president of the International Advertising Association, area director, Chile.

DENMARK

Organizing for Self-Regulation

At present, there is no voluntary self-regulation in Denmark. Instead, there is a consumer ombudsman, whose office was established in May 1975. Before that, the Dansk Reklame Naevn (Danish Advertising Standards Authority, DASA) governed advertising self-regulation. This organization was founded in 1971 to replace a previous advisory board organized by the Danish Advertising Association.

The consumer ombudsman is responsible for controlling compliance with the Danish Marketing Act. On his or her own initiative, or following complaints or applications from other persons or groups, the consumer ombudsman endeavors through negotiations to influence business firms to act in accordance with the Marketing Act. The ombudsman is entitled to take action to obtain injunctions against infringement of the law, and—when necessary—to impose a temporary ban, pending the decision of the court—normally, the Maritime and Commercial Court of Copenhagen. The activity of the consumer ombudsman in any other respect is supervised by the minister of industry.

Functioning of Self-Regulation

After creation of the ombudsman system, the character of cases coming to DASA for adjudication changed considerably. Complaints, even those from competitors, which used to be brought to DASA, were now presented to the ombudsman. This shift was due in part to the fee that DASA customarily charged for handling each case, whereas the ombudsman reviews cases without any charges whatsoever. Over time, the total number of cases dealt with in a given period decreased, after the original backlog of cases that developed in the office of the Ombudsman.

In addition, members of DASA had also invented ways to circumvent the law rather than to prescreen their commercials through DASA. Given this situation, the chairman of DASA found it advisable, with the concurrence of all sponsoring organizations, to discontinue in 1975 all prescreening of commercials.

Consequently, since December 31, 1975, there has been, for all intents and purposes, no self-regulation of advertising in Denmark. Nor is there in the Danish community any form of the "responsible advertiser" (ARU) as there is in Swedish agencies—someone who is presented with all materials in each advertising agency for judgment, prior to publication or release to a client. Advertisements can be presented to the Danish consumer ombudsman for review and decision prior to publication, but this procedure is time-consuming, and the ombudsman's opinions are not binding.

Although DASA's sponsoring organizations failed to institute a system comparable to Sweden's "responsible advertiser" system in Danish advertising agencies, two of these sponsoring organizations tried a different approach to the problems at hand. The Danish Advertising Agencies Association and the Danish Daily Publishers Association took seriously the rising confusion created for their members by the consumer ombudsman, whose office issued a constant stream of decisions, all in photocopy form and without comment or cross-referencing.

After discussions, the former secretary of DASA agreed to serve the two associations as an adviser and legal consultant. With the former secretary as editor, the two associations now publish from two to four information bulletins a year, where the most important decisions of the consumer ombudsman are presented and discussed. These bulletins are distributed to member advertising agencies as well as to the advertising departments of newspapers.

The editor of these bulletins functions also as an adviser and legal consultant to those advertising agencies and newspapers who ask for advice. For this service, the editor charges a fee comparable to that levied in Sweden for analogous consultations by the Konsultbyrån för Marknadsrätt (Marketing Law Consultancy), with which he maintains very close contacts.

A close, though informal, cooperation also exists between this editor/adviser/consultant and the consumer ombudsman. They maintain regular contacts and ask for each other's advice. The consumer ombudsman subscribes to the aforementioned information bulletins based on the ombudsman's decisions.

It must be added that the various codes of the International Chamber of Commerce have inspired the activities of the Danish advertising industry for over fifty years. Various industries (alcohol, tobacco, pharmaceuticals) have developed advertising guidelines. There is also an Advertising Council (Reklameradet) to handle competitors' complaints.

The Consumer Movement

Throughout Denmark, some six or seven consumer groups are active. By its statutes, DASA is required to include a consumer representative on its board of directors. An official representative of one consumer group, the Consumer Association, had earlier sought, without success, this seat on DASA's board. Because the Consumer Association felt it should have representation that was equal—50 percent of the voting power—to that of industry members, it has refused to recognize DASA's consumer board member, who continues to serve as a private individual.

Government Involvement

From the establishment of the first advisory board in 1949 up to 1974, there was no government involvement in advertising regulation, except for laws concerning unfair competition. What regulations did exist originated in the voluntary actions of the advertising industry.

On June 10, 1974, the Danish Parliament, in response to the requests of consumerist organizations, enacted a law to bring advertising and marketing under governmental control through a consumer ombudsman, similar to those active in Sweden and Norway.

This 1975 Marketing Act has been the principal legal text bearing on marketing and advertising. In January 1990, the Minister of Industry put forward amendments to this act to the effect of abolishing Sections 6-8a and inserting a new section dealing with "safety requirements for toys and any other products the appearance of which can be mistaken for food." The main purpose of this amendment is to enable the implementation of an EC-directive covering these products.

According to this amendment, Sections 6-8a in respect to gifts, trading stamps, prize competitions, and interest-free credit are to be taken out of the act; while the general clause of Section 1, about proper marketing practices, is to form the sole basis of future evaluation and judgment in cases concerning the promotional activities mentioned above. In the notes to the bill, it is pointed out that such evaluation and judgment will require the consumer ombudsman to initiate negotiations with trade and consumer organizations about the guidelines to be applied in the use of gifts, trading stamps, and competitions for marketing purposes.

Other acts influencing advertising control include the Pharmacy Act of 1975, the Trademarks Act of 1959, the Competition Act of 1989, the Copyright Act of 1961, and the Food Act of 1973. The most restrictive act is the Pharmacy Act, prohibiting advertising for medicines on TV, radio, film, and outdoors. Advertising is permitted only with the approval of the Medical and Health Board as to the nature, form, and contents of the advertisements.

The Broadcasting Act includes restrictions such as a ban on the advertising of pharmaceutical products and of alcoholic beverages (with an alcoholic content of 2.25 percent or more). Tobacco advertising is also forbidden. Advertising for economic interest groups and for religious and political beliefs is permitted only on local radio but not on TV.

In compliance with the Broadcasting Act, a TV advertising tribunal has been set up with the authority to take action in case of violations of the rules in force. This tribunal also acts as an adviser to the relevant minister on the contents of TV and radio advertising.

Trend

Discussions are going on to relax the advertising ban for certain pharmaceutical products, in view of the recent EC broadcasting directive.

Information for this section has been updated by Mr. Bent Vindelin-Pedersen, director of the Dansk Annoncørforening (Association of Danish Advertisers).

FINLAND

Organizing for Self-Regulation

There is no central self-regulatory body in Finland, but there is a commercial television company, established in 1957, which regulates its own practices:

> MTV Finland
> Ilmalantori 2
> 00240 Helsinki

MTV has Television Advertising Terms and Conditions, created and published by the company itself, which basically follow the ICC International Code of Advertising Practice. All television commercials are pre-screened before they are aired. The board of MTV reviews manuscripts and story boards, and it hands its decisions to the agency or advertiser. In 1990, the company reviewed 1,622 submissions. A privately owned company, MTV Finland operates nationwide; and it also takes care of the pre-clearance of commercials for its subsidiary, the Third Channel (Oy Kolmostelevisio Ab), which started in 1987 and works on a commercial basis. In 1990, there were 2,346 reviewed submissions for the Third Channel.

The Consumer Movement

There are two major consumer groups in operation in Finland—Suomen Kuluttajaliitto (Finland's Consumers' Union) and Kuluttajat ry (Consumers' Association). Each exerts only moderate influence on the public and the government. A council supervising sex equality in advertising was started by the Finnish Periodical Publishers' Association, the Association of Finnish Advertisers, the Finnish Association of Advertising Agencies, and the Finnish Newspapers Publishers' Association. Its chairperson is nominated by the Central Chamber of Commerce.

Government Involvement

The government of Finland prohibits the advertising of tobacco and liquor. Also, the Kuluttajasuojalaki law to protect consumers contains marketing guidelines. A consumer ombudsman ensures that the law is followed. According to the MTV Code, the unnecessary use of children in commercials should be avoided.

Trend

MTV Finland is preparing a Code of Green Advertising on television.

Information for this section was supplied by Raimo Ruohisto, vice-president of MTV Finland.

FRANCE

Organizing for Self-Regulation

A central body exists in France for the self-regulation of advertising. Because of the government role in broadcasting, its self-regulatory activities have covered all forms of media advertising outside of broadcasting. However, since January 1991, TV commercials are being previewed by the jurists of the Advertising Control Bureau when agencies request it.

Bureau de Vérification de la Publicité (BVP)
(Advertising Control Bureau)
5 rue Jean Mermoz
75008 Paris

The BVP, founded in 1953, was reorganized in 1971 at the invitation of the government in order to give greater weight to self-regulation. Since that date, there has been a marked expansion in membership and activity. Of particular importance has been the affiliation of major industry, trade and professional associations on a "correspondent" basis.

The membership of the BVP consists of fee-paying advertisers, advertising practitioners, and the media. Advertisers subscribe to the BVP under their own firm's name, and include most major French marketing firms. Advertising agencies are usually members of the Association des Agences-Conseils en Communication (AACC), but there are also independent agencies and counselors or consultants. Individual print media (the daily press and periodicals of a consumer, trade, industrial, and technical nature) are members of the BVP, as are representatives of the radio/cinema and outdoor/poster media. The BVP's board of directors also include three representatives of the National Consumers Institute (INC).

Functioning of Self-Regulation

The BVP functions as a voluntary organization and applies existing laws and regulations as well as the ICC international codes of advertising practice and sales promotion. It also applies its own general and sectoral guidelines (*recommandations*).

In a vigorous effort to anticipate regulatory needs, the BVP carries out the following program:

- consultation prior to appearance of the advertisement;
- verification after appearance of the advertisement through BVP monitoring and outside requests from competitors or consumers; and
- response to consumer complaints.

In 1990, 4,334 investigations were handled by the BVP (compared with 2,181 in 1987), with 2,398 of them requested by consumers. These investigations by the BVP's staff of four lawyers do not include non-binding consultations and opinions constantly provided by phone and visit. In its procedures, the BVP makes specific reference to its own guidelines and to relevant government laws and regulations. Intervention after the appearance of the advertisement consists of recommending that the advertising be withdrawn or modified, if found in violation of the existing guidelines, statutes, and regulations. The BVP asks the media to stop publication in cases of noncompliance. Information concerning the cases examined is circulated to the entire BVP membership and to the press, in a summary fashion, with no names disclosed.

The BVP works with trade and professional associations to develop specific guidelines for the self-regulation of their members' advertising activities. In addition, executives of the BVP carry on an external public-information program consisting of lectures, conferences, meetings with major advertising agencies and staffs, and appearances on radio and television.

The Consumer Movement

Consumer awareness of advertising problems is communicated through a dozen organizations, one of which is government owned. These organizations publish magazines for their memberships, pursue active public-relations programs with the press and television, and engage in other kinds of public activity. The major institution is the Institut National de la Consommation (INC). It is a government-owned institution in which several consumer organizations are represented. One of them is the Union Fédérale des Consommateurs (UFC).

> Institut National de la Consommation
> (National Consumers Institute)
> 80 rue Lecourbe
> 75015 Paris

> Union Fédérale des Consommateurs
> (Federal Union of Consumers)
> 18 rue Victor Massé
> 75009 Paris

Government Involvement

An overall law (Loi Royer of 1973, as amended in 1978 and 1991) prohibiting misleading advertising, plus about twenty-five specific laws covering various industrial sectors (drugs, alcoholic drinks, tobacco, stock shares, and investment companies), protect consumers and competitors. Comparison advertising was allowed in 1991, although with major restrictions. Government control over all public and private broadcasting within the territorial border of France gives a new state body (CSA, Conseil Supérieur de l'Audiovisuel) control over the amount, length, frequency, and content of television commercials:

> Conseil Supérieur de l'Audiovisuel
> (High Council for the Audiovisual Media)
> 56 rue Jacob
> 75006 Paris

The BVP was charged in 1991 with the administration of the statutory CSA rules.

Trend

Active cooperation among the advertising industry, the government, and consumer organizations to promote self-regulation continues to be evident in France. Nonetheless, the trend to government regulation of advertising continues, as expressed in legislation enacted in 1973 giving the courts the right to impose "corrective advertising" (that is, messages contradicting information previously communicated by advertisements). However, this has happened only once during the past four years. While attributing overall legal responsibility for incorrect messages to the advertiser, the law implicates the agency and media producing and publishing the advertising as accomplices. While such government regulation can make a positive contribution by helping eliminate deliberately false advertising, self-discipline has been strongly supported by recent government administrations.

The steady increase in the collaboration of major advertisers, agencies, and the media with the BVP is taken as a favorable indication that self-regulation may render unnecessary any further, more stringent government regulation, although tobacco and liquor advertising will soon be banned almost entirely.

Information for this section was supplied by Françoise Assère of the Association des Agences-Conseils en Communication (AACC), Lucien Bouis, director of the Bureau de Vérification de la Publicité, and Françoise Perucki of the Bureau de Vérification de la Publicité.

GERMANY

Organizing for Self-Regulation

Self-regulation of advertising in Germany falls under the authority of a central nationwide organization:

> Zentralausschuss der Werbewirtschaft (ZAW)
> (Advertising Federation)
> Villichgasse 17
> Postfach 20 14 14
> 5300 Bonn 2

The ZAW, founded in 1949, is a voluntary association of federations from all fields of advertising. It is quadripartite, the four components being advertisers, media, agencies, and a separate category of professionals (consultants and technicians with recognized status). The ZAW treats all questions that affect these groups and works as a "round table" toward the solution of common problems of advertising practice and technique. The ZAW's General Assembly (Praesidialrat) and Executive Committee (Praesidium) are the top deliberative and administrative levels. Beneath them function a number of expert committees, dealing with questions concerning special sectors or issues in advertising.

The Deutscher Werberat (German Advertising Council) is the self-regulatory body of the ZAW. It is responsible for questions concerning the broad area of unfair and misleading advertising, including the so-called "gray zones at the limit of the law" (e.g., taste-and-opinion issues). It is composed of twelve members of the ZAW Council: four representatives of advertisers, three of media, two of agencies, and one from the professional category. Additionally, two women from the advertising industry became members in 1988 because of the increasing number of complaints concerning the alleged discrimination against women in advertising.

The ZAW cooperates closely with the International Chamber of Commerce. In 1967, it officially adopted the ICC International Code of Advertising Practice.

Functioning of Self-Regulation

The Advertising Council bases its work on the ICC Code and the declarations of the European Economic Community of February 1972 concerning advertising self-regulation. It reviews individual cases on its own initiative or as a result of complaints for the public, from members of the ZAW, or from competitors of the advertiser being challenged. The council, which can also act on its own initiative, meets according to need.

Where legal violations are found, the Advertising Council does not take action itself, but turns such cases over to the independent Central Organization Against Unfair Competition (ZBUW). In cases where the advertising is not legally actionable but is nevertheless considered undesirable, the Advertising Council seeks to obtain withdrawal or modification on an informal basis, contacting the advertisers and the media. With few exceptions, this procedure has been successful. The German law implementing the 1989 EC Broadcasting Directive has left the control of this sector to the Advertising Council.

The self-regulatory activities of the ZAW are reported, along with its extensive efforts in all sectors of advertising development, in the ZAW Annual Report and other publications made available to the public. Information about specific cases investigated or discussed is communicated to the public; the persons and firms involved are not identified.

As a general rule, the Advertising Council does not give prepublication advice since this could be perceived as censorship, which is forbidden by the German Constitution.

The Consumer Movement

One major consumer organization dominates the picture in Germany, the AgV (Arbeitsgemeinschaft der Verbraucher, Consumer Association), with headquarters in Bonn. Financed principally by the government, this consumer association has its impact chiefly through liaison and consultation with various government ministries.

Following the basic principle of "concerted action," the ZAW formed a joint Coordinating Committee on Consumer Advertising with the AgV to improve mutual understanding and to discuss complaints, but meetings have been rare on account of diverging philosophies and interests.

Government Involvement

Advertising in Germany is subject to the effective Law Against Unfair Competition (UWG) and to special laws concerning food, cigarettes, and pharmaceuticals, for example. Consumers and competitors usually take legal action because these laws lend themselves readily to the handling of complaints.

The ZAW functions as the official voice of the German advertising industry to all national and international governmental bodies. In the past several years, the government has asked for opinions from the ZAW on laws under consideration, covering unfair competition, food, cosmetics and pharmaceuticals advertising, cartels, the regional control of outdoor advertising, and the European Community's efforts to harmonize legislation covering advertising.

Trend

At present, there are few legislative initiatives at the national level in Germany. However, the European Community is developing a number of directives that will have a strong impact on the German advertising industry after they are adopted. This includes new regulations on broadcast advertising, pharmaceuticals, food, tobacco, and data protection. However, before being enforced in a member country, EC directives have to be translated into national laws—at which point national organizations become involved in negotiations about their implementation.

Information for this section was updated by Georg Wronka and Irene Wind of the ZAW.

GREECE

Organizing for Self-Regulation

One of the main objectives of the Greek Advertising Agencies Association (GAAA), founded in 1969, was a Code of Advertising Practice. The Code, an adaptation of the ICC Code, was officially adopted in 1977 by all the members of the GAAA, now numbering thirty-nine.

> Greek Advertising Agencies Association
> 12 Ravine Street
> 115-21 Athens

The Code has since been adopted by the following:

- the Greek Advertisers Association and its members (GAA);
- the Federation of Greek Industry (FGI);
- the Association of Athens Daily Newspapers;
- consumer and specialized magazines;
- the Commercial Chamber of Athens;
- the Institute for the Protection of the Consumer which, on many occasions, has publicly praised the GAAA for the results of its self-regulatory efforts;
- municipal and private radio and television stations; and
- non-GAAA members.

Although the two national channels of the Greek Radio and Television Corporation (ERT) have not officially signed the Code, they are in close cooperation with the GAAA and its two committees on self-regulation—on one of which they are represented. Also, according to the basic law for national television (Law 1730 of August 18, 1987), the ERT is required to draft its own code of advertising practice—a task already undertaken by a special committee in which the GAAA representative was instrumental. However, the last draft submitted by the working party has not been finalized yet, due mostly to the constant changes in the administration of the ERT.

Until December 1987, the board of directors of the GAAA was the body responsible for self-regulation. Since then, two committees have been set up, one consisting of two members from the GAAA and two from the FGI, and one made up of one representative each from GAAA, GAA, the Newspapers Association, magazines, and the national radio and television channels.

The rules under which they operate have recently been revised by a working party from the agencies' and the advertisers' associations, on the

basis of the experience gained so far (based on over 350 cases), and they
have been approved by the respective boards of both associations. The
second committee has been increased by three more members, representing the Ministry of Commerce (Consumer Protection) and the independent radio and television industry.

The first committee handles complaints and provides prepublication
advice, while the second committee deals with appeals. In the case of
noncompliance, the media are asked to discontinue the advertisement,
and all relevant members are informed.

The Consumer Movement

A consumer-protection organization (Consumer Association, INKA)
came into being in 1970. Thus far, however, it has not concerned itself
with advertising questions.

Government Involvement

Law 1730 of August 18, 1987, made official the advertising ban on cigarettes and tobacco products on radio and television; it also banned toy
advertising. An amendment to that law was passed in March 1991, restricting the ban to war toys. A bill on television stations was enacted as
Law 1866 on October 6, 1989, after the formation of the National Council
on Radio and Television and on the issue of licensing the creation and
operation of private television channels. In its present form, it makes no
specific reference to the content of advertising—there is only a vague
wording that advertising time and content are expected to follow the
patterns prevailing on national channels. Restrictions still stand regarding
over-the-counter pharmaceutical products, for which special approval
must be given by the National Organization of Pharmaceutical Firms.

A ministerial decree (5206/89) on misleading advertising was issued
recently, acknowledging self-regulatory bodies.

Trend

A draft law on consumer protection has been submitted to Parliament
by the minister of commerce. It contains articles on misleading, unfair,
and comparative advertising.

*Information for this section was supplied by Maro Cambouris, director of the
Greek Advertising Agencies Association.*

HONG KONG

Organizing for Self-Regulation

The body governing the self-regulation of advertising in Hong Kong is the following:

> The Association of Accredited Advertising Agents of Hong Kong
>   (AAAA)
> 504-505 Dominion Centre
> 43-59A Queen's Road Central
> Hong Kong

Established in 1957, the AAAA consists of the twenty top advertising agencies in Hong Kong. The Association is primarily involved with issues of professional or financial relevance to their members and, as such, conducts research on various advertising issues. Although the association does handle complaints, it does so only on issues involving its own members. Sometimes though, the association is called upon to consult on issues at the request of the Television and Entertainment Licensing Authority, the government department responsible for handling complaints. Should a member choose not to comply with a decision of the association, its membership may be revoked. However, situations can occur when government codes permit advertising to run despite its contravention to the association's self-regulatory code.

The code upon which the AAAA bases its activities is the Standards of Practice of the Association of Accredited Advertising Agents of Hong Kong. This Code of Practice is, in some cases, considered more restrictive than the government's code.

The other agencies involved in the self-regulation of advertising are the Consumer Council and the Television and Entertainment Licensing Authority (TELA). The Consumer Council is a statutory body that was formed under the Consumer Council Ordinance of 1977. It is charged with protecting and promoting the interests of consumers with regard to goods and services. TELA is a government agency whose main responsibility is to enforce the advertising and technical standards imposed on the two Hong Kong licensed television stations (TVB, ATV).

> Consumer Council
> 1 Hennessy Road
> 3/F Asian House
> Wanchai, Hong Kong

Television and Entertainment Licensing Authority
9/F National Mutual Centre
151 Gloucester Road
Hong Kong

Functioning of Self-Regulation

Although the official body responsible for adjudicating television advertising complaints is currently TELA, the government is extremely keen to move this responsibility onto the shoulders of the two commercial television stations (TVB, ATV). Strong negotiations are underway between the television stations, the advertisers' association and the Association of Accredited Advertising Agents of Hong Kong, on the one hand, and the government, on the other, in order to resist these proposed changes.

The recent formation of a supreme body called the Broadcasting Authority has relegated TELA to the role of adviser. Complaints are sent directly to the Broadcasting Authority's Complaints Committee, which meets regularly. The Complaints Committee is comprised of members of government, leaders of the community, and members of TELA. Rulings on complaints involving commercials or film materials are decided at these meetings and then conveyed to the plaintiff/defendant by TELA. If ruled against, the advertiser has the right to appeal.

The Consumer Movement

Currently, the Consumer Council is the sole consumer group in Hong Kong. It has conducted a number of surveys in order to raise consumer awareness and to highlight major problem areas in advertising. A teaching kit titled "Advertising and the Consumer" was recently produced for use in schools and youth organizations. The council also receives and acts on complaints from the public concerning deceitful advertisements.

The council has been active in proposing several changes to current advertising regulations. It has advocated that a single piece of legislation, embracing all existing legislations that have a bearing on advertising and covering all media, be enacted and enforced by a government authority. The council has also proposed the structuring of a body, composed of representatives from all concerned parties (i.e., advertisers, advertising agencies, media, related government agencies, and the Consumer Council), to receive and deal with complaints. Such a body would possess real sanctioning powers if the parties against which complaints are brought are found guilty.

Other areas of concern include the advertising of products containing tobacco and alcohol, as well as the social issue of advertising to children.

Government Involvement

Major laws affecting advertising are the Trade Descriptions Ordinance and the Undesirable Medical Advertisements Ordinance. All media are strongly controlled by the government through rigorous licensing controls, among others. The government owns a medium called Radio Television Hong Kong, which operates a radio network and produces programs for the commercial television stations.

Trend

Despite the apparent lack of cohesion, advertising agencies and the media have functioned quite well under the existing system. A number of media developments, including the introduction of cable television plus the review of existing television and radio licenses, have provided a fertile ground for consumer activists to lobby for tighter restrictions on several product categories and substantive issues.

Information for this section was supplied by Kim Walker, vice-chairman of the Association of Accredited Advertising Agents of Hong Kong.

HUNGARY

Organizing for Self-Regulation

The body governing advertising self-regulation in Hungary is:

Magyar Reklamszövetseg
(The Committee for Ethics in Advertising of the Hungarian
　Advertising Association)
Dob u. 45
1074 Budapest

Organized in 1975, the Ethics Committee includes advertisers, consumer representatives, and experts in the field of law and advertising. It is primarily responsible for promoting and publicizing the self-regulatory system, monitoring and prescreening ads to ensure that they conform with accepted norms, and providing preadvertising information and advice to advertising practitioners. The committee bases its activities on general principles and guidelines of good advertising behavior, as well as on its own detailed code (the Ethical Code of Hungarian Advertising), which is based on the ICC's codes. The Ethics Committee hears and decides about alleged violations of its code.

Functioning of Self-Regulation

The Ethics Committee receives complaints from consumers, consumer organizations, competing advertisers, trade associations, governmental bodies, and the media, as well as on the basis of the self-regulatory body's own internal monitoring.

Initially, the chairman of the committee examines the complaint, then contacts the parties concerned. Thereafter, a meeting of these parties is arranged, and experts are called, if needed. At the open session, the participants explain their standpoint, while the committee adopts a resolution at a closed session. If necessary, a second session is held after full verification of the information. The decision of the committee is then sent to all interested parties, and sometimes to the press.

In the event that an advertisement is found to violate the provisions of the code, the Ethics Committee seeks to have the advertisement modified or recommends that the media refuse it. Advertisers are not permitted to appeal the decisions of the Ethics Committee. In recent years, the most frequent investigations have involved advertisements for cosmetics and other personal-care products, as well as the imitation of advertising ideas (plagiarism).

The self-regulatory system in Hungary is quite effective. Most complaints received refer to misleading advertising, advertising for unavailable goods, or the unlawful use of a competitor's advertising ideas. Practically without exception, the disputing parties accept the standpoint or decisions of the Ethics Committee. Moreover, in many cases the parties arrive at an agreement through the mediation of the committee. The committee is often consulted in advance by advertisers, agencies, media owners, and, especially, by the Hungarian television network.

The Consumer Movement

Currently, there is only one consumer group in Hungary, the National Council for Consumer Protection. Its main purpose is to submit suggestions for self-regulation and to ask the Ethics Committee for decisions on actual complaints.

Recently, consumer groups have raised the idea of softening the ban on the advertising for alcoholic beverages in order to promote the consumption of beer and wine instead of spirits.

Government Involvement

Television and radio are mostly government-owned and controlled, but local television and radio stations as well as cable television now exist in many parts of the country.

The major laws and restrictions affecting advertising in Hungary today include (1) laws prohibiting the use of pornography in advertisements, (2) laws prohibiting misleading advertising, as well as advertising for alcoholic beverages, cigarettes, and dangerous products, (3) laws restricting the use of comparison advertising, (4) laws prohibiting advertising for human medications, and (5) laws protecting the use of registered trademarks, copyrights, and industrial property.

Trend

For the time being, market conditions are developing and competition is growing in several sectors in Hungary, contributing to the increasing number of inquiries and complaints submitted to the Ethics Committee. This trend is likely to increase the importance and effectiveness of advertising self-regulation in Hungary.

Information for this section was supplied by Peter Nagy, secretary general of the Hungarian Advertising Association.

INDIA

Organizing for Self-Regulation

The central advertising self-regulatory body in India is the following:

The Advertising Standards Council of India (ASCI)
2nd Floor, Bakhtawar, Nariman Point
Bombay 400 021

The Advertising Standards Council of India was registered as a nonprofit organization on October 21, 1985. The council is governed by a board of governors consisting of sixteen people, four each from the following four categories:

- advertisers of goods or services;
- publishers of newspapers or periodicals;
- advertising agencies; and
- hoarding (billboard) contractors, film producers, printers, and other types of allied trades and professions who assist in the creation or placement of advertising or are concerned with advertising.

The ASCI has adopted a Code for Self-Regulation in Advertising. This code has been drawn up to ensure the truthfulness and honesty of representations and claims made by advertisers, to safeguard against misleading advertisements, and to ensure that advertisements are not offensive to generally accepted standards of public decency.

Until the formation of the Advertising Standards Council of India, there was no uniform self-regulatory body for the entire advertising industry. Individual industry associations and groups such as the Advertising Agencies Association of India (AAAI), the National Council of Advertising Agencies (NCAA), the Indian Society of Advertisers (ISA), the India Newspaper Society, and the Radio and Television Advertising Practitioners Association of India followed their own codes of practice.

The AAAI, a representative body of advertising agencies, was established in 1945. Its membership is open to any organization, firm, or company engaged in advertising and having a permanent office in India. The NCAA is a representative body of accredited advertising agencies that was established in 1967. Its membership is restricted to organizations and companies that carry advertising and are Indian-owned. The NCAA sponsored the First National Advertising Congress, which was held at New Delhi in 1973.

The ISA was founded in September 1952 as an organization of national advertisers. Its purposes are to promote, maintain, and uphold sound ethical and economic advertising principles. It publishes a monthly bulletin, *Nutshell*, and maintains a library of books and media materials on advertising, industry statistics, and relevant governmental acts, rules, and regulations, as well as a clipping service for the benefit of its members. Each year, the society awards an ISA-Khatau Gold Medal to a person or company for making outstanding contributions in the field of advertising or public relations.

The India Newspaper Society has its own code of standards for the acceptance of advertisements and the payment of commissions. The Radio and Television Advertising Practitioners Association of India came into being in the mid-1970s and was incorporated as a limited company in 1979. It is comprised of professionals concerned with promotion on radio and television, and it includes advertising agencies in the same line. Advertising campaigns are governed by the advertising codes of the relevant radio and television media.

Advertising Agencies Association of India
35 Maker Towers F
Cuffe Parade
Colaba
Bombay 400 005

National Council of Advertising Agencies
45 Panchkuin Road
New Delhi 110 001

Indian Society of Advertisers
148 Mahatma Gandhi Road
Bombay 400 001

The India Newspaper Society
I.N.S. Building
Rafi Marg
New Delhi

Radio and Television Advertising Practitioners Association of India
305 Neelam Building, Worli
Bombay 400 018

Functioning of Self-Regulation

The ASCI has set up a Consumer Complaints Council (CCC) as an independent unit to evaluate consumer complaints against advertisements appearing in the press, television, radio, and outdoor media. The Consumer Complaints Council consists of fourteen members with varied professional backgrounds. To date, the CCC has processed close to 650 complaints. It meets each month. From April 1990 to March 1991, the CCC dealt with 283 complaints (compared to 213 the previous year).

If a complaint is upheld, the Advertising Standards Council of India will try to ensure that the offending advertisement is either suitably modified or withdrawn. The ASCI of India can point these instances out to the advertisers concerned, and invite them to explain, substantiate, amend, or withdraw the offending advertisement. If this is not effective, it can publicly disclose the instances through the media and special publications to serve as a guideline for future "dos and don'ts." Finally, in situations where, even after detailed discussions and debate, an advertisement is still found to be objectionable and no correction is forthcoming, it may refer the case to the media for suspension of the advertisement, to the government for legal prosecution, to consumer organizations for public boycott, or to trade organizations for expulsion from membership.

The Consumer Movement

The 1980s have seen the emergence and growth of several consumer activist groups. Two organizations stand out:

The Consumer Guidance Society of India
Hutment J. Mahapaika Marg
Bombay 400 001

Consumer Education and Research Society
Thakkorebhai Desai Smarak Bhavan
Ahmedabad 380 006

Several smaller organizations exist in metropolitan areas and in smaller towns. The ASCI is in touch with many of them.

Government Involvement

The Monopolies and Restrictive Trade Practices Act and the Consumer Protection Act (1986) provide wide powers against false and unfair advertising. In 1987, a law was passed against the indecent representation of women in the media. There is adequate legislation at both the central and state levels to protect the consumer. Low awareness of the law has hampered recourse to remedial measures, however.

Trend

The ASCI recently completed a national advertising campaign informing the public of the existence of a body for the self-regulation of advertising. The response both in terms of interest and of complaints received has been encouraging.

In September 1990, the ASCI held its first All-India Seminar to inform both the industry and the public about the work of the council and the problems it faces. The ASCI has published three volumes of cases handled by the Consumer Complaints Council. These publications are made available to members, and sold to the public.

Information for this section was supplied by Karl P. Mehta, former honorary general secretary of the ASCI; Roger C. B. Pereira, chairman of Roger Pereira Communications, Private Ltd., and Teresa Viju James, executive secretary of the ASCI.

INDONESIA

Organizing for Self-Regulation

The central body for self-regulation of advertising in Indonesia is:

Komisi Tata Krama Dan Tata Cara Periklanan Indonesia
(Indonesian Advertising Standards Commission)
23, Jl. Taman Tanah Abang III
Jakarta 10160

The Indonesian Advertising Standards Commission was founded in 1981 as a result of the government's increasingly active role in the regulation of advertising. The association is comprised of representatives from the various fields of advertising, including advertisers, agencies, and all types of media:

- Serikat Penerbit Surat Kabar (Indonesian Newspaper Publishers Association)
- Persatuan Perusahaan Periklanan Indonesia (Indonesian Association of Advertising Agencies)
- Persatuan Radio Siaran Swasta Niaga Indonesia (Association of Commercial Radio Broadcasters of Indonesia)
- Asosiasi Pemrakarsa dan Penyantun Iklan Indonesia (The Advertisers Association of Indonesia)
- Gabungan Pengusaha Bioskop Seluruh Indonesia (Association of Cinema Owners in Indonesia)
- RCTI—Rajawali Citra Televisi Indonesia

The main functions of the Indonesian Advertising Standards Commission are to (1) monitor ads to ensure their conformity to accepted norms, (2) prescreen commercials, (3) provide preadvertising information and advice to advertisers, and (4) broaden public awareness of the self-regulatory system.

On September 17, 1981, the Code of Ethics and Code of Practice of Advertising was adopted by the Indonesian advertising industry as a basis for directing and managing advertising activities. The Commission on the Indonesian Advertising Code of Ethics was formed to overlook the implementation of the Code of Ethics.

In addition, individual industry groups have their respective codes of professional behavior or standards of practice that deal with advertising. There are two associations with such codes—the Indonesian Association of Advertising Agencies, with the Code of Ethics for Advertising Agencies in Indonesia, and the Indonesia Newspaper Publishers Association, with the Code of Ethics for Press Advertising.

Functioning of Self-Regulation

Complaints from consumers, competitors, government institutions, as well as cases generated by the self-regulatory body's own internal monitoring are handled by the Indonesian Advertising Standards Commission. Cases are presented to the Sub-Commission of Ethics or the Sub-Commission of Practice. If found guilty, the advertiser or agency and media are reprimanded. The advertisement itself must be corrected; otherwise, it cannot be inserted again.

The Consumer Movement

There are a few organized consumer groups in Indonesia. One such group is called the Lembaga Konsumen Indonesia (Indonesian Consumers Association). However, none of these consumer groups are very influential, and they exert little or no pressure on the advertising industry to modify its promotional campaigns.

Government Involvement

At present, the government regulates some parts of advertising. Specifically, the government of Indonesia prohibits all forms of nudity in all media. Also, the government-controlled television networks do not accept commercials for alcoholic beverages (including beer) and for cigarettes. However, the 450-odd privately owned commercial radio stations may accept beer and cigarette commercials.

Trend

The Indonesian Advertising Standards Commission has been inactive for the past four years. During this period, at least three major violations of the Code of Ethics and Code of Practice have taken place. So far, the Indonesian Association of Advertising Agencies (PPPI) has managed to handle these cases.

The commission is now being reactivated. The Code of Ethics and Code of Practice are currently being reviewed and updated for improvements. The newly revised codes will soon be in effect.

Information for this section was supplied by H. M. Napis, secretary of the Indonesian Advertising Standards Commission.

IRELAND

Organizing for Self-Regulation

The self-regulation of advertising is based on the Code of Advertising Standards for Ireland. The code, which incorporates the principles of the ICC's International Code of Advertising Practice as well as the best European standards in self-regulatory advertising controls, is administered by the following:

> The Advertising Standards Authority for Ireland (ASAI)
> IPC House, 35/39 Shelbourne Road
> Dublin 4

The ASAI also administers the Code of Sales Promotion Practice, published in 1988.

Established in April 1981, ASAI replaced and extended the work of the former Advertising Standards Committee. Its membership consists of individual advertisers, agencies, and media. It is fully supported and financed by the advertising industry—advertisers, media, and advertising agencies. The main source of revenue is a levy of 0.2 percent on advertising expenditures, collected by advertising agencies and remitted quarterly to the ASAI. The main features of the system include public access, consumer representation, prepublication advice, and the monitoring of advertisements. All members undertake not to use advertisements that contravene the code. ASAI regularly publishes case reports on investigated complaints.

Structure of the ASAI

The ASAI Board consists of thirteen members, three panels of four each, representing advertisers, agencies, and the media, together with an independent chairperson. The chairperson, an eminent lawyer with experience of business and public service, is entirely unconnected with the advertising business and is appointed by the board.

The Board of the ASAI is the custodian of policy, oversees the work of the Authority, and ensures that the Code of Advertising Standards is adapted from time to time in the public interest in order to meet changes in advertising practice.

The Complaints Committee is responsible for dealing with complaints and for initiating corrective action when necessary. Its eleven members include four consumer representatives, nominated by the director of Consumer Affairs and Fair Trade. Only three members represent advertising-industry interests. The board can take disciplinary action if required.

The chief executive implements the policies and decisions of the Authority. In addition, he is Secretary to both the Board and to the Complaints Committee.

Functioning of Self-Regulation

All advertising is subject to the Code of Advertising Standards for Ireland, modeled after the ICC and British Codes. The principal objective of the code is to promote and enforce the highest standards of honesty, decency, truthfulness, and legality in advertising in all media.

One of the Authority's main tasks is to investigate complaints of advertisements believed to be in breach of the Code. The Authority receives and investigates complaints from members of the public, public bodies and consumer representatives, and from competing advertisers.

Complaints about advertisements have to be submitted in writing to the Secretary of the Advertising Standards Authority for Ireland. Whenever possible, a copy of the advertisement in question should be enclosed, together with details of the publication in which it appeared and the date of issue. If this is not possible, a description of the advertisement and where and when it was seen should be given. A short explanation of the nature of the complaint is also required.

The monitoring of advertisements is ongoing, and the prepublication advisory service is widely used by advertisers, agencies, and media.

When it is decided that an advertisement contravenes the code (whether as a result of a complaint or through monitoring action), the advertiser is asked to withdraw or amend the advertisement. In the great majority of cases, an agreement to do so is freely given and conscientiously adhered to. Otherwise, the ASAI Board may impose sanctions including a fine, suspension of membership, or expulsion from the ASAI.

The Consumer Movement

The major consumer group in Ireland, which is active in influencing advertising regulations is as follows:

Consumers' Association of Ireland Ltd. (CAI)
45 Upper Mount Street
Dublin 2

This association was founded in 1966 as a wholly independent association to protect and educate the Irish consumer. Membership is open to all. It publishes *Consumer Choice* and distributes the *Which?* magazine in Ireland to CAI Members. CAI handles publications, surveys, lectures, and a consumers' advisory service. CAI is a full member of Bureau Européen des Unions de Consommateurs (Brussels) and of the International Organization of Consumers Unions (The Hague). The ordinary members elect its council annually.

Government Involvement

Statutory regulation of advertising exists in a number of specific areas, such as tobacco, medical preparations, credit services, and employment agencies.

The director of Consumer Affairs and Fair Trade, an independent statutory officer appointed under the Consumer Information Act of 1978, has functions in the areas of consumer protection, trading standards, and competition laws, including laws on trading practices, food labeling, and price displays. The office of the director also enforces the 1988 regulations that give effect to the European Community's Misleading Advertising Directive.

> Director of Consumer Affairs and Fair Trade
> Fourth Floor
> Shelbourne House
> Shelbourne Road
> Dublin 4

Advertising on Radio Telefis Eireann (the Irish Radio and Television Organization, RTE) comes under the Broadcasting Authority Act of 1960, the Broadcasting Authority (Amendment) Act of 1976, and the Broadcasting Act of 1990, and it is regulated by the Ministry of Tourism, Transport and Communications. RTE and the Independent Radio Television Commission (IRTC, established by the Radio and Television Act of 1988) are represented as participating bodies of the ASAI.

Under the terms of the Broadcasting Authority (Amendment) Act of 1976, the Broadcasting Complaints Commission was established, which, among other responsibilities, examines specific complaints relating to breaches of RTE's Code of Advertising Standards.

Under the terms of the Broadcasting Act of 1990, the Ministry of Tourism, Transport and Communications is to issue new codes to govern standards in advertising and sponsorship. These new codes will supersede the RTE advertising code and will apply to all broadcast services—both those of RTE and of stations licensed by the IRTC.

Trend

In Ireland, the advertising industry's self-regulatory system has developed so as to complement legal controls. It provides an alternative and sometimes only means of resolving disputes about advertisements. It encourages advertisers' acceptance of standards of practice that, in a number of areas, go beyond what is or can sensibly be required by law, while the flexible and informal characteristics of self-regulation enable it to overcome some of the difficulties limiting the application of legal controls.

The Code of Advertising Standards can be adapted to changing circumstances more easily and more rapidly than is normally possible with legislation. The self-regulatory system makes possible an investigatory process that encourages the advertiser to accept full responsibility for demonstrating that an advertisement conforms to the code. The advertiser must produce adequate justification both for what is said and for how it is said. If the advertiser cannot or chooses not to justify, then the advertisement may be declared contrary to the code.

The code emphasizes that advertisements should satisfy all legal requirements and should avoid anything that might have the effect of bringing the law into disrepute. Self-regulation is not a means of law enforcement. Complaints are not pursued under the code if they concern matters that should be resolved in a court of law.

The ASAI has the task of publicizing the Code of Advertising Standards and how it is enforced. This involves making sure that its own role as an independent investigator of complaints is both widely known and generally accepted. Through the generosity of the media, ASAI has been able to undertake substantial annual advertising campaigns. A recent Awareness Survey disclosed that one-third of the population knew of ASAI.

The Federation of Irish Chemical Industries has long operated a code of advertising practice for proprietary home medicines and another one for the promotion and advertising of veterinary medicinal products. More recently, the Irish Association of Investment Managers introduced a Code of Advertising Practice for its members, while the Irish Insurance Federation has prepared Recommendations on the Content of Advertising and Sales Literature for its members. Thus, there is clearly a growing awareness of the value of self-regulation in a number of commercial sectors in Ireland.

Information for this section was supplied by Kevin O'Doherty, former chief executive of the Advertising Standards Authority for Ireland, and by Jim Nolan, director of the Institute of Advertising Practitioners in Ireland. It was updated by Noel McMahon, chief executive of the Advertising Standards Authority for Ireland.

ISRAEL

Organizing for Self-Regulation

Self-regulatory action in Israel is based on a joint declaration signed in 1972 by the Israel Advertising Association and the Advertisers Association of Israel, binding their members to standards concerning truth and ethics in advertising. The agreement was developed in cooperation with the Israel Consumers Council.

While self-regulation is the joint domain of these two groups, additional organizations are peripherally associated in the voluntary regulation of certain aspects of advertising. These include (1) the Audit Bureau of Circulation (ABC), whose members are the Israel Advertising Association, Advertisers Association of Israel, and Daily Newspapers Managers Association, and (2) MABAF, a media organization for publications other than newspapers whose members include the Israel Advertising Association and the Advertisers Association of Israel, as well as representatives of other print media. Both of these bodies concern themselves mainly with questions of circulation and distribution.

Functioning of Self-Regulation

Since the issuance of the 1972 declaration, the volume of complaints has been quite low, an average of two a month. All cases have been successfully settled.

The Consumer Movement

As noted, the Consumers Council participated in the development of the self-regulatory agreement.

Government Involvement

No government regulations concerning advertising exist, and no serious government activity toward regulation is reported.

Since radio is a government monopoly in Israel, the Israeli Broadcasting Authority at one point claimed the right to control the content and wording of all commercials. This question was reconciled without difficulty by the inclusion in the Authority of a representative of the Israel Advertising Association.

Trend

No trend toward increased government regulation is evident, since strict adherence to high ethical standards by the advertising industry, as established by the two parallel associations, has rendered such government intervention superfluous.

A significant change concerning the outdoor advertising of tobacco products is in the making. Additionally, cable television will soon be available, but there is no official regulation for cable television advertising.

Information for this section was updated by Eli Warshavsky, president of the Israeli Chapter of the International Advertising Association.

ITALY

Organizing for Self-Regulation

The central advertising self-regulatory body in Italy is:

Istituto dell'Autodisciplina Pubblicitaria (IAP)
(Institute for Advertising Self-Regulation)
Via Larga 15
20122 Milan

A voluntary control system and a self-disciplinary code have been in effect since 1966. The code (Codice di Autodisciplina Pubblicitaria) was developed by the Italian advertising industry in response to the International Chamber of Commerce's code.

The fourteen sponsoring organizations (two of them joined in 1990) of the IAP are:

- Associazione Consulenti Pubblicitari Italiani (ACIP) (Association of Advertising Consultants)
- Associazione Italiana Creativi Communicazione Visiva (AIAP) (Association of Creative People)
- Associazione Italiana Pubblicita Stampa (AIPS) (Association of Press Advertising Media)
- Unione Televisioni Private (UTEPA) (Independent Television Association)
- National Association of Audiovisual Advertising Companies (ANIPA)
- Italian Association of Professional Organizations (OTEP)
- Italian Association of Full-Service Advertising and Marketing Agencies (ASSAP)
- Italian Association of Advertising Practitioners (TP)
- Federazione Italiana Editori Giornali (FIEG) (Italian Federation of Newspaper Publishers)
- Radiotelevisione Italiana (RAI) (Italian Radio-Television)
- Societa Italiana Pubblicita per Azioni (SIPRA) (RAI-owned advertising concessionaire)
- Associazione Aziende Pubblicitarie Italiane (AAPI) (Association of Outdoor Advertising Concerns)
- Association of Sales Promotion Agencies (ASP)
- Utenti Pubblicita Associati (UPA) (Association of Advertisers)

The IAP has a three-tiered structure. The *Jury* is composed of fourteen outside members nominated by IAP and chosen from particularly well-qualified jurists and from experts in consumer problems and in advertising communication. Since 1966, the president has always been a magistrate. The Jury's task is to examine the advertisements submitted by the Control Committee, a private plaintiff or a competitor, and to decide whether they do infringe the Code of Advertising Self-Regulation.

The *Committee for the Control of Advertising Claims* is composed of eleven members nominated by the IAP and chosen from experts in advertising, consumerism, and law. Its roles are to uncover false or misleading advertisements, to request that such ads be substantiated or modified, to negotiate and settle cases with advertisers by mutual consent and, if this fails, to bring them before the Jury. This committee also provides pre-advertising advisory opinions at the request of advertisers, agencies, and media, for a fee. Positive advice is binding on the committee not to intervene against the advertisement thus approved.

The *Secretary's Office* is a permanent administrative unit appointed by the IAP and located in Milan, operating in support of both the Jury and the Control Committee.

Functioning of Self-Regulation

The structure is governed by a code for self-discipline developed along the lines of the ICC Code, but adapted to Italian conditions. In some ways, the Italian code is considered to be stricter than its ICC prototype.

Since the first edition of the code in 1966, there have been sixteen revisions. Besides general rules, this code also covers the advertising of specific kinds of sales, such as credit sales, direct-mail sales, sales of unsolicited goods, special and clearance sales, and sales contests, as well as specific kinds of products such as alcoholic beverages, cosmetics, physical and aesthetic treatments, medicinal products, curative treatments, courses of instruction, methods of study and teaching, financial instruments, real estate, and organized travel tours. Many other provisions were added during the past few years, concerning advertising for children, toys, and dietetic foods.

A regulatory investigation can be initiated in two ways: (1) the Control Committee can initiate an action as a result of its monitoring activity or (2) a complainant, whether consumer, competitor, or any other party, can initiate action by a written request containing a statement of facts. If the complainant is a business firm, the request must be accompanied by a fixed fee.

The Jury and the Control Committee meet as necessary to handle the cases presented to them, usually once or twice a month. Their members operate as independent individuals and not as representatives of the bodies appointing them. Deliberations are conducted in private, and decisions are taken by majority vote. Parties to a dispute are present for the discussion and can be advised or represented by their lawyers. At the request of an interested party, the Control Committee can render an advisory opinion on whether or not a finished-but-not-yet-published piece of advertising violates the code. The committee can invite an advertiser to modify a piece of advertising already published if it is judged not to comply with the rules of the code.

A decision of the Jury is usually issued within a month of initiation of action and is immediately communicated to the interested parties. Within ten days of its decision, the Jury files its verdict in writing with the Secretariat, which then sends a copy to each party concerned and also to the IAP members. The IAP sees that appropriate publicity is given to the Jury's decision. The Jury's decision is final, and has to be enforced. If it confirms that there has been a violation of the code, the advertisement must be stopped at once. To date, all Jury decisions have been adhered to.

The case law developed by the Jury shows not only severity but also a good deal of common sense, based on profound knowledge of social sensitivity and human behavior. On several occasions, the Jury has displayed uncommon open-mindedness and moderation. Thus, the Jury has ruled that advertisements dealing with topical social issues must not be judged to offend the beliefs of a certain part of the public when the message does not suggest any pattern of denigration, depravity, or gratuitous exploitation of the worst aspects of human nature. A similar equanimity has been displayed regarding television campaigns where unruly children were involved, where the Jury has ruled that advertising cannot conceal what happens in everyday life. Also, in the case of commercials containing horrifying characters, the Jury held that self-regulation must not interfere with good or bad taste and has to accept the preferences of a certain part of the public.

Many of the criticisms of the Jury's decisions from advertisers and professionals do not address the core of the problem, which often pertains to the content of the rules rather than the outsiders who apply them.

If the Jury has sometimes gone beyond the traditional limits of advertising self-regulation and has ruled on trademarks or promotions, this must not be ascribed to an abuse of power on the part of outsiders involved in the system but to the Italian Code of Advertising Practice, which gives the broadest possible definition to the term "advertising" as including every form of presenting products to the public, including trademarks, packages and sales promotions.

In addition, the way in which the process works does not depend on outsiders, since they did not establish the procedural rules. The code was set up by the Institute, whose main concern has been to prove that self-regulation works fast and is able to stop a campaign while it is still in progress. Outsiders have tried to temper some of the most controversial aspects of the self-regulatory process by applying many principles borrowed from the Italian Codes of Civil and Penal Procedures. Such principles now form some sort of informal guidelines that are usually followed in the hearings by the Jury, and they help protect some basic guarantees of due process of law.

The Consumer Movement

There are now three major consumer groups in Italy. The participation of outsiders has meant that the self-regulatory rules have been applied with greater severity. This may be noted in the activities of the Control Committee. Independent consumerists play a leading role in this body, which accounts for the strictness and even inflexibility that it displays in carrying out its functions. Advertisers have difficulty negotiating and settling a case by mutual consent with this committee. Consequently, they often prefer to wait until the campaign is referred to the Jury and to face its decision, hoping that it will not be too severe.

As for the Jury, no consumerist influences can be observed. This body is made up principally of experienced jurists of great reputation and is known for its fairness. Yet, broad outside participation means greater severity. Figures show that complaints are upheld by the Jury in about 80 percent of the cases, and only 20 percent of the cases are dismissed. Orders for publication of its decisions have almost quadrupled.

Government Involvement

The government does not interfere in the functioning of the self-regulatory system. Several laws affect advertising, however. Prior to WW II, the Police Law of 1931 required that all advertisements be approved in advance by the Questore (chief of police). At the same time, separate laws were enacted to deal with the advertising of particular types of products or services. The Police Law, as well as a 1936 law establishing a censorship system for the advertising of clearance sales, were repealed after the war.

Other prewar laws have remained in effect, however. The 1934 law on drugs and medical preparations submitted all advertisements for health products to prior authorization by the Ministry of Health. Similar provisions were applied to the advertising of other products and services such as mineral waters, disinfecting detergents, insecticides, medicated toothpastes, medical treatments and services, spas, and physiotherapy treatments. In 1938, the law on premiums, gifts, and competitions made such promotions conditional upon prior authorization by the Ministry of Finance.

Postwar laws have regulated other products. A 1953 decree was enacted to regulate advertising for baby foods and dietetic products. A 1962 law prohibited false and misleading advertising for foodstuffs and beverages. Another banned the advertising of cigarettes and tobacco, mainly to protect local brands, but its enforcement was stepped up in 1982. The marketing of textile products was regulated in 1973, while a 1980 law dealt with the advertising of promotional sales. A 1982 law made the advertising regulations of foodstuffs and beverages conform with EC directives.

In 1990, the Parliament mandated the government to issue by the end of 1991 a law to enforce the EC directive on misleading advertising (EC

Directive No. 84/450 of 10 September 1984). A draft law has proposed the creation of a special government authority to handle misleading advertising. However, this authority would be made to wait for the Jury's decision (around one month) before issuing a judgment. It is the first time in Italy that the self-regulatory system would be made part of a law. On its part, the IAP has put forward a number of proposals to improve this draft law.

Trend

The Italian self-regulatory system keeps enjoying a generally good reputation among consumers. The Control Committee is active in carrying out its tasks. The number of cases handled by the Jury is increasing year by year. With few exceptions, the whole mechanism functions well, so much so that the public does not seem to feel the need for further government regulation of advertising.

Information for this section was supplied by Roberto Cortopassi, director of the Istituto dell'Autodisciplina Pubblicitaria, and by Avv. Maurizio Fusi.

JAPAN

Organizing for Self-Regulation

The central body for self-regulation of advertising is:

The Japan Advertising Review Organization (JARO)
Kosan No. 3 Building
16-7, Ginza 2, Chuo-ku
Tokyo 104

JARO was established in October of 1974 to coordinate the activities of the nine individual self-regulatory bodies existing within the industry. These organizations have dealt with complaints that concern their own areas of specialization:

Advertising Federation of Japan (1953)
4-8-12 Ginza
Kochiwa Building
Tokyo

Japan Advertisers' Association (1957)
4-8-12 Ginza
Kochiwa Building
Tokyo

Japan Advertising Agencies Association (1970)
4-8-12 Ginza
Kochiwa Building
Tokyo

Japan Newspaper Association (1946)
Japan Press Center Building
2-2-1 Uchisaiwai-Cho
Chiyoda-ku
Tokyo

Newspaper Advertising Review Council (1971)
6-7-16 Ginza
Iwatsuki Building
Tokyo

Japan Magazine Advertising Association (1946)
1-7 Surugadai, Kanda
Chiyoda-ku
Tokyo

Japan Commercial Broadcasters Association (1952)
3 Kioicho, Chiyoda-ku
Tokyo

All-Japan Radio and TV Commercial Council (1960)
2-3 Kojimachi
Chiyoda-ku
Hanabusa Building
Tokyo

Federation of All-Japan Outdoor Advertising
Organizations (1958)
1-17-14 Kamezawa
Sumida-ku
Tokyo

Japan Mail Order Association
Mori No. 32 Building
Shiba Park 3-4-30, Minato-ku
Tokyo

Japan Over-the-Counter Drug Industry Association
Honcho 3-9-7, Nihonbashi
Chuo-ku
Tokyo

Japan Association of Travel Agents
Zen-nitsu Building
Kasumigaseki 3-3-3, Chiyoda-ku
Tokyo

Each of the above organizations has its own advertising code. JARO's membership has more than tripled since the inauguration of the organization in 1974. In 1990 alone, more than 40 companies became JARO members. Most of the leading newspapers, magazines, broadcasting companies, advertising agencies, and many of the major advertisers are members of JARO. Recently, its membership included 893 companies, representing the following sectors of the advertising industry:

Advertisers	417
Newspapers	85
Broadcasters	132
Magazines	54
Advertising Agencies	166
Advertising Suppliers	39

Functioning of Self-Regulation

The functions of JARO as an advertising self-regulation body are:

- to assist advertisers, the media, and advertising agencies in their efforts to cooperate with one another on issues relative to self-regulation and the common goal of joint and individual public responsibility
- to protect the interests of consumers by responding to their criticisms, by considering their demands, and by assisting in consumer education in any way that seems appropriate for JARO's breadth of influence
- to undertake the necessary coordination with the government regarding consumer protection policies, while keeping legislative control at a minimum and self-regulation as effective as possible. This is achieved by:
  a. cooperating with the self-regulatory organizations in coordinating the efforts of advertisers, media, and advertising agencies;
  b. developing codes or standards for advertising and labeling;
  c. maintaining cooperation and contact with the related governmental authorities and consumer groups;

d. providing educational activities for business as well as for consumers in general; and

e. establishing JARO as an information center.

JARO consists of a dual system led by a board of directors and review committees, which are connected by a Secretariat. The overall management of JARO is undertaken by its board of directors and subordinate committees of general affairs, finance, and public relations. On the other side, a Final Review Committee, together with a Primary Review Committee and its five subcommittees, deal with complaints from consumers, the business community, the media, and advertising agencies, with the objective of instituting policies of self-regulation in the advertising industry.

Review Structure

JARO's Final Review Committee is operated by a chairman and six committee members, but the chairman of JARO's board of directors, with approval of the board, may commission men of learning and experience from outside the organization to review advertisements and descriptions of a product or service from a neutral, independent and fair-minded point of view.

JARO's Primary Review Committee is composed of well-qualified people selected from among the advertising directors of the regular members of JARO to represent each type of business; the head of this committee is appointed by the chairman of the board. As a group of specialists on advertising, their primary responsibility is in the area of self-regulation, but they also deal with the settlement of specific complaints.

Review Procedure

An office to receive complaints, inquiries, and disputes is established within the Secretariat, where simple cases can be settled directly. Cases that need more than simple clerical settlement are referred to the appropriate advertiser for answer or substantiation. Next, the evidence and the answers submitted by the advertiser are examined, and if the Secretariat finds it impossible to obtain agreement among all parties concerned, the matter is submitted to one of the subcommittees.

At sessions of the subcommittee, the replies from the advertiser or his representative are questioned, and the submitted evidence is reviewed. After deliberating, the subcommittee drafts a recommendation, which is sent to the advertiser and other interested parties. The case is then forwarded to the Primary Review Committee for confirmation.

The Primary Review Committee discusses the matter and the proposed recommendation submitted by the subcommittee. If necessary, a member may be assigned to any problem that requires specialized examination. After a thorough investigation, the Primary Review Committee approves the recommendation under its own name to settle the case; otherwise, it submits its findings to the Final Review Committee.

If one of the parties concerned does not agree with the findings of the Primary Review Committee, the Final Review Committee takes over the case and decides on an appropriate solution.

In 1990, JARO received twenty-nine complaints. They were referred to the Primary Review Committee and settled. On the other hand, 1,978 inquiries were logged that included unqualified complaints and requests for various information and assistance.

The Consumer Movement

There are more than ten national consumer organizations and over 2,000 regional organizations. These groups, as well as individual consumers, can complain to the individual advertising associations concerning specific advertisements. Some of the consumer organizations are in favor of increased direct government regulation. Over 11 million Japanese (10 percent of the population) belong to these groups. The All-Japan Consumers Convention is held once a year to promote the consumer movement.

Consumer groups exert pressure on a government agency or members of Congress concerned with an issue so that it may be handled under a new law or legislation. An example was the Consumer Protection Fundamental Act, which was enacted on the basis of the specific interests and demands of consumer groups. As far as advertising regulation is concerned, however, there have been few cases where the consumer movement successfully led to rule-making by the government.

Several years ago, consumer groups urged the Fair Trade Commission to set regulations on television commercials as a whole. The FTC eventually gave up its rule-making efforts after realizing the benefits of a self-regulatory system by broadcasters versus a strict regulatory system that would have required the FTC to keep a constant watchful eye on broadcasters.

As a result of severe pressure from consumers, the Ministry of International Trade and Industry introduced new advertising and business regulations in the area of mortgage-policy transactions in order to put a stop to a recent wave of fraudulent consumer schemes.

Government Involvement

Government regulatory activities are handled by the Fair Trade Commission and sixteen administrative departments and agencies.

The laws directly relating to the advertising industry can be classified into two groups: general regulatory laws and specific laws applied to industry groups and consumer protection.

General Regulatory Laws. The basic law regulating advertising as a whole in general terms is the Premiums and Representations Act, and it comes under the jurisdiction of the Fair Trade Commission. Enacted in 1962 against unjustifiable premiums and misleading representations, the law is the core of various measures regulating advertising. In 1934, the Act Pertaining to the Prevention of Unfair Competition was enacted. Its purpose is to maintain order in transactions by eliminating false advertising and business practices that might adversely affect competitive enterprises. A third general regulatory law is the Minor Offenses Act. Under this 1948 act, advertising likely to mislead or cheat people concerning merchandise and services is prohibited.

Specific Laws. A number of separate laws and regulations aimed at protecting the interests of consumers relate to advertising in one way or the other. Thus, there are the Drugs, Cosmetics and Medical Instruments Act; the Food Sanitation Act; the Act Pertaining to Transactions for Residential Land and Structures; the Hire-Purchase Act; the Act Relating to Door-to-Door Sales; and the Act Pertaining to Materials for Outdoor Advertising.

Since 1974, ordinances aimed at protecting the interests of consumers have come to be passed by local public entities in various places across the country. Such ordinances are now in effect in thirty-four prefectures and five cities especially designated by a Cabinet order. Most ordinances enacted in recent years contain a clause concerning the proper handling of advertisements.

Trend

In recent years, legal regulations concerning advertising have become quite strict, but the scope of such regulations is limited.

The establishment of rules for self-regulation is essential in the advertising world, which relies on a liberal use of originality to create effective advertisements. Recently, much more importance has been attached to self-regulation, and the number of such voluntary controls has increased yearly. As a result, these self-imposed regulations have become as important as the legal regulations.

Recent pressure from Western countries has forced the Japanese government to deregulate its domestic rules that hamper international trade competition, thereby forcing the advertising industry to respond to this trend. Thus, in response to the Fair Trade Commission's guidelines for comparative advertising issued in 1986, the automobiles, cosmetics, agriculture, and fishing industries revised their rules of fair trade to allow comparative advertising.

Magazine publishers recently withdrew restrictions regarding the use of discount coupons in magazines. Currently, the newspaper industry is looking to follow in the footsteps of the magazine industry by removing the ban on coupon advertising in newspapers.

Recently, local tobacco marketers decided to restrict the amount of television commercials in anticipation of adverse reactions by antismoking interest groups. This self-induced industry regulation has caused much friction between local and foreign tobacco marketers. Foreign tobacco marketers have disregarded these restrictions and are promoting their brands aggressively in all media.

The FTC has modified the premium-offer rules, removing the maximum value limit (10 percent of the price of the good) of a premium item offered, as long as it is the same as the product that is being advertised. The ceiling was also lifted on the compensation amount of sales competitions offered to retailers by manufacturers. More than four dozen of the Fair Trade Rules will be modified to accommodate these new changes. Currently, the industry is adjusting to this new move toward more self-regulation combined with government deregulation.

On March 1, 1991, advertising for banks on television was voluntarily deregulated, and advertisements for a single banking institution are now allowed, besides the previously authorized cooperative ads—it does not have to be for a co-op anymore. However, the time for each bank is still limited to 375 seconds a month, or 2,700 seconds a year; and the sponsoring of any TV program is forbidden. Now, banks are also allowed to use any new media without the approval of the National Federation of Bank Associations. Advertising for banks on radio has been free since 1990.

As a result of U.S.–Japan Structural Impediments Initiatives, the maximum value of premiums given to consumers was raised in nine industries: biscuit, chocolate, chewing gum, dog food, curry and pepper, camera manufacturing, camera wholesaling, processed tofu, and newspaper coupon-advertising. This was achieved by revising the Fair Competition Rules of these industries.

Information for this section was supplied by Chiaki Shimada of the Japan Advertising Review Organization's public-relations unit.

REPUBLIC OF KOREA

Organizing for Self-Regulation

Although the advertising industry lacks a single self-regulatory body, two separate industry associations do exist and regulate their own activities quite rigorously. They are as follows:

Broadcasting Advertising Review Committee, Korea Broadcasting
  Commission
The Korea Press Center
25 Taepyongro 1-ka, Chung-ku
Seoul

The Korea Press Ethics Commission
The Korea Press Center
25 Taepyongro 1-ka, Chung-ku
Seoul

The Korean Broadcasting Commission (KBC) was established under
the Korea Broadcasting Law (No. 3978, 28 November 1987) and its Enforcement Decree (No. 12432 Presidential Order, 19 April 1988). KBC is
comprised of twelve members, four of whom are proposed by the speaker
of the Congress, four by the government, and four by the chief justice of
the Supreme Court. The chairperson of KBC appoints thirty broadcasting
review committee members. Nine of these serve on the Broadcasting Advertising Review Committee comprised of academics in mass communication as well as representatives from the advertising industry, consumer
organizations, the pharmaceutical industry, and youth-guidance organizations. The Broadcasting Advertising Review Committee meets twice a
week to preview all radio and television commercials. This preview is
mandatory.

Advertising in newspapers is subject to voluntary self-regulation administered by the Korea Press Ethics Commission. This commission is
comprised of a board of directors and an Ethics Committee. The board
consists of senior members of the mass media and academicians. The
board has a rather ceremonial function when it comes to newspaper advertising ethics. The Ethics Committee consists of a chairperson and
twelve other members. The thirteen members hold tenure for two years.
The Chairperson is chosen from the Korea Bar Association. Two members
each are drawn from the Korea Newspaper Publishers Association, the
Korea Newspaper Editors Association, the Korea Journalists Association,
the National Assembly, and writers. One member is also chosen from both
the Korea Federation of Educators and the Korea Newspaper Advertising
Directors Council.

The Ethics Committee holds a monthly meeting to discuss and study
cases presented to it by a permanent deliberation committee. It makes
final decisions about both newspaper editorial matters and advertising.

The Consumer Movement

The National Council of Consumer Protection Organizations, comprised of nine associations, leads the consumer movement on matters

relating to advertising. The most active are the Young Women's Christian Association, the Citizens' Alliance for the Consumer Protection of Korea, the Consumers Union of Korea, and the Korean Women's Association. Their concerns about advertising range from the use of women in advertising to misleading pharmaceutical advertising. The consumer movement receives continuous support from the daily press.

Government Involvement

By law, the amount of broadcast time allocated to commercials is limited to 8 percent of the total broadcasting hours. The Fair Trade Commission, under the Economic Planning Board, reviews unfair trade practices, including advertising and sales-promotion activities. The Home Ministry regulates conditions for outdoor advertising. The Consumer Protection Board (CPB), established in 1987, also monitors trade practices, including advertising operating under the rules of the Consumer Advice Division. The CPB, however, has no legal power.

Trend

The advertising industry perceives some need for a self-regulatory body governing print media. The overall trend appears to be toward less government regulation and more self-regulation. Further unified actions by the advertising industry to organize self-regulation are required, however.

Information for this section was supplied by In Sup Shin, group media director of Korad Ogilvy & Mather.

LUXEMBOURG

Organizing for Self-Regulation

There is no voluntary self-regulation in Luxembourg. The advertising sector in this country is little structured, with no professional association in that field.

Government Involvement

Restriction comes from the government, which passed a law on November 27, 1986, regulating various commercial practices and penalizing "unfair competition." This expression refers to "honest practices" that attempt or result in taking away a competitor's clientele or in harming its competitive ability.

That law applies to any advertisement inciting actions considered to amount to unfair competition as enumerated in its Title II, Section 1— even if the action on which the advertisement is based has taken place in a country where it is allowed. This law also forbids comparison advertising.

The agency that aired the ad is held responsible in case of conflict. If this agency is not located in Luxembourg, the editor or distributor of the ad in Luxembourg can be incriminated.

There are also laws bearing on the advertising of tobacco products, medicinal products, and foodstuffs. A 1991 law on the electronic media rules the Radio Television Luxembourg (RTL) Company, which also obeys the laws and voluntary restrictions of the countries to which its commercials are broadcast.

Information in this section was supplied by Emmanuel Servais, inspecteur principal, Ministère d'Etat in Luxembourg City.

MALAYSIA

Organizing for Self-Regulation

The body governing self-regulation in Malaysia is:

> The Advertising Standards Authority Malaysia
> c/o Corporate Secretarius Sdn. Bhd.
> Goonting & Chew Management Consultants Sdn. Bhd.
> Lot 403, 4th Floor, Wisma Mirama
> Jalan Wisma Putra
> 50460 Kuala Lumpur

The Advertising Standards Authority was established in 1974 as a voluntary body by the Malaysian Advertisers Association, the Association of Accredited Advertising Agents Malaysia, and the Malaysian Newspaper Publishers Association.

The self-regulatory body's main functions are to monitor advertisements to ensure that they conform to accepted norms, and to adjudicate complaints.

Functioning of Self-Regulation

The Malaysian Code of Advertising Practice, administered by the Advertising Standards Authority Malaysia, is a fundamental part of the system of control by which Malaysian advertising regulates its activities. The code is supplemented by special conditions imposed by individual media. Television and radio have their own codes and are under the control of Radio Television Malaysia (RTM), which is under the Ministry of Information.

The Authority maintains close contact with central and local government departments, consumer organizations, and trade associations; and it deals with complaints received through them or directly from the public. In the event that an advertisement is found to violate the provisions of the code, advertising space or time is withheld from the advertisers.

The Consumer Movement

The Consumers Association of Penang is a major consumer organization in Malaysia, but it has had little influence in the regulation of advertising.

Government Involvement

The following are the major laws and legislation regarding the regulation of advertising. The Trade Description Act of 1972 is aimed at the prevention of goods being incorrectly named, described, or portrayed. The Trade Description Act of 1987 regulates cheap sales. It makes it mandatory to provide for a fixed period of time during which stocks must be available. In 1952, the Lotteries Act established guidelines under which lotteries may be held (e.g., license must be obtained). Games of chance are prohibited.

According to food regulations passed in 1985, no copy text can make any advertising claim. All texts must be descriptive of what the product is, with a full description of ingredients, manufacturer's name and address, and the expiration date. In 1984, Guidelines for Medicines Advertising were enacted. These include guidelines laid down by the board of advertising of the Ministry of Health. It is applicable mainly to the pharmaceutical industry and is designed to protect the public from misleading claims.

Trend

Currently, advertising regulations in Malaysia are heavily influenced by politically based national aspirations and Islamic principles.

Information for this section was supplied by the Corporate Secretarius Sdn. Bhd. of the Advertising Standards Authority of Malaysia.

NETHERLANDS

Organizing for Self-Regulation

Until 1987, the regulatory and complaint-handling functions for television and radio advertising self-regulation were exercised by the Reclameraad (Advertising Council), the partly state-controlled broadcasting authority, and by the self-regulatory Stichting Reclame Code (SRC, Advertising Code Foundation), which, through its Reclame Code Commissie (Advertising Code Commission), handled all other media. Due to the introduction of new media legislation, the Reclameraad ceased to exist in January 1988, and its regulatory and complaint-handling functions were taken over by the SRC.

Stichting Reclame Code
Paasheuvelweg 15
1105 BE Amsterdam

The SRC is the parent organization for the various code commissions that operate within its structure. The first such commission was formed in 1964. Today, the Advertising Code Commission operates in four sections: one for direct marketing, one for broadcast advertising, and two for all other media. The commissions are made up of representatives from all sectors of the advertising industry, plus consumer representatives from eleven organizations, including:

- Dutch Advertisers Association
- Direct Marketing Institute
- Television and Radio Advertising Foundation (STER)
- Cinema Advertising Organizations
- Dutch Advertising Agencies Association
- Daily Press Association
- Magazines Association
- Consumentenbond
- Konsumenten Kontakt

In practice, the Advertising Code Commission members, nominated by their respective organizations, participate on a rotating basis, functioning as a committee of five members with a chairperson who is a professional judge.

Functioning of Self-Regulation

Regulations are based on the Dutch Advertising Code, adapted from the ICC International Code of Advertising Practice. Inquiries can be initiated on the basis of complaints. A Secretariat reviews such complaints and asks for the advertiser's point of view. If the complaint is found valid and the advertiser refuses to withdraw or modify the advertisement, the relevant commission can make a public recommendation, as well as a recommendation that the advertisement not be accepted by the media. The norm, however, is that the commission will make a private recommendation before a public one is made. The agencies, the daily press, and all print and audiovisual media have agreed to accept the rulings of the commission as binding. If a complainant or advertiser finds a ruling unsatisfactory, he can put his case before a body of appeal (College van Beroep).

The Code of Broadcast Advertising, drawn up by the former Reclameraad, has been integrated into the SRC's Dutch Advertising Code as of 1992. The Television and Radio Advertising Foundation (STER) has become a member and cofinancier of SRC. As mentioned above, complaints are dealt with by a separate Committee for Broadcast Advertising. The Television and Radio Advertising Foundation has agreed, however, to comply with the recommendations of the Code Commission, and it continues to review commercials prior to broadcast.

Special codes have been developed with the cooperation of particular industries (alcohol, tobacco, sugar confectioneries, direct marketing, and casino gambling). Fines and corrective advertisements may be imposed in cases of violation of these special codes.

A separate self-regulatory body (Keuringsraad Openbare Aanprijzing Geneesmiddelen/Keuringsraad Aanprijzing Medische Aspecten) exists to check, prior to publication, advertisements for pharmaceutical products, medical claims, and general health claims for all products. Members of the body include advertisers, advertising agencies, members of the pharmaceutical industry, and individuals from the print media industry.

The Consumer Movement

The two leading consumer organizations, the Consumentenbond (Consumers Union) and Konsumenten Kontakt (Consumers Contact), participate in the structure and functioning of the SRC and, at the same time, maintain their own role as protectors of the consumer interest.

Government Involvement

The Dutch government participates strongly in the regulation of advertising via a variety of statutes, legislative actions, and ministerial rulings empowered by statute. While a competitor or consumer in the Netherlands can go to the extreme of taking an advertiser to court for "misleading advertising" with the allegation that such advertising has caused him "economic damage," this kind of recourse to the judiciary is rare.

Trend

In view of impending legislation regarding alcohol and tobacco, the SRC has refined the existing self-regulatory codes for alcohol and tobacco advertising.

Information in this section was supplied by Dr. G. J. Ribbink, Secretary of Nederlandse Vereniging van Erkende Reclame-Adviesbureaus and T. I. Kamphuisen-van der Schaaf, former director of the Stichting Reclame Code.

NEW ZEALAND

Organizing for Self-Regulation

The organizations responsible for self-regulation in New Zealand are the Advertising Standards Authority and the Advertising Standards Complaints Board:

> Advertising Standards Authority (ASA)
> P.O. Box 10-675
> Wellington 1
>
> Advertising Standards Complaints Board (ASCB)
> P.O. Box 10-675
> Wellington 1

The ASA is made up of all the media bodies in New Zealand, print and electronic, and it is widening its membership to include outdoor and direct marketing. It also includes advertiser and agency associations:

- Television New Zealand Ltd.
- Radio New Zealand Ltd.
- TV3 Ltd.
- Newspaper Publishers' Association of New Zealand
- Advertising Agencies Association of New Zealand
- Independent Broadcasters' Association
- Magazine Publishers' Association

- Association of New Zealand Advertisers
- Community Newspapers Association
- Cinema Advertising Council of New Zealand

The ASA was formed in 1973 as the industry's self-regulatory body. Its main functions are (1) to encourage self-regulation in all advertising matters by media and advertising groups, (2) to maintain generally accepted standards for advertising, ensuring that advertising is not misleading or deceptive, either by statement or implication, and (3) where appropriate, to introduce codes of advertising practice for specific categories of advertising.

Besides the general Advertising Code of Ethics, there are now codes regulating liquor and cigarette advertising, baldness or hair-loss claims, driving and petrol consumption claims, financial advertising, and the way people are portrayed in advertising. Slimming or weight-loss claims, the reproduction of banknote images, farm-safety, and environmental claims are also covered by various codes.

The role of ASA has been expanded with its establishment of the Advertising Standards Complaints Board (ASCB) in 1988. Its main functions are:

- to adjudicate on complaints received about advertisements or commercials that may be in breach of the ASA's codes of advertising practice;
- to advise ASA on the interpretation and possible improvement of the codes; and
- to report to ASA on any aspect of advertising that is causing concern.

The key feature of the ASCB is that four of its eight members, including the chairperson, are public representatives with no connection to the media or advertising groups. This public representation is further endorsed by allowing the chairperson, where appropriate, the right to cast a vote.

Functioning of Self-Regulation

Complaints can be introduced to the Advertising Standards Complaints Board by consumers, consumer organizations, competing advertisers, trade associations, governmental bodies, and the media.

Complaints should be addressed directly to the secretary of the Advertising Standards Complaints Board. Complaints must be submitted in writing and signed. The complainant must supply a copy of the advertisement, or indicate where it can be located or observed. The chairperson then determines whether the complaint is within the Complaints Board's jurisdiction. If it is, opinions and comments are sought from all parties concerned. Last, the ASCB determines whether the codes of advertising practice have been contravened, and all parties are informed of the outcome. Sanctions normally involve modification or withdrawal of the ad. Before accepting jurisdiction, the ASCB requires an agreement from the complainant that the complaint will not be pursued in any other forum.

In addition to the ASA, the main media bodies have their own self-regulatory review systems.

The Consumer Movement

Consumers are active in New Zealand, and they have formed various groups to protect their interests. The main one, the Consumers' Institute, publishes reports outlining good values, ratings of products, and so on. The major consumer-oriented groups are the Ministry of Women's Affairs, the Ministry of Consumer Affairs, the Department of Health, the Consumers' Institute, the Broadcasting Standards Authority, the Alcohol Liquor Advertising Council, the Ministry of Transport, and the Ministry of the Environment.

Government Involvement

Apart from the Fair Trading Act of 1986, there are regulations prohibiting the advertising of certain products in the media. All tobacco advertising was banned in 1990 by the Smoke-free Environments Bill, including point-of-sale advertising. Brand-liquor advertising is now allowed on television, as well as liquor sponsorship advertising, albeit under very strict rules.

Trend

Self-regulation is growing, with groups like the Ministry of Women's Affairs and the Ministry of Consumer Affairs maintaining a monitoring role. There is increased pressure against liquor advertising, as well as about the way women, children, and minority groups as well as environmental and green claims are presented in advertising. The statutory body that controls broadcast program and advertising standards, the Broadcasting Authority, is now investigating liquor sponsorship advertising on television and radio.

Information in this section was supplied by Chris R. Ineson, executive director of the Advertising Agencies' Association of New Zealand (Wellington).

NIGERIA

Organizing for Self-Regulation

The self-regulatory body for advertising in Nigeria is the following:

Association of Advertising Practitioners of Nigeria (AAPN)
18 Amore Street, Ikeja
P.M.B. 1054, Ebute-Metta
Lagos

Established in 1972, the Association of Advertising Practitioners of Nigeria is comprised of advertising agencies. The main objective of the association is to promote and advance the effective management of advertising through a code of conduct established in the best interest of the industry and the public, the Nigerian Code of Advertising Practice. No other individual industry groups have codes of professional behavior or standards of practice that deal with advertising.

Functioning of Self-Regulation

One of the main activities of the Association of Advertising Practitioners of Nigeria is adjudicating complaints. They can be introduced to the complaint-handling body by consumers, consumer organizations, competing advertisers, trade associations, governmental bodies, the media, or the self-regulatory body itself as a result of its own monitoring.

In the event that a complaint is made against an advertisement, the agency handling the account will be identified, whether or not it is a member agency. If it is a member agency, the Professional Practices Subcommittee investigates the complaint and makes its findings and recommendations known to the Executive Committee of the AAPN, which in turn acts on these findings and recommendations. In most cases, evidence from all sides concerned is taken into consideration.

If an advertisement is found in violation of existing statutes and regulations, the committee may (1) issue cautions, warnings, or reprimands as the committee considers necessary, (2) require from such member any specific or general undertaking as to such practitioner's future conduct, (3) recommend the termination or suspension of the membership of any such practitioners, and/or (4) publish notice of any such action taken by the committee.

The Professional Practices Subcommittee and the Executive Committee determine what measures a member must take to reverse a termination or suspension of membership. Appeals related to any decision of the Professional Practices Subcommittee must be filed within thirty days of such decision to the Executive Committee and within a further thirty days thereafter to a general conference of the AAPN. In proceedings before the Executive Committee or the General Conference, legal representations are not allowed.

The Consumer Movement

At present, there are no important consumer groups exercising influence over advertising regulatory activity.

Government Involvement

Various advertising practices come within the province of The Companies Act of 1968 — for example, Sections 44 and 45 make it illegal to publish a prospectus for the sale of slaves, and to promote securities through false statements or misrepresentations. The Sale of Goods Law of 1973 of Lagos State contains several provisions for the protection of consumers from false or misleading advertising.

The Food and Drugs Act of 1974 particularly regulates the advertisement of foods, drugs, and cosmetics. The Special Military Tribunal Decrees of 1986 (Miscellaneous Offenses Amendment) prohibits the advertisement of adulterated petroleum products, food or drink, and the advertisement of prohibited goods. In addition, the Enabling Law Decree for the Advertising Practitioners Council of Nigeria (APCON) empowers APCON to regulate and control the practice of advertising in all its aspects and ramifications.

Information in this section was supplied by Chief O. O. Odukoya, administrative secretary of the Association of Advertising Practitioners of Nigeria.

NORWAY

Organizing for Self-Regulation

The activities that fall under a self-regulatory structure in other countries are fulfilled by a consumer-ombud system instituted by law in Norway in January 1973. The consumer ombudsman (Forbrukerombudet), who functions independently, is actually a government functionary.

Functioning of Self-Regulation

The self-regulatory functions in Norway are handled by three bodies: the Bureau for Legal Affairs in Marketing, the Better Business Council, and the Norwegian Association of Advertising Agencies.

Bureau for Legal Affairs in Marketing (Naeringslivets Servicekontor for Markedsrett). This private bureau provides extensive services, giving advice and recommendations as to how regulations (under the 1972 act that instituted the ombud sytem) should be interpreted, when applied to specific cases of proposed advertisements. The Bureau assists in negotiating with the consumer ombudsman and government agencies. The registered subscribers of the Bureau are also invited to a number of seminars, lectures, and meetings. The Bureau distributes a news bulletin and publishes the reference book *Rett og Kutyme i Markdsforingen* as well as other materials relating to marketing law.

The Bureau for Legal Affairs in Marketing was established by the Norwegian Marketing Federation (Norges Marketsforbund). Later on, the Federation of Norwegian Industries (today called the Confederation of Norwegian Business and Industry) joined. The Norwegian Bankers Association (Dennorske Bankforening), the Norwegian Savings Banks Association (Sparebankforeningen i Norge), and the Federation of Norwegian Commercial Associations (Norges Handelsstands Forbund) are now also co-owners.

A large number of Norwegian companies, including most of the advertising agencies, subscribe to the services of the Bureau. The registered subscribers pay an annual fee, with additional fees for more extensive services. They automatically obtain advice by telephone on questions regarding marketing law. Nonregistered subscribers may also receive assistance, but they must pay higher fees, including a fee for telephone consultations.

The Better Business Council (Konkurranseutvalget). This council, created in 1970, is concerned with competitive disputes between firms, including those that involve advertising. It is sponsored by its member associations, which are represented on the council. These associations include the Norwegian Marketing Federation, other business federations, and private and cooperative commercial associations.

In addition to general principles and practices of good marketing and advertising behavior, the Better Business Council bases its activities on the Marketing Law of 1972. The complaint-handling process is wholly based on written statements from the parties involved in each dispute.

It should be noted that, within advertising agencies that are members of the Norwegian Advertising Agencies Association, one executive is assigned to review and approve every advertisement produced to ensure that it is in accordance with the law. As a visible sign of this verification, each advertisement includes the letters "RRA." This "responsible executive" is expected to be well-versed in both the provisions of the law and the decisions made since passage of the legislation. The Bureau for Legal Affairs in Marketing is the main source for information in this connection.

The Norwegian Association of Advertising Agencies (RF). The RF is a self-regulatory body governing all its member agencies and their advertising practices. The association's Ethics Committee rules on all questions of ethics in advertising on the basis of the association's own Code of Ethics, the ICC codes, and Norwegian laws. Its rulings are binding for the members, and may include measures such as fines or loss of membership.

The Consumer Movement

There are three consumer representatives on the Market Council (see below). At present, there is one major consumer group in Norway, the Consumer Council (Forbrukerradet). Currently, this group is not proposing anything in particular in the way of further regulation of advertising. Still, the consumer ombudsman has recently asked the legislature for the power to enforce fines automatically when the law is broken in serious cases.

Government Involvement

In June 1972, the Act for Control of Marketing Practices was passed by the Norwegian Parliament. It took effect in January 1973. The law bears upon all kinds of marketing practices, including advertising communications. It replaced a law dating from 1922, which concentrated chiefly on the regulation of competitive disputes. The 1972 act places increased emphasis on consumer protection, particularly as it involves the truth, fairness, and adequacy of advertising information.

The act introduced two supervisory bodies: (1) the consumer ombudsman as investigator and arbitrator and (2) the Market Council, which has the power of a court of law. Both are state-financed agents of the government. These two bodies have in practice taken over all functions of advertising regulation, except those of review prior to publication and of business-to-business conflicts, which are handled, as explained above, by institutions set up by business.

The consumer ombudsman is assisted by a staff that receives complaints from consumers, competitors, and public-interest organizations, concerning advertising and marketing activities. The ombudsman is also responsible for continuously monitoring advertising campaigns and marketing practices. Where advertising does not conform to the Marketing Practices Act, the ombudsman negotiates with the advertiser to bring about its modification or termination. The ombudsman has no enforcement power, except where urgent need justifies issuing a direct injunction, which can be appealed.

The Market Council is the body to which the ombudsman refers matters not settled through negotiation and to which injunctions are appealed. Its nine members are appointed by the King-in-Council and include three business members, three consumer members, and three representatives of other interests such as the judiciary, science, and government. The Market Council has the legal power to prohibit any advertising contrary to the Marketing Practices Act and thus deemed to be against the consumer interest. Deliberate violation of the Marketing Practices Act is punishable by fines or imprisonment.

An important aspect of the Norwegian system is the "negative burden of proof," whereby the advertiser under investigation is required to substantiate that the charges against the advertisement are without merit.

A recent amendment to the Marketing Act allows the consumer ombudsman to bring cases before the Market Court even after an advertisement has been discontinued. Tobacco and liquor advertising have been banned for quite some time.

Trend

The advertising industry of Norway has accepted the market-control system created by the Stortinget (Norway's Parliament). However, some possible modifications of the system in the direction of increased self-regulation are foreseen.

Information in this section was supplied by Svein Erik Andersen, president of the Norwegian Association of Advertising Agencies, and by Kjell Salbu, director of Norges Markedsforbund.

PERU

Organizing for Self-Regulation

Self-regulation of advertising in Peru falls under the authority of:

Consejo Nacional de Publicidad (CONAPU)
(National Advertising Council)
Alberto Lynch 164
Lima 27

CONAPU was formed in 1986; it is currently awaiting official recognition from the government. Four members comprise the self-regulatory body:

- Asociacion de Realizadores de Comerciales (ARCO) (Commercials Producers Association)
- Asociacion de Publicitarios (Association of the Advertising Industry)
- Asociation Peruana de Agencias de Publicidad (APAP) (Advertising Agencies Association)
- Asociacion de Anunciantes de Peru (AAP) (Advertisers Association)

CONAPU bases its activities on the Codigo de Etica Publicitaria (Code of Advertising Ethics), which closely follows the codes of other countries. The main functions of CONAPU include lobbying government bodies and handling complaints.

The main advertising associations involved in self-regulation are as follows:

>Asociacion de Anunciantes de Peru
>(Advertisers Association of Peru)
>Ap. 3848
>Lima 100

>Asociacion Peruana de Agencias de Publicidad
>(Advertising Agencies Association of Peru)
>Alberto Lynch 164
>Lima 27

Functioning of Self-Regulation

Complaints can be introduced to CONAPU by consumers, consumer organizations, competing advertisers, trade associations, government bodies, the media, and CONAPU itself as a result of its own monitoring.

Complaints are directed to the Ethics Committee of CONAPU. This committee investigates and confronts all parties involved (if necessary) within a few weeks of receiving the complaint.

In the event that an advertisement is found to violate the provisions of the Code, CONAPU seeks to have the advertisement modified, recommends that the media refuse the advertisement, publicizes the case with or without the name of the advertiser, and/or notifies the government. The advertiser has the right to appeal to CONAPU's Directive Committee.

The Consumer Movement

Peruvians do not have much information about self-regulation and consumer-protection groups, and the work of the government is just beginning. The major consumer groups are the Asociacion de Consumidores de Lince (Lima); Asociacion de Consumidores y Usuarios (Lima); Organizacion de Consumidores y Usuarios (Lima); Instituto de Estudios del

Consumidor—IEC (Lima); and Asociacion de Protección del Consumidor (Arequipa).

These groups are trying to form a coalition to better protect consumer rights. In the first quarter of 1991, the IEC introduced successfully legal petitions against five companies because of their false and misleading advertising. These initiatives marked the beginning of the consumer movement in Peru, but the government's CONASUP unit is now the main agent in protecting consumers, as far as advertising is concerned.

Government Involvement

A consumer-protection law was passed in 1983 (Decreto Supremo No. 036-83-Jus). Protection of the consumer fell under the authority of the Ministerio de Industria, Commercio Interior, Turismo e Integracion's Direccion General de Defensa del Consumidor, which was formed in 1987. This Directorate General was dedicated to give consumers all the necessary information about their rights and the way the law protects them, but it was eliminated in 1990.

An advertising law was enacted in 1981 (Decreto Supremo No. 002-81-OCI/OAJ). This law ordered that complaints should be presented to the Instituto Nacional de Comunicación Social (INACOMS), which provided an inexpensive and fast procedure. However, this administrative authority was also abolished, in 1991.

The amended Criminal Code (Codigo Penal, Decreto Legislativo 635) of April 3, 1991, prescribes in its Articles 238 and 239 that false advertising constitutes an economic crime, while Article 240 covers cases of confusion and denigration in advertising. Complaints must now be introduced before a criminal court rather than an administrative body (like the former INACOMS). Judiciary procedures, however, are long and expensive, and judges are often not familiar with advertising matters.

New advertising rules to protect consumers were enacted on November 5, 1991 (Normas de Publicidad en Defensa del Consumidor, Decreto Legislativo 691). It contains thirty-one articles, prescribing among others that advertising practice must respect the Constitution and the law (Art. 3), that advertisements cannot be false or misleading (Art. 4), that advertisements must respect the rules of fair (loyal) market competition (Art. 7), and that comparison advertising is authorized (Art. 8).

Advertising matters now fall under the administrative authority of the Consejo (Council) Nacional de Supervision de la Publicidad (CONASUP) within the Ministry of Industry, Domestic Commerce, Tourism, and Integration. CONASUP has the powers to warn, to issue cease-and-desist injunctions, to fine, and to order corrective advertisements (Art. 16). Recourse to CONASUP is inexpensive and fast. Its Directorate includes six members: two from government, two from the advertising industry, and two from the consumer movement (Art. 27).

There are also new consumer-protection rules (Normas sobre Protección al Consumidor, Decreto Legislativo 716 of November 9, 1991). Title IV (Articles 15-23) deals with the information to be provided in connection with the offer of goods and services, including the requirement that advertisements must be truthful. This legislative decree is also administered by the Ministry of Industry, Domestic Commerce, Tourism, and Integration under its Directorate General for Consumer Protection, which can advise and penalize business firms under simple and fast administrative procedures.

All advertising materials must be produced in Peru and in Spanish. New advertising systems cannot be patented, but advertising copy and illustrations may be copyrighted. In addition, foods and drugs are ruled by a governmental entity similar to the U.S. Food and Drug Administration. This entity preauthorizes all advertising material for these products. Producers are allowed to conduct promotions, subject to governmental authorization and the payment of corresponding taxes. Food and drug manufacturers may not conduct promotions, however. Outdoor advertising (posters, billboards, etc.) is regulated by municipal governments.

The govenment owns or controls Channel 7 TV and Radio Nacional and the newspaper *El Peruano*.

Trend

CONAPU is still awaiting formal recognition from the government. It provides, however, a major recourse for any advertising issue, and the government is now relying considerably on CONAPU to settle these issues.

Information in this section was supplied by Eduardo Orbegoso, former president of the Asociacion de Anunciantes de Peru, and it was updated by Crisológo Cáceres Valle of the Instituto de Estudios del Consumidor (IEC).

PHILIPPINES

Organizing for Self-Regulation

The central organization for voluntary self-regulation of the advertising industry in the Philippines is the following:

Advertising Board of the Philippines (Adboard)
Second Floor, L&F Building
107 Aguirre Street, Legaspi Village
Makati, Metro Manila

Adboard is a unified organization that dates back to 1974. It consists of advertising practitioners from various national associations. Participating organizations include the following:

- Philippine Association of National Advertisers (PANA). This is the association of domestic and transnational corporations (with a recent membership of 217 companies) which manufacture and market nationally advertised brands.
- Association of Accredited Advertising Agencies—Philippines (4 As). It includes sixty-one of the leading and well-established professional agencies.
- Association of Broadcasters in the Philippines (KBP). It includes the major radio and television stations/networks (101).
- Print Media Organization (PRIMO). Print marketing executives from 24 of the leading nationally circulated newspapers/magazines comprise PRIMO.
- Outdoor Advertising Association of the Philippines (OAAP). This body includes 36 major outdoor-sign companies represented by their owners or general managers.
- Cinema Advertising Association of the Philippines (CAAP). The 5 major cinema-commercial bookers are in CAAP.
- Advertising Suppliers Association of the Philippines (ASAP). The ASAP includes major accredited suppliers for advertising services (printers/typesetters, production houses, audio-video processors, photographers, talent agencies, etc.).
- Marketing & Opinion Research Society of the Philippines (MORES). This is the professional association of 58 marketing and opinion-research specialists from the country's principal research firms and national marketing companies.
- Public Relations Society of the Philippines (PRSP). It is comprised of 115 company members and independent public-relations practitioners.

Functioning of Self-Regulation

The main objectives of the Adboard are to promote the development of the advertising industry through self-regulation and in harmony with national goals and to institute reforms and enhance professional standards.

In April 1976, the Adboard promulgated and adopted a code of ethics, rules, and regulations for advertising and sales promotions. The code was last revised in October 1990.

The Adboard operates primarily through its four Professional Practice Committees. The Advertising Content Regulation Committee (ACRC) interprets and implements provisions of the Code of Ethics that bear on advertising content. The Trade Practices and Conduct Committee (TPCC) formulates, interprets, and implements intersectoral and interassociation agreements relating to advertising trade practices and conduct. The Research Committee (RC) undertakes the gathering, processing, and dissemination of data and information relating to the advertising industry.

The Industry Development Committee (IDC) develops, maintains, and implements programs aimed at maximizing the growth potential of the advertising industry.

Alleged or potential violations of the Code of Ethics are presented to a Screening Panel of the Advertising Content Regulation Committee (ACRC), or to the ACRC itself. It is composed of members from the three sectors represented in the Adboard, namely advertisers, advertising agencies, and media.

Complaints leading to investigations normally originate from three main sources—an advertiser's competitors, the government passing along constituent complaints, and the Adboard ACRC/screening committee, which prescreens or postscreens about three hundred broadcast commercials each month.

The Consumer Movement

At the present there are three active consumer groups in the Philippines—Kapinsanan na Mamimili sa Pilipinas (Philippine Buyers Association) in charge of consumer protection, the Consumer Union of the Philippines Association, and the Consumers Federated Groups of the Philippines.

Government Involvement

The Adboard has maintained excellent relations with the Department of Trade and Industry's Bureau of Domestic Trade, and with the Department of Health, particularly the Bureau of Food and Drugs. Informal consultations take place about complaints received by these bureaus and transmitted by them to Adboard. The departments are also consulted about Adboard Code revisions and regulatory proposals. Government officials used to sit on Adboard screening panels but no longer do. The Bureau of Food and Drugs is supposed to approve all relevant advertisements but, in fact, has delegated this task to the Adboard. More significant is the bureaus' basic trust in the Adboard and its functions. According to the Bureau of Domestic Trade, the government hardly intervenes because the Adboard has done a good job policing its members. Government action is a last resort.

Various bills have been introduced in both the Senate and House of Representatives to ban the advertising of tobacco and alcohol products as well as outdoor advertising along national highways; to require health warnings and government preclearance in the case of food, drug, and cosmetic ads; to restrict television advertising, and even to create a Philippine Advertising Council or a Consumers Board of Advertising, involving consumer representatives. No regulatory changes, however, have been made to date.

Information in this section was supplied by Vivian T. Tomada, executive secretary of the Association of Accredited Advertising Agencies—Philippines; Stella S. Villegas, executive director of the Advertising Board of the Philippines (Adboard); Ruben Nuñez, executive director of the previous Philippine Board of Advertising; and Chérie Mijares, vice-president of Corporate Affairs at Advertising and Marketing Associates (Manila).

PORTUGAL

Organizing for Self-Regulation

The Portuguese Association of Advertising Agencies (APAP) has been operational since 1978. It was first made up of full-service agencies, but it has recently changed its statutes so that different kinds of companies can be included: direct marketing, sales promotion, public relations, institutional communication, creativity, and media management.

> Associação Portuguesa das Agencias de Publicidade (APAP)
> Rua Rodrigo de Fonseca 204-4-D
> 1000 Lisbon

Until recently, there was no self-regulatory system. But the APAP, together with the Portuguese Association of Advertisers, the media, and consumer associations established an advertising self-regulatory system (ICAP) in October 1991. It is composed of advertisers, advertising agencies, media, and consumer members.

> Instituto Civil da Autodisciplina da Publicidade (ICAP)
> (Civil Institute for Advertising Self-regulation)
> Avenida da Republica, 62F, 6°
> 1000 Lisbon

The creation of ICAP was encouraged by the Secretary of State for Social Communication as an effort to deregulate the industry and to reduce delays in court actions. ICAP has issued a Code of Conduct based on the International Chamber of Commerce code. It is ruled by a Management Body consisting of one advertiser, one advertising agency, and one media representative. There is also a Jury made up of these three members and chaired by a well-known lawyer. A junior lawyer provides the Secretariat. The Jury provides prepublication advice and investigates complaints on the basis of the Code of Conduct.

The Consumer Movement

There are two consumer organizations. According to law, there is an Advertising Council where the whole range of interests bearing on advertising is represented, including those of the consumer groups. In general, consumer groups want more regulations, and current laws are being revised to handle consumer complaints.

Government Involvement

Government legislation has emphasized consumer protection through the use of correct descriptive labeling, the size of lettering in clearly defined proportions, the definition of product ingredients, the specification of weights, and so on. A new Advertising Code was legislated on October 23, 1990.

Alcohol advertising is restricted; there are specific laws banning the advertising of medicine, medical treatments, and pharmaceutical products; the promotion of tobacco products has been banned since 1983; and car advertising is restricted by law. Advertising to children is restricted, as are political and religious advertising, pornography, sexism, and the use of foreign idioms.

Investigations are carried out by the National Institute for Consumer Protection. Proceedings can be initiated following a complaint by a member of the public or by the Advertising Council, a body under the authority of the Secretary of State for the Environment.

Trend

Currently, television stations and some newspapers are government-owned but this situation will soon change. Two or three private television channels will be available.

Information in this section was supplied by Nuno Tavora, executive secretary of Associação Portuguesa das Agencias de Publicidade.

SINGAPORE

Organizing for Self-Regulation

Advertising self-regulation is applied by advertising practitioners and the media on the basis of guidelines provided by the Singapore Code of Advertising Practice. This code serves as a criterion for professional conduct and is the basis for arbitration and resolution in case of a dispute. It is updated and administered by a central organization for voluntary self-regulation of the advertising industry in Singapore:

Advertising Standards Authority of Singapore (ASAS)
Block 164, No. 04-3625
Bukit Merah Central
Singapore 0316

The ASAS is an advisory council of the Consumers Association of Singapore (CASE). ASAS comprises members drawn from the media owners, advertisers, advertising agencies, trade and professional associations, relevant government departments, and the CASE. The institutions represented in the ASAS are as follows:

- Singapore Advertisers Association (SAA)
- Association of Accredited Advertising Agents of Singapore
- Consumers Association of Singapore (CASE)
- Advertising Media Owners Association of Singapore
- Singapore Manufacturers Association
- Singapore Medical Association
- Pharmaceutical Society of Singapore
- Singapore Association of Pharmaceutical Industries
- Ministry of Health
- Ministry of the Environment
- Singapore Broadcasting Corporation
- Direct Marketing Association of Singapore

Functioning of Self-Regulation

ASAS applies the Singapore Code of Advertising Practice. It was introduced in 1976 as the successor to the Malaysian and Singapore Code of Advertising Practices, last published in 1972. This code is based on the British Code of Advertising Practice.

The main objectives of ASAS and its code are to lay down criteria for professional conduct, to have practitioners (advertisers, agencies, and media) follow them and to improve the image of advertising among members of the public or by those representing them.

Complaints can be initiated by the public, but all complaints must be in writing and addressed to ASAS' chairperson. In the case of competitor complaints, it is recommended that the complainant raise the issue with the offending party in writing so that the offending party may have the opportunity of defending its actions.

ASAS may call upon either party to the dispute, or upon any outside independent party, for further information. Members of ASAS, other than the chairperson, have one vote, and all the decisions are by a simple majority vote. In the event of the votes being divided, the chairperson casts the deciding vote. Any member of ASAS who has a vested interest in a dispute must immediately declare that interest and sit out of all deliberations. The decision reached in each case is handed to the interested parties in writing; and each is advised of any action that is required to be taken.

The working head of the ASAS is the chairperson, who convenes meetings, appoints committees, and notifies individual members of the deliberations or outcomes of complaints. ASAS meets monthly to consider complaints. The chair of the ASAS is rotated every three years among the representatives of the media owners, advertisers, and advertising agents. CASE provides the secretariat.

Even though ASAS prescreens some advertising materials, responsibility for observing the Singapore Code rests primarily on each advertiser. ASAS also offers free advice to advertisers, advertising agencies, and media owners on the interpretation of the code. About seventy complaints are handled each year.

Government Involvement

The government of Singapore is very concerned with the advertising industry, which it controls directly through legislation (such as a ban on cigarette advertising and restrictions on the advertising of alcoholic beverages and medical products) and informally through the ASAS. The government is supportive of the self-regulatory body and guides it on occasion. It is represented in ASAS by officers from the Ministry of Health and the Ministry of the Environment.

Trend

The trend in Singapore is for more cooperation between the government and industry, and for maintenance of a high level of advertising standards. So far, ASAS has been quite successful, and it is probable that the existing pattern will continue for some time to come.

The information in this section was revised by Ng Ah Kan, acting general manager, Marketing Support, of the Singapore Press Holdings Group.

SOUTH AFRICA

Organizing for Self-Regulation

The self-regulatory body for advertising in South Africa is the following:

> Advertising Standards Authority of South Africa (ASA)
> P.O. Box 91550
> Auckland Park 2006

The ASA was founded at a meeting of advertising interests held in June 1969 in order to bring about a consolidated policy toward self-regulation by eliminating the discrepancies and confusion arising from the acceptance procedures of various media.

The founding organizations of the ASA were as follows:

- Association of Advertising Agencies (AAA)
- Association of Marketers (AOM)
- Cinemark Limited
- Newspaper Press Union of South Africa (NPU) (including magazine publishers)
- Outdoor Advertising Association of South Africa (OAASA)
- South African Broadcasting Corporation (SABC)
- South African Direct Marketing Association (SADMA)
- SA Printing and Allied Industries Federation

Membership in the ASA is open to any trade organization whose members are involved in preparing, printing, and disseminating any type of advertising. An individual company may be admitted directly to membership if there is no trade organization to represent its activity. New members are thus being added, so that the composition of the ASA is continually widening without expanding the membership beyond the advertising community or to bodies directly affected by advertising.

The Copy Committee, as indicated below, has both regular and cooptable members. The latter, while representing constituent member bodies, do not have a permanent sitting on the Copy Committee but have the right, after studying the agenda of any given meeting, of requesting cooption if they feel that any matter to be discussed affects their members' interests.

Since its formation, the following organizations have also taken up membership in the ASA:

- The Specialist Press Association (SPA)
- The Grocery Manufacturers' Association of South Africa (GMA)
- The Pharmaceutical Manufacturers' Association of South Africa (PASA)
- The Proprietary Association of South Africa (PMA)
- The Sales Promotion and Design Institute of South Africa
- The Namibia Broadcasting Corporation (NBC)
- The Furniture Traders' Association (FTA)
- The Agricultural and Veterinary Chemicals' Association (AVCA)
- The SA Coordinating Consumer Council (SACCC)
- The South African Chamber of Business (SACOB)
- The Motor Industries' Federation
- The Electronic Media Network, Ltd. (MNet)
- The Timeshare Institute of South Africa (TISA)
- Bophuthatswana Commercial Radio (Radio 702)
- The SA Franchise Association

The ASA functions through a series of committees that meet as circum-stances warrant. The topmost tier is the General Assembly, in which all member bodies are represented. The next tier is the Executive Committee, consisting of representatives of media member organizations, the agencies and marketers organizations, the Consumer Council, and three members elected from the remaining organizations.

Beneath the Executive Committee, three committees function—the Copy Committee, the Advertising Properties Committee, and the Appeals Committee.

The Copy Committee consists of full-time representatives of the AAA, AOM, SABC, Cinemark, NPU, SA Coordinating Consumer Council, and co-opted members from any of the remaining members whose interests may be affected by, or who can bring expertise to bear on, the point under consideration. This committee deals with all complaints referred to it, except those relating to imitation and goodwill.

The Advertising Properties Committee deals only with complaints relating to imitation and goodwill. It consists of seven representatives drawn from the Association of Marketers and the Association of Advertis-ing Agencies, and one representative each from the NPU and the elec-tronic media. The Appeals Committee hears appeals arising from the decisions of the above two committees.

The only other parties that may attend Copy or Advertising Properties Committee meetings are the litigant parties (advertisers and/or their agencies), who will be admitted to the meeting while their matter is being considered in order to give verbal evidence and to answer questions. They are required to recuse themselves before the matter is finally discussed and the decision taken.

Legal representation is only permitted when complaints relating to imitation or goodwill are taken on appeal. Then, the president of the ASA (a jurist) presides at the Appeals Committee hearing. At all other appeal hearings, the chairperson of the ASA presides. However, the restriction on legal representation does not preclude litigants from submitting written legal opinions in support of their cases to any of the committees. Organizations that are not members of the ASA may not attend meetings.

The president of the ASA has always been a distinguished jurist. The present incumbent is a retired judge of the Appeal Court. The full-time Secretariat of the Authority is headed by an executive director, who deals with many of the complaints on an administrative basis.

The ASA has gained wide acceptance as the coordinating body for advertising control in South Africa. Its representation on the committee set up to help enact the Trade Practices Act (now repealed and replaced) put the seal of government approval on its status; and its services are widely called upon by government departments.

Self-regulation by separate bodies continues to be significant. Prior to the formation of the ASA, each component had its own mechanisms, and these continue to apply. Newspapers and magazines have their own long-standing code of conduct, as do radio and television companies. Cinema advertising is carefully checked before screening and is subject to the approval of the Publications Control Board. Advertising practitioners are bound not only by the ASA Code but by their own code of ethics.

Within each advertising agency, there is a system of code enforcement. Executives who are responsible for giving guidance to the copy, art, and production departments are also charged with determining in the first instance what is permissible under the ASA Code and other applicable codes.

Functioning of Self-Regulation

The ASA bases its activities on its Code of Advertising Practice (this code includes packaging in the concept of advertising). The code, while embodying the main features of the ICC's Code and a number of others, is specially conceived to take into consideration the protection of consumers at different levels of sophistication. This is necessary because of the unique population structure of South Africa. Regulations are considered by the ASA to be vital to protect those of a lower standard of sophistication than is normally found in Europe and the United States.

A complaint received by the ASA under its code, from either consumer or competitor, is first referred to the advertiser for comment (except in isolated cases where the complaint is so illogical that it can be dismissed out of hand). Once the response has been received, it is decided whether the issue is sufficiently clearcut to be dealt with administratively or whether it should be referred to the Copy Committee. In the former case, the party against whom a ruling is given is always informed of the right to ask that the ruling be reviewed by the Copy Committee. All matters that are borderline cases or that involve a matter of principle or review are referred to the Copy Committee. The committee deliberates and makes a ruling, which is then enforced by the Secretariat. In 1990, 1,027 complaints were received, of which only 147 were referred to the Copy Committee.

If ruled against, the advertiser has the right of appeal to the Appeals Committee. Once a ruling has been given by the ASA, it must be conformed to. The ASA has the powers necessary to impose sanctions on the advertisers who refuse to conform. As all the major media are members and are committed to support ASA decisions, such sanctions take the form of a request that they accept no further advertising from the advertiser in question until the problem has been resolved. Since the SA Printing and Allied Industries Federation is also a constituent member, these sanctions also extend to the printing of advertising material.

The ASA may require prepublication approval, for a specified period of time, of all future advertising from an advertiser who persistently contravenes the code.

Every effort is made to handle complaints and appeals promptly, within one to two weeks. Decisions are communicated only among members of the ASA, but designated officers can offer comments to the media on ASA decisions. Unless immediate suspension of an advertisement is required, a time period for compliance with a decision against an advertiser is clearly established as part of any decision.

Beyond its self-regulatory functions, the ASA works actively with government bodies and organizations from other industries to promote the self-regulation of advertising.

The Consumer Movement

The South African Coordinating Consumer Council, with full support of the government, is active in South Africa. This body is a constituent member of the ASA, has representation on its committees, and plays an important role in its affairs.

With regard to complaints, there is a close working relationship between this council and the ASA. Complaints relating to each other's activities are referred to the other body on receipt. Because of this ongoing cooperation, the Joint Liaison Committee with consumer interests has fallen into abeyance.

Government Involvement

A considerable amount of statutory regulation governing or affecting advertising exists in the Republic of South Africa. However, government departments vested with powers in terms of this legislation are tending to make more and more use of the services of the ASA rather than take other steps to regulate unacceptable advertising. The ASA has recently been invited to serve on a committee reviewing regulations related to cosmetics advertising in South Africa.

In addition, the SABC, a semi-state public-utility corporation responsible for most of the broadcast media, was a founder member of the ASA and applies its code. Its participation in the ASA is vital in ensuring full participation of all the major media in the enforcement of self-regulatory standards.

There is no law in South Africa that deals specifically with advertising. However, at least twenty-three laws contain references to advertising to a greater or lesser degree. The most important ones are the following:

1. *The Harmful Business Act.* Act 71 of 1988 provides for a committee to investigate harmful business practices (including advertising). It replaced the former Trade Practices Act, which was almost entirely repealed.
2. *The Medicines and Related Substances Act.* Act 101 of 1965 makes all medicines liable for registration and contains specific provisions relating to labeling and advertising.
3. *The Foodstuffs, Cosmetics and Disinfectants Act.* Act 54 of 1972 has one section dealing with false and misleading advertising and descriptions.
4. *The Credit Agreements Act.* Act 75 of 1980 allows the minister to regulate the manner in which the price of any good or service must be displayed or advertised.
5. *The Marketing Act.* Act 59 of 1988 contains provisions that relate to the labeling and advertising of foodstuffs—particularly fruits.

An excellent working relationship has been established between the ASA and the government departments responsible for the enforcement of these and other acts. Advertising infringements are referred to the ASA for resolution rather than to the courts because of the ASA's ability to deal with the matter quickly and effectively. Only one case relating to advertising has surfaced before South African courts in the past ten years.

Trend

The ASA continues to use every possible opportunity to impress upon the government that effective self-regulation is preferable to legislation. Still, laws and regulations containing references to advertising continue to be enacted. There is, however, a continually growing recognition of the effectiveness of the ASA. There is also an increasing tendency by lawyers to turn to the ASA rather than to the courts for relief in matters relating to advertising.

Although the recent Unacceptable Business Practices Act contained provisions relating to advertising, assurances were given at the ministerial level that the intention was not to interfere with the functions of self-regulation.

Information in this section was supplied by J.G.C. Seibert, former executive director of the Advertising Standards Authority of South Africa.

SPAIN

Organizing for Self-Regulation

The central body for self-regulation of advertising in Spain is as follows:

Autocontrol de la Publicidad, S.A.
(Advertising Self-regulation)
Avenida de Burgos 14, Torre III 2B
28036 Madrid

The body was established in 1977 through the efforts of the Spanish Advertisers Association. It consists of representatives from all fields of advertising, including advertisers, advertising agencies, and the media.

The basic objectives of the body are to protect consumers against misleading, irresponsible, and disrespectful advertising; to protect advertisers, advertising agencies, and the media against unfair competition; to help industry maintain a level of standards that is acceptable to the government; and to improve the social image of advertising. Its main activities are to develop codes and standards, monitor advertisements, prescreen advertisements, promote the self-regulatory system, and lobby government bodies.

In addition to the ICC's International Code of Advertising Practice, which Autocontrol officially adopted in 1977, it bases its activities on advertising codes regarding children, foods, alcoholic beverages, cosmetics, and testimonials.

The structure of Autocontrol consists of a board, a Secretariat, and a Judicial Commission. The latter is made up of Autocontrol members, and it provides prepublication advice, handles complaints, and develops guidelines.

Functioning of Self-Regulation

Investigations or complaints can be initiated by a member of Auto-control, a consumer, or the Judicial Commission of Autocontrol, after scanning or monitoring the media. As a rule, Autocontrol handles false and misleading advertising as well as advertisements that are unfair to competitors or to consumers, such as religious disparagement.

When, after due inquiry, Autocontrol has found an advertisement to contravene its standards, it usually asks the advertiser to stop or modify the advertisement. Sometimes, Autocontrol will notify the agency as well, but the media and other members of Autocontrol are rarely notified. If the advertiser does not comply, the media is asked to stop showing the advertisement (they comply in about 70-80 percent of the cases), the case is publicized to members of the Autocontrol, and the member may be expelled from Autocontrol. Occasionally, the government is notified.

The normal length of the complaint-handling process is one month. There is an appeal process that also takes one month.

The Consumer Movement

In recent years, a greater number of consumer groups have been formed in the country. Even though they are not very effective, their presence is felt in the advertising field. The three most active consumer groups in Spain are the Union de Consumidores de España, Federacion Nacional de Asociaciones de Amas de Hogar, and Organizacion de Consumidores y Usuarios.

Government Involvement

The Spanish government regulates the advertising industry quite extensively. Its regulations can be classified into two major groups: (1) the Advertising General Law, a law of 1988 that regulates advertising activities, mainly false and misleading ads, and (2) special regulations that are directed at specific product categories like alcohol, tobacco, pharmaceutical products or at outdoor advertising, and those that concern the admission of commercials on the government-owned television network. The 1988 Advertising General Law now recognizes Autocontrol when mentioning the complaints procedure to be followed. Its Title IV contains the provisions relating to sanctions and control of illegal advertising "without prejudice to voluntary control of advertising exercised by existing self-regulatory bodies." It lays down that "competent administrative bodies, consumer and user associations, natural or legal persons affected, and, in general, any person with a subjective right or legitimate interest can demand from an advertiser to stop or, if appropriate, to correct an illegal advertisement." In case the advertiser refuses to comply with such a demand, the complainant may submit his complaint to the usual judiciary bodies.

Trend

Overall, government control of advertising, including bans, is increasing, as are actions against the industry by consumer activist groups.

Information in this section was supplied by Rafael Lopez-Vivié, director general of Autocontrol de la Publicidad.

SWEDEN

Organizing for Self-Regulation

The regulation of advertising in Sweden is handled under the ombudsman system. Although the Swedish Konsumentombudsman is an official appointed by the government, this Commissioner for Consumers is voluntarily accepted by the advertising industry as an impartial investigator and arbitrator of advertising complaints and competitive disputes.

Consumer Ombudsman
P.O. Box 502
162 15 Vällingby

The ombudsman is also director general of the National Board for Consumer Policies (NBCP—KOV in Swedish). Its main role is to deal with matters referred to it under the Marketing Practices Act, the Improper Contract Terms Act, and the Consumer Credit Act. In this context, the NBCP monitors marketing practices, identifies violators of the above laws, and negotiates with the implicated firms, while the ombudsman petitions the Market Court for injunctions and fines against uncooperative wrongdoers. A complaint against a decision of the ombudsman can be made to the Fiscal Court of Appeal.

The Swedish system, with its NBCP and consumer ombudsman, is regarded by Swedish industry as state regulation because the NBCP is fully state-controlled and has law-enforcement capacity, which no self-regulatory body has.

The Market Court (a special court to which the ombudsman can refer cases not resolved through its entreaties) has nine members representing business (three each from manufacturing, wholesaling, and retailing), three from labor and consumer organizations, one independent expert on consumer affairs, and an independent chairman and vice-chairman with judicial experience. The Market Court can force an advertiser to stop an incriminated practice through cease-and-desist injunctions and prohibitions, and it can require more information in advertisements and labels. These decisions are enforceable with fines if the Market Court's orders are violated, and they cannot be appealed. Unlike traditional courts, the Market Court is not limited to prevailing standards but can refer to emerging ones. Its task is to make the market better for the future since it can only enjoin business firms from repeating past offenses.

In their administration of the Marketing Practices Act, the consumer ombudsman and the Market Court take into account, among other legal and administrative materials, the ICC's International Code of Advertising Practice. Any breach of the act deemed serious can be passed by the consumer ombudsman to a public prosecutor for legal proceedings, which can result in fines or even imprisonment. Thus, the Marketing Practices Act functions like the ICC Code and its adaptations in various countries, but it is backed by the force of law.

The 1970 Marketing Practices Act, as amended, is rooted in a few general clauses. Section 2 prohibits marketing practices that adversely affect consumers or businesses. Section 3 requires businesses, as part of their marketing activities, to supply information important for consumers. Section 4 prohibits the sale to consumers of dangerous products and services, as well as those manifestly unfit for their main purpose. These general clauses are given more specific meaning through guidelines negotiated with trade associations, and which are used in the Market Court as generally accepted practices that all businesses should observe.

Several other self-regulatory bodies have been established in the past few years, in specific product areas of sensitive character to the consumer. One example is the Ethical Business Council Against Sex Discrimination in Advertising (ERK), which is run jointly by advertisers, agencies, and the media. This council accepts complaints from consumers and others, and it issues verdicts that then become standards for similar cases in the future. There are currently thirty-five to forty self-regulatory councils. The Swedish pharmaceutical associations (LIF, RUFI) control the advertising of medicinal products.

Functioning of Regulation and Self-Regulation

Complaints are received by the National Board of Consumer Policies from individual consumers, business firms, regional and local authorities, and associations, but problems are also detected through the monitoring of advertisements. The National Board then determines whether the advertising in question is in fact faulty, and whether the ombudsman has jurisdiction. If these criteria are satisfied, the board takes up the matter with the advertiser, pointing out where the problem lies, requesting justification or explanation, and asking that it be corrected. In over 95 percent of the cases, the marketer or advertiser agrees, and the matter stops there. Informal persuasion is thus the first technique used, while having the ombudsman present a case before the Market Court is a last resort.

It is difficult to keep track of how many complaints are received by the new self-regulatory bodies, as it varies from one product area to the other. Regarding sex discrimination in advertising, for instance, some 600 complaints were received in two-and-a-half years. Out of them, only twenty-five advertisements have actually been found to be discriminatory.

Advertising firms must include a person responsible for the overall legality of the ads produced. Special private legal advisory consultants are available, as in Norway, to advise advertisers and agencies.

The Consumer Movement

There is no leading organization representing all or most of the Swedish consumer bodies. Consumer representatives on the National Board for Consumer Policies' Governing Council and on the Market Court are typically drawn from the cooperative union (Kooperativa Forbundet), the Confederation of Trade Unions, and the Central Organization of Salaried Employees. These organizations are economically and politically powerful, largely because of their size. This situation has allowed them to dominate the representation of consumer interests, although their multiple missions do not make them ideal consumer representatives. At times, they antagonize other more independent consumer organizations.

There are smaller consumer associations focusing on the specific concerns of handicapped people, tenants and homeowners, car and boat owners, and so on. These are influential when their interests are at stake, but they do not work in unison, as does business, which is much better organized. Active, vocal, and even radical individual consumerists are found everywhere in this well-organized society — in the Parliament, the unions, the Ombudsman Secretariat, the press, the media, and the broadcasting networks.

Altogether, these fragments of the Swedish consumerist movement add up to a powerful constituency in terms of defining and supporting broad pro-consumer goals. However, they appear to have had less influence than business in the development of the National Board's guidelines that interpret the law and in the decisions of the Market Court, where the law is given meaning.

Government Involvement

The ombudsman is responsible for insuring the observance of two laws: (1) The Marketing Practices Act, which prohibits in general marketing activities unfair to consumers or to competitors and, more explicitly, prohibits misleading advertising, certain types of trading stamps and certain kinds of offers and (2) The Act Prohibiting Improper Contract Terms, which aims to protect consumers by eliminating contracts that improperly favor the seller at the expense of the purchaser.

These two acts provide the ombudsman and the Market Court with powers of legal enforcement in cases where arbitration fails.

Trend

In recent years, public consumer policy has placed greater emphasis on the responsibilities of trade and industry to take their own initiatives in order to prevent and resolve consumer problems of various kinds—for instance, by establishing rules of ethics for marketing activities. A detailed explanation of this development is given in Parliament Bill No. 1985/1986:121, where it is stressed that ethical standards for marketing are a matter of public concern. It is felt that, in cases where self-regulation has failed, there must be means for necessary intervention by consumer-affairs authorities.

The Swedish government is about to propose a new law against sex discrimination in advertising. The advertising community is very concerned about that new law. It will create enormous problems for the agencies and advertisers, because the borderlines of sex discrimination are very difficult to define.

Information in this section was supplied by Svante Sköldberg, president of the Swedish Advertisers Association.

SWITZERLAND

Organizing for Self-Regulation

The central organization for voluntary self-regulation of advertising industry in Switzerland is the following:

Schweizerische Kommission für die Lauterkeit in der Werbung/
Commission Suisse pour la Loyauté en Publicité
(Swiss Commission for Fair Practices in Advertising)

Kappelergasse 14
Postfach 4675
8022 Zurich

The Advertising Fair-Practices Arbitration Commission was initiated by the Swiss Advertising Association and the Fédération Romande de Publicité in 1966-67. Revised statutes reflecting current practice were issued effective September 1973.

This commission, now renamed, is composed of a neutral chairperson, representatives of the tripartite Swiss Advertising Association (two representatives each from the advertiser, media, and specialist sectors), three consumer representatives, and three representatives from related fields such as publishing, education, and environmental protection. Representation of the German, French, and Italian communities is ensured in the commission's membership. Editors of the advertising review, *Werbung/ Publicité*, serve as consultants, and the use of experts is authorized.

The commission is located at the headquarters of the Swiss Advertising Association, which bears routine administrative costs. Exceptional expenses, such as expert testimony, if required, are borne by one or both sides in a complaint.

Functioning of Self-Regulation

Activities of the commission are based on the International Chamber of Commerce codes, together with various interpretations and applications recording particular practices, products, and services.

The commission deals with its business in plenary meeting or in three chambers. The latter are composed of a chairman, two representatives of the advertising world, and a neutral member. There is also a secretary, whose tasks are to promulgate provisional decisions, to reject unfounded complaints, and to forward well-founded complaints to the chambers. The secretary may provide prepublication advice, but this is non-binding on the commission. The Control Bureau, composed of the chairmen of the commission and the chambers, controls the activities of the secretary, decides on the sanctions necessary to maintain compliance with existing provisional decisions, and deals with complaints against the secretary.

The commission's main tasks are as follows:

- to evaluate whether the advertising campaigns submitted to it or those it decides to examine itself are in compliance with the dispositions and the spirit of the ICC code (only post-publication), and

- to take measures to remedy the situation when a breach of the code has been demonstrated.

Complaints are accepted from anyone about advertising alleged to violate the ICC codes, and they are treated as confidential. On receipt of a complaint, the secretary has the power to initiate immediate action to stop an advertisement if it is obviously in violation of these codes. Where action is called for, discussion of a case by the commission or its chambers is scheduled. The advertiser (or other party) responsible for the advertising under scrutiny is entitled to be heard personally, but the burden of proof rests with the advertiser.

The commission's conclusion is determined by a two-thirds majority vote. If a violation is found, the advertiser will be requested to terminate the advertisement, and a short written justification will be provided. Parties to a commission decision have the right of appeal to the Control Bureau or to the full commission.

Should the advertiser refuse to conform to a commission decision, the following sanctions are possible:

- publication of the commission's decision, with full identification of the offending advertiser;
- recommendation to the media that they refuse the advertising found to be unacceptable;
- recommendation that the advertiser's firm be excluded from membership in the relevant trade or industrial associations; and
- revocation of the recognition of the agency/consultant by the Swiss Advertising Association, and withdrawal of the right to receive commissions on advertising.

The statutes of the commission provide for an annual report to be published in advertising-industry magazines, summing up its activities, but preserving the confidentiality of advertisers against whom complaints were lodged.

The Consumer Movement

Consumer interest groups are represented in the self-regulation system by three members of the Swiss Consumer Organizations (Vertretner des Schweizerische Konsumenten-Organizationen) on the commission.

Government Involvement

A large number of federal, cantonal, and municipal laws and regulations pertain to advertising—particularly, the Federal Law Against Unfair Competition. In general, the commission has not been involved in enforcing voluntary conformity to these laws, or in anticipating possible conflict over them. Nor is the Swiss government represented in the regulatory activities of the commission.

In 1973, however, the commission modified its policy to some extent. It formed a working group to regulate the advertising of pharmaceutical and cosmetic products, and it included in its structure representatives of federal and intercantonal authorities. Also, the commission has concluded voluntary agreements with Swiss manufacturers, importers, and agents who advertise alcoholic beverages, detergents, and soap powders.

Information in this section was updated by René R. Hürlimann and Gery Heller of the International Advertising Association's Swiss chapter.

TAIWAN

Organizing for Self-Regulation

There is no central self-regulatory body in Taiwan that regulates the total industry. However, three bodies are active in this field:

> The Taipei Association of Advertising Agencies
> 2nd Floor, No. 4-1, Lane 217, Alley 3
> Chung-Shiao East Road, Section 3
> Taipei

This body consists of 142 advertising agencies. It sponsors the annual convention, holds the monthly meeting of the Standing Committee of Directors and Trustees, edits and issues the Advertising Statistics Monthly Report, and cosponsors, with *China Times*, the annual advertising awards.

Other bodies regulating advertising in Taiwan are as follows:

> The National Press Council of the Republic of China
> 3rd Floor, No. 4
> Lane 9, Nan Cheong Street, Section 1
> Taipei

> The Television Academy of Arts and Sciences of the Republic
>   of China
> 120 Chung-Yang Road
> Nan-Kang
> Taipei

Functioning of Self-Regulation

The body responsible for adjudicating complaints is the National Press Council (R.O.C.). Complaints can be introduced by consumers, consumer organizations, competing advertisers, government bodies, the media, and the self-regulatory body itself as a result of its own internal monitoring. Once this council makes an adjudication, it publishes its comments, together with the facts of the complaint, in its monthly journal.

The Consumer Movement

The Taipei Consumer Foundation publishes a Consumer Report (monthly) and occasional product-testing reports. However, it does not propose any specific recommendations in regard to advertising regulations.

Government Involvement

Both the Government Information Bureau (equivalent to the U.S. Federal Communications Commission) and the Health Bureau (equivalent to the U.S. Food and Drug Administration) have issued advertising codes and regulations. Usually, commercials will be submitted to the Government Information Bureau for censorship. If the commercials deal with food, cosmetics, or medicines, they have to be submitted to both the Government Information Bureau and the Health Bureau.

Outdoor advertising is regulated by the local police. Newspaper ads are precleared by the respective newspapers.

Trend

Government organizations issue regulations often. The local advertising industry is keenly aware of the necessity of self-regulation. However, there is no concerted effort in setting up effective codes for the entire industry.

Information in this section was supplied by Peter Yi-Chih Liu, consultant to the Taipei Association of Advertising Agencies.

TURKEY

Organizing for Self-Regulation

There is no central, self-regulatory body in Turkey at this time, and none is likely in the near future. However, some professional bodies exercise self-regulatory control over advertising practices. They are the following: the Turkish Advertising Agencies Association, the IAA Turkish Chapter, and the Istanbul Chamber of Commerce.

Reklamcilar Dernegi (RD)
(Turkish Advertising Agencies Association)
Yildiz Posta Caddesi, No. 26 A-Blok, D.18
Gayrettepe
80280 Istanbul

The main activities of this association are to conduct research on various advertising issues, to lobby government bodies, and to adjudicate public-interest complaints.

When the association receives a complaint, it first investigates its worth. Then interested parties (agency, advertiser, media) are notified about the complaint, and justification and/or clarification is requested. The issue is discussed at board meetings, and this board decides whether the complaint is justified. If so, modification of the advertisement is recommended to the complainant. In some cases, the complaints are forwarded to the Istanbul Chamber of Commerce's Advertising Evaluation Committee.

Although the International Advertising Association's (IAA) Turkish Chapter was established in 1972, it gained legal status as an association only in 1989, according to Turkish laws.

Uluslararasi Reklamcilik Dernergi
(IAA Turkish Chapter)
Büyükdere Cad. Ecza Sokak No:6
Gültepe
80498 Istanbul

Both associations and their members have adopted the self-regulatory advertising codes of international (e.g., ICC) and European origins; and advertising self-regulation is achieved by the goodwill of the advertising industry.

The Istanbul Chamber of Commerce has two committees performing self-regulatory functions over advertising practices. The Arbitration Committee consists of three members: one advertising person representing advertising agencies, one lawyer, and one businessman. The committee acts as, and has the power of, a court dealing with conflicts and arbitrating them. It can be solicited by the parties in conflict before they go to a regular court.

The second committee is the Advertising Evaluation Board. This is the body responsible for enforcing the compulsory Professional Code of Fair Advertising Practices. The Turkish Advertising Agencies Association is represented by a board member.

The Consumer Movement

Consumerism is not very powerful in Turkey. Consumer organizations are rather isolated and have no real impact. The media are trying to create consumer awareness and to increase consumer involvement. Local administrations and the Istanbul Chamber of Commerce are also becoming more sensitive about consumer protection, and involved in it.

Government Involvement

The state-owned television and radio authorities exercise a regulatory function in the form of continuous screening of advertising commercials and scripts. Comparison advertising is forbidden, and claims must be supported by documents based on authoritative sources.

The state monopoly on broadcasting has been broken. A private TV company, Magic Box, started broadcasting in 1990, but the broadcasts are made from Germany, because the legislation preventing private TV broadcasting has not yet been changed. Radical changes in this direction and the proliferation of TV stations are expected.

Trend

The Turkish Standardization Institute is circulating a draft copy of a Turkish standard for advertising: the Required Conditions for Advertising. The views of various experts are being collected.

The emergence of private TV broadcasting is leading to a liberalization in advertising regulations. This has also resulted in a shift of advertising budgets to private TV channels. In order to maintain its advertising income, the state-owned television network will have to be more flexible in its advertising rules.

Information in this section was supplied by Sönmez Taner, general coordinator of the Turkish Advertising Agencies Association.

UNITED KINGDOM

Organizing for Self-Regulation

The self-regulatory structure in the United Kingdom is a "tripartite, two-tier system," devised to give the fullest effect to the British Code of Advertising Practice. The latter was developed from the International Chamber of Commerce's code, which has been adopted in the United Kingdom, but elaborated into the British code to meet national needs. In addition, a separate code has been developed to cover sales-promotion techniques. This is administered in the same way as the advertising code.

In practice, the overall self-regulatory structure is concerned primarily with nonbroadcast advertising (press, posters, cinema, direct mail, etc.) and sales promotion, since acceptance of television, radio, and cable commercials falls under statutory regulations and bodies established to govern broadcasting according to their own codes.

The two tiers of overall self-regulation are the Advertising Standards Authority (ASA) and the Committee of Advertising Practice (CAP).

The Advertising Standards Authority. The ASA is a limited company, financed through a levy of 0.1 percent of billings on all forms of nonbroadcast advertising, but wholly independent in its actions and functioning. Its chairperson, who is salaried, is appointed by the Advertising Standards Board of Finance, the industry body that raises the levy, after consulting widely. The chairperson must be wholly independent of all advertising interests. The appointment is for three years and is renewable.

The chairperson appoints the eleven other members of ASA's Council. At least two-thirds must be completely independent of all advertising interests, while up to one-third may be persons with advertising skills. The chairperson of the Committee of Advertising Practice (CAP), by invitation, also attends ASA Council meetings.

The ASA was established in 1962. Prior to that time, the advertising industry in Britain had already successfully established an internal system of self-regulation. In the conviction that public confidence required a system with an independent mechanism of verification, the advertising industry, on its own initiative, established a higher level of authority in the form of ASA. The members of ASA's Council, furthermore, are expected to act as individuals and to exercise moral authority rather than to act as representatives of any particular industry or interest.

The function of ASA is to supervise the entire control system, ensuring that the code is kept under continuous review, is properly and fairly applied, and that the CAP functions effectively and smoothly. In particular, the ASA is responsible for the investigation of complaints from the public that advertisements contravene the code, and for monitoring the overall quality of advertisements.

> Advertising Standards Authority
> Brook House
> 2-16 Torrington Place
> London WC1E 7HN

Committee of Advertising Practice. The CAP consists of representatives of twenty-three advertising organizations, including advertisers, agencies, and all types of media. The television companies are represented by their association (the Independent Television Association), even though these media are controlled by a public body, the Independent Television Commission. The chairperson of ASA is invited to attend CAP meetings. This committee, which is responsible for reviewing the British Codes of Advertising Practice and of Sales Promotion Practice, has a number of special-purpose subcommittees or panels that meet as needed to consider specific subject matters.

The ASA and CAP share the same premises, Secretariat (with about sixty employees), and chief executive. The Secretariat, which in practice constitutes a third tier, performs four functions. It provides prepublication guidance on copy, investigates complaints prior to adjudication by ASA or CAP, prevets advertisements in mandatory areas (e.g., cigarette advertising), and monitors advertising and sales promotions.

> Committee of Advertising Practice
> Brook House
> 2-16 Torrington Place
> London WC1E 7HN

Functioning of Self-Regulation

Complaints are considered initially by the staff of the ASA/CAP Committee Secretariat. Complaints from the public are dealt with by ASA. They may concern the content of specific advertisements or, in the case of mail orders, the behavior of advertisers. Evidence of the advertisement itself, or sufficient details to identify it, must be supplied by the complainant, and the complaint must be made in writing. In most cases, a preliminary evaluation is possible at staff level. In more complicated or controversial matters, issues may be referred to the Copy Advisory Panel or to one of ASA's expert advisers. All cases are eventually submitted to ASA's Council for final adjudication. Whatever is decided, the advertiser is informed and must abide by any adverse decision.

Complaints from competitors are dealt with by CAP. They generally fall into one of two categories: complaints that competitive copy claims are incorrect or cannot be substantiated, and complaints of denigration or unfair product comparison. As with public complaints, the advertiser or agency responsible is asked to substantiate or justify the claims. If this cannot be done, the copy must be changed or the advertisement withdrawn. Difficult or controversial cases are referred to the Copy Advisory Panel, a section of which is available to meet weekly. Appeals against a decision of CAP may, if the chairpersons of ASA and CAP agree, go to the ASA Council for final adjudication.

The ASA monitors a statistically reliable sample of newspapers and magazines, supplemented by occasional full-scale checks on "sensitive areas." Where a violation of the code or a marginal situation is discovered, the procedure is essentially the same as that for a complaint generated from outside the ASA structure, although monitored cases do not appear in the ASA Case Reports. A separate monitoring operation, based on in-store checks, covers sales promotions.

CAP provides extensive guidance and consultation in two forms: (1) bulletins and leaflets supplying guidelines on rule changes, new rules, and interpretation of controversial points, and (2) confidential review of advertisements prior to publication.

In recent years, as a result of publicity campaigns to increase public awareness of ASA, the number of complaints received from members of the public has increased steadily to 9,700 in 1990 (compared to 8,800 in 1987). One-third of the complaints do not warrant investigation because they relate to matters outside the remit of ASA or to advertisements that appear to conform to the codes. Of the complaints requiring investigation, about 11 percent relate to the non-receipt of goods ordered in response to mail-order advertisements, and the vast majority of these are resolved by delivery of goods or refund of money. Fewer than half of the complaints are upheld.

Complaints concerning copy claims are predominantly on the grounds that the advertisement is generally misleading either through omission, exaggeration, or layout. This category is closely followed by specific claim challenges in relation to taste and decency, price claims, comparisons, and availability of advertised products. Sales promotions have increasingly become the subject of complaint, and these are dealt with under the British Code of Sales Promotion Practice, which sets out to improve the manner in which sales-promotion terms are quoted.

Following complaint investigation, where complaints are upheld, subsequent advertisements are amended or withdrawn. The primary sanction for breaches of the code is nonpublication by the media. Each of the six press-media bodies circulates confidential memoranda to its members. If a particular advertisement does not conform to the code, no member will accept the advertisement. Similar arrangements apply in other media. Each month, ASA issues to the press and other enforcement agencies a summary of the cases with which it has dealt; and where complaints are upheld, the resulting adverse publicity also acts as an important sanction against offending advertisers.

In order to publicize both its self-regulatory system and its procedures for resolving complaints against advertisements—a procedure free of cost to a complainant—the ASA has, since 1975, conducted a regular advertising campaign. Most space is donated by the advertising business (a value of well over one million British pounds in recent years).

ASA also maintains an active program publicizing its work to the educational field. The staff of ASA lecture and instruct at a large number

of universities, colleges, and business schools each year; and they participate in seminars, courses, and dialogues.

The Consumer Movement

Consumer awareness has been high in Britain for many years. Consumer interest is well organized, even to the extent that at least one specialized newsletter and service exists to describe the evolution of consumerism itself. Three groups are recognized: the Consumers Association
(overwhelmingly the largest), the National Federation of Consumer
Groups (40 regional member groups), and the Consumer Standards Advisory Committee of the British Standards Institution. In addition, a government agency, the National Consumer Council, represents consumers
in the same way that the Confederation of British Industry represents
employers and the Trade Union Congress represents workers. Much consumerist feeling is expressed through political channels, without regard to
party.

The ASA is constituted to include nonadvertising members in its Council (two-thirds of the total membership) who, while they act as individuals, by their objectivity provide consumer representation. In addition,
the ASA at the Secretariat level maintains close liaison with consumer
bodies and social organizations such as the Charity Commission and the
Citizens' Advice Bureaux. It also cooperates with associations that apply
their own codes (e.g., for nonprescription medicines and mail-order firms).

Government Involvement

As in many large markets, the government of the United Kingdom has
enacted a great deal of legislation that, in regulating products and markets, affects advertising practice. Beyond this, overall legislation covering
trading and marketing practices has been enacted or is contemplated.

Statutory control of certain media (notably television, radio, and cable)
is established by an act of Parliament. Regulations also restrict outdoor-
advertising locations and practices. Cigarette advertising is prohibited on
broadcast media and cinema; and the scheduling of advertisements for alcoholic beverages on television is restricted, with the advertising of spirits
(hard liquor) being prohibited. Investment advertising is under the control of a new regulatory body, The Securities and Investment Board.

The voluntary ASA operation maintains close liaison with all pertinent
government bodies. These include the Office of Fair Trading (OFT),
which, under the Fair Trading Act of 1973, was given wide powers to regulate advertising and marketing practices and practitioners. In 1988 the
OFT acquired, under regulations based on a 1984 European Community
directive, a "long-stop" power to seek injunctions to prevent the publication

of misleading advertisements that could not be dealt with by any other method. The ASA is one of the "established means" recognized by the Court.

The ASA also has a liaison with the Department of Trade and Industry, the Home Office, the Department of Health, and the Ministry of Agriculture, Fisheries, and Food. In addition, ASA has close links with the Trading Standards officers of local authorities—some 128 in number, who represent a "grass roots" contact for ASA—as well as with chambers of commerce, trade councils, and the Citizens' Advice Bureaux.

Trend

There is no basic disagreement, in terms of consumer protection and interest, between the principles of the Code of Advertising Practice and the statutory regulations of the United Kingdom.

Increasingly, consumer concern is focusing on issues other than the accuracy of advertisements, which monitoring shows to be overwhelmingly truthful and honest. Such matters as the alleged obtrusiveness and wastefulness of direct-mail advertising and the lack of taste of advertisements offering sex-related services are current topics of concern, as are the environment, timeshares, homework schemes, and the whole issue of the manner in which women are depicted and referred to in advertising. The ASA has completed two major research surveys on this last topic.

The Independent Television Commission has recently replaced the Independent Broadcasting Authority to control both television and cable, while radio will be under the separate control of the Radio Authority. These new bodies have their own codes for advertising and program sponsorship.

Information in this section was originally supplied by Peter Thomson, former director general of the Advertising Standards Authority. It was updated by Enid Cassin, former acting director at the Advertising Standards Authority, and by Matti Alderson, current director general of the ASA.

UNITED STATES

Organizing for Self-Regulation

In 1971, in the face of increased government controls and growing consumer criticism, the advertising industry formed a centralized mechanism for self-regulation embodied in the National Advertising Division (NAD) of the Council of Better Business Bureaus (CBBB), and the National Advertising Review Board (NARB). The objective was and remains today to promote the highest standards of truth and accuracy in national advertising. This is seen to have two primary benefits. It ensures that the marketplace where advertisers compete is not corrupted by false product claims, and it defends advertisers against excessive government restrictions that would severely limit their ability to function in a competitive business environment. It enables consumers to make informed purchase decisions, fostering confidence in the business community as a whole.

NAD/NARB
845 Third Avenue
New York, NY 10022

The sponsoring body of the NARB is the National Advertising Review Council (NARC). NARC is a nonprofit organization that was founded by the American Association of Advertising Agencies (AAAA), the American Advertising Federation (AAF), the Association of National Advertisers (ANA), and the Council of Better Business Bureaus, Inc. (CBBB). NAD is a division of the CBBB. The board of directors of NARC, consisting of the presidents and current chairs of the four organizations, provides advice and counsel on basic operating policies and also selects the chairperson and members of the NARB.

The NAD and NARB work on the basis of voluntary industry cooperation and do not have legal authority to enforce their judgments. However, in their review procedures, NAD/NARB are autonomous and completely independent of any or all other persons and organizations, and they have considerable influence within the advertising industry through reports published at the conclusion of their investigations.

As the active investigative unit, NAD has a staff of full-time professional reviewers who monitor national consumer advertising, respond to complaints, select cases for formal inquiry, evaluate data supplied by advertisers, and decide whether claims are adequately substantiated. When NAD does not agree with an advertiser that the substantiation is adequate, the advertiser is asked to withdraw or modify the claims in question. If the advertiser does not comply, the matter is referred for resolution to a panel drawn from NARB.

The NARB is structured differently from the NAD. Every effort has been made to provide a balanced system to provide advertisers with a combined peer review and appeal process. The NARB is comprised of fifty members. Thirty of them are drawn from companies that do national advertising, ten are from advertising agencies, and ten are distinguished educators, attorneys, and other public authorities who represent the public at large. Ten alternate members from advertising agencies are available to serve when a possible conflict of interest might disqualify an agency member from participating in a panel. Individual NARB members are "answerable to no one for the decisions reached and actions taken by the NARB or any panel thereof," and they serve on a voluntary basis.

NAD publishes the results of its investigations in a press release in which the issues are outlined and agreements with advertisers noted. NAD also publishes *NAD Case Report*, compiling all the decisions for a month. NARB publishes reports of its decisions individually.

Individual efforts at nongovernment regulation are much older than the NAD/NARB.

Media Control. Newspapers and magazines have been setting standards and controls on a voluntary basis since 1911. However, the standards vary from one publication to another on the basis of each publication's audience and management. The broadcast media are much more involved with advertising review because the stations licensed by the Federal Communications Commission are subject to FCC regulations. Each of the major networks maintains a staff to prescreen commercials.

Advertiser Control. Many industries have their own voluntary guidelines. Some industry trade associations, such as the automobile dealers and liquor distillers, issue their own codes of advertising. Most of these associations use moral persuasion to encourage their members to follow the applicable code. The CBBB, through its Better Business Bureaus' Code of Advertising, has no basis for requiring compliance.

Advertising Agency Control. Before the inception of the NAD/NARB, self-regulation in advertising was handled by advertising trade associations. The major trade associations are the American Association of Advertising Agencies, the American Advertising Federation, and the Association of National Advertisers. The bulk of such self-regulation for national advertising has now been passed to the NAD/NARB. However, each organization continues to conduct some self-regulatory activity within its membership. Local Better Business Bureaus continue to handle local advertising complaints.

Company Self-Discipline. Besides the above groups, most major companies administer their own codes of advertising standards and ethics, ensuring both compliance with the law and attention to matters of public taste and welfare not covered by law. Advertising agencies serving such advertisers maintain legal departments or consult counsel routinely in order to ensure that their advertising complies with these internal codes as well as with all legal requirements.

Functioning of Self-Regulation

The NAD/NARB process begins with a complaint brought by an individual, organization, or competitor, or with an inquiry initiated by NAD as a result of its own monitoring of broadcast, cable, and print advertising. Complaints must be addressed to the NAD. If they are submitted to the NARB, they are acknowledged and referred immediately to NAD, where the review process begins.

NAD's specific mandate covers complaints, challenges, and questions concerning the truth or accuracy of an advertisement, or its capacity to mislead. Complaints about issues other than truth and accuracy, such as taste or social responsibility, are considered only if they concern broadly applicable questions or involve techniques or concepts in frequent use. In such cases, NAD will refer the questions to NARB for study by a consultative panel.

NAD initiates or accepts a case and records it only after it has been determined that it meets the criteria for pursuing an investigation. Frivolous complaints are rejected, as are "fishing expeditions." Having recorded the complaint, NAD forwards the complaint to the advertiser, asking for substantiation that, in the advertiser's view, supports the claim in question. If, in the judgment of the NAD, the material submitted is adequate, the case is published in the *NAD Case Report* under the heading "Advertising Substantiated."

If the NAD finds the substantiation to be inadequate, the advertiser is asked to modify or discontinue the disputed advertising. If the advertiser agrees to do so, the case is published under the heading "Advertising Modified or Discontinued."

If, however, NAD and the advertiser are unable to negotiate a satisfactory settlement of the complaint, then either the NAD or the advertiser has the right to appeal the NAD decision to an NARB panel. If the original complainant disagrees with NAD's decision, the complainant may request an appeal. In the latter instance, the NARB chairperson studies the complainant's request and determines whether or not it will be reviewed by an NARB panel.

In the case of an appeal, the chairperson of the NARB designates a panel of five members to judge the case, with the panel membership comprised in the same ratio as NARB itself: three drawn from advertiser members, one from advertising-agency members, and one from "public" members. The NAD investigation file is made available to the panel, which then holds a hearing to assess the NAD findings as well as to obtain pertinent testimony and facts from the advertiser. The panel aims for informality and speed.

An NARB panel may reverse a negative NAD finding and hold that a challenged claim has been adequately substantiated. If, on the other hand, the panel upholds a complaint against the advertiser, as has occurred in most cases in recent history, the advertiser is requested to modify or discontinue the questionable claims. In both cases, the NARB publishes its findings and recommendations in a separate NARB Report.

If, however, the panel upholds the complaint and the advertiser is still unwilling to modify or eliminate the advertising, the NARB chairperson is empowered to issue a notice of intent to the advertiser, explaining that, if the advertiser fails to respond or comply with the decision of the panel within ten days, the chairperson will inform the appropriate government agency by letter, turn over the complete NARB file upon that agency's request, and publicly release the letter to the government agency. In such an instance, the matter will be reported in the NAD Case Report as "Advertising Referred to Government Agency." To date, NARB has taken such an action only once.

As mentioned earlier, although confidentiality during an investigation and any subsequent review procedure is emphasized, the NAD/NARB have a policy to publicly disclose their findings and recommendations at the conclusion of an inquiry, with the name of the advertiser being disclosed. In addition to a press release issued immediately thereafter, the *NAD Case Report* is issued monthly, listing all cases closed during the preceding month under five separate headings: Advertising Substantiated, Advertising Modified or Discontinued, Advertising Referred to the NARB, Advertising Referred to Government Agency, and No Substantiation Received. The report also carries any comment advertisers might wish to make concerning their cases. Currently, distribution numbers 6,000 copies nationally, to corporations, advertising agencies, government offices, law firms, universities, libraries, and the media.

NARB Panel Reports also are made public, each covering in some depth the nature of the complaint and the NAD investigation and decision, pertinent information developed in the panel hearing, and the panel decision and reasons supporting it.

Since 1971, the NAD has published over 2,500 cases: 42 percent were "substantiated," 56 percent "modified or discontinued," and approximately 2 percent "referred to the NARB."

To date, the NAD/NARB review function has been confined largely to consumer advertising, as distinct from trade or "business-to-business" advertising. While many of the complaints received by NAD during the first few years of operation were from consumers, a significant shift has occurred, with an increasing number of complaints being filed by competitors.

In 1974, a special unit was established within NAD—the Children's Advertising Review Unit (CARU)—to respond to public concerns and to promote responsible children's advertising, not only with regard to issues of truth and accuracy but also in the area of safety. CARU publishes the *Self-Regulatory Guidelines for Children's Advertising* to help advertisers and agencies deal sensitively and honestly with appeals to children. These guidelines undergo periodic revisions to reflect the latest trends and research in marketing to children.

CARU monitors advertising directed to children under the age of twelve, and responds to challenges from competitors as well as consumer complaints. It conducts inquiries, effects changes through the voluntary cooperation of advertisers, and publishes these agreements in the *NAD Case Report*. In addition, CARU provides a general advisory service to consumers, educators, professional associations, government agencies, and the press. CARU staff members meet frequently with advertisers to exchange views on current trends in advertising to children, and to conduct workshops for marketing and advertising personnel.

In areas extending beyond truth and accuracy, the NARC authorized NARB in 1972 to organize "Consultative Panels." Operating in a confidential manner, the consultative panels of five members each confer with appropriate industry and academic sources to arrive at general conclusions, but they do not direct formal inquiries to specific advertisers, nor do they hear individual complaints. Panel findings are published, when this is deemed desirable, in the form of position papers.

The first of these papers, released in mid-1974, was titled *Product Advertising and Consumer Safety*, and it contained recommended procedures for advertisers and agencies to follow in preparing any kind of advertising involving questions or issues of safety. Other panel reports include *Advertising and Women* and *Identifying Competitors in Advertising*.

The Local Advertising Review Programs (LARP), founded to reinforce the grass-roots level of self-regulation provided for many years by local Better Business Bureaus, have been established in many communities and market regions of the United States. If the local BBB—in exercising the NAD function of receiving, initiating, and evaluating local complaints—fails to elicit voluntary cooperation from any party, such unresolved cases are referred to LARP Panels for final consideration and appropriate action. The BBB/LARP structures parallel the NAD/NARB activity, with strong insistence on public presentations in deliberations and meaningful enforcement procedures.

Each LARP is comprised of local advertisers, agencies, and public members. The actual size of the review panels varies, depending on the size of the city, the workload, and the availability of participants. In some cases, there is media representation in the LARP structure.

NAD/NARB operations are financed solely by advertisers and advertising agencies through membership dues paid to the CBBB. The operations of the LARP are funded as part of the operating costs of their constituent bodies, with much activity undertaken on an unpaid, volunteer basis. The Council of Better Business Bureaus makes grants to local BBBs to aid them in expanding the review of advertisements in their communities and to help establish LARPs. These structures are wholly independent of national, state, or local government.

Funding of LARP operations underlines a problem basic to self-regulation in the United States. By law, local, regional, and national businesses cannot be compelled to participate in self-regulatory activity. Extension of the process to LARP is, in fact, paid for by including its cost in the operating budgets of the local BBB and advertising club. This poses two problems: adequate funding to sustain effective operations, and disproportionate representation of certain local interests in the funding.

The Consumer Movement

Consumer protection has been an important issue in the United States at least since 1911, when the "truth in advertising" movement was founded. Having proliferated since the mid-1960s, it is now difficult to list all the organizations and their chosen sectors of activity, or to classify those whose interests are more than local or peripheral.

Some consumerist organizations place heavy emphasis on the importance of advertising to their areas of interest—for example, the former Action for Children's Television (ACT) organization expressed concern over the impact of television commercials on children; nutritionists manifest concern about promotion of heavily sugared ready-to-eat breakfast cereals; and vehicle-safety advocates criticize the presentation in automotive advertisements of high-speed driving. However, no major consumerist organization concentrates its attention solely on advertising as a potentially anti-consumer force. This is apparently due to the general feeling, even among the most ardent consumer advocates, that advertising is not per se contrary to the public interest, and that only specific abuses must be restrained.

Contact between consumer groups and the advertising industry takes the form of participation and confrontation in numerous conferences, including congressional hearings. Advertising self-regulation has, like government, sought to enlist prominent consumerists in its structures, although with limited success.

Though the consumer activist groups have grown in the United States, the general public's opinion about advertising has not changed much, which is in itself a positive element for the industry. Studies done in 1974 revealed that, when consumers are asked to pick "the things that most need immediate attention and change" among their concerns with institutions, only 11 percent indicated advertising, as opposed to 70 percent for government, 36 percent for education, and 29 percent for big business. In this same study, 88 percent of all U.S. consumers agreed that "advertising is essential," but about 41 percent of the consumers had a negative attitude toward advertising. A 1985 survey by Ogilvy & Mather revealed fairly similar feelings, with ambivalence still the order of the day.

Government Involvement

Few sectors of business in the United States are subjected to so many types of federal, state, and local legislation as is the advertising industry. This is true even though no other business sector has had a longer history or range of self-regulatory activities.

In Washington, D.C., alone, more than twenty different federal administrative bodies exercise controls over advertising. Those with major jurisdiction or influence include the Federal Trade Commission (FTC), the Food and Drug Administration (FDA), the U.S. Postal Service, the Federal Communications Commission (FCC), the Bureau of Alcohol, Tobacco and Firearms of the Internal Revenue Service (IRS), and the Securities and Exchange Commission (SEC).

In general, agencies of the federal government enforce legislation against advertising deemed to be (1) fraudulent, deceptive, or misleading in a material sense, (2) unfair in its methods of competition, or (3) injurious to public safety or health.

In their efforts to ensure fair-trade practices, it is a paradox that government regulatory bodies in the United States find themselves required by anti-trust law to prohibit the kinds of industry-wide agreements and sanctions upon which the self-regulation of advertising is based in other countries.

In addition to action by agencies of the executive branch of the federal government (with possible enforcement by the courts), committees of the Senate and House of Representatives exert increasing influence on advertising. Not only do they exercise their responsibilities for overseeing the activities of the regulatory agencies (hence involving themselves in continuing reappraisal of the judgments these agencies make and the laws on which they are based), but they have undertaken a series of searching inquiries into marketing practices, communication functions, and specific categories of products, and even into specific industries.

Consumer groups and their campaigns against certain kinds of advertising have moved Congress to pass legislation and the FTC to monitor, question, and appraise the advertising industry. Legislation also authorizes the FTC to issue Trade Regulation Rules (TRRs) for advertising standards and other related business activities. A relatively recent phenomenon has been the increased involvement of the National Association of Attorneys General (NAAG). NAAG has strongly urged the FTC to step up its efforts to bring complaints against advertisers, and it takes action itself when, in NAAG's opinion, the FTC does not move fast enough.

State and local laws involve an even greater variety of regulations. It is difficult to generalize but, in a majority of states, there is legislation that forbids advertising to carry any statement or representation of fact that is untrue, deceptive, or misleading. This kind of legislation provides the

Better Business Bureaus and the Local Advertising Review Programs with legal recourse at the grass-roots level.

In addition, protection of the public interest has taken the form of appointed "consumer representatives" at all levels of government. At state and local levels, such consumer advocates serve as watchdogs for many kinds of business practices, including advertising. At the national level, the White House and major executive departments have similar offices — for example, the Bureau of Consumer Protection of the FTC, and a Special Assistant to the President for Consumer Affairs.

It appears to be the consensus of both government and the advertising industry that they have identical objectives, but they vary in their programs of achieving these objectives.

Trend

The NAD/NARB structure is engaged in increasing its effectiveness, in making its activities known to the public, and in building consumer awareness and confidence. In this effort, it has instituted strict time constraints for resolving an individual case, and it has increased its efforts to publicize its decisions while preserving confidentiality during the investigation and negotiation stages.

The movement toward increasing government regulation of advertising in the United States, temporarily diverted by deregulation since the mid-1970s, appears to be resuming. While proposals for increased government regulation usually center on specific substantive issues (health claims, environmental claims, safety claims, and children's television advertising now being among the most prominent), each specific proposal contains within it the germs of future generalized legislation.

The forecast is complicated, on the one hand, by the lack of clear-cut philosophy among the advocates of government regulation — they agree on the need for such regulation, but not on a common rationale or goal — and, on the other hand, by a similar lack of unity among the defenders of freedom from government regulation about the means by which self-regulation can be strengthened without becoming as burdensome as government intervention.

Information in this section was supplied by Mary-Jane Raphael, former senior vice-president, NAD; and it was updated by Phyllis E. Dubrow, attorney/senior advertising review specialist, NAD.

Appendix 1

The Role of Advertising and the Need for Regulation

Sir Gordon Borrie, Director General,
Office of Fair Trading, U.K.

The advertising industry, like The Advertising Association itself, is usually thought of as consisting of 3 parts: the advertisers, the agencies and the media. The first two of those parts have been well represented by very articulate spokespersons this afternoon. They have made some powerful comments about the value of advertising, within the marketing mix, as a vital ingredient of a developing free enterprise economy. No doubt the media too would enthuse about their role in marketing strategy as well as the essential contribution that advertising revenue makes to the viability of a free press. Martin Sorrell has in any case made that point.

I might seem to be the 'odd man out', the party pooper who spoils everything. For those among you who want a scrap, I am afraid I shall be something of a disappointment because I find myself in agreement with much of what has already been written. I share the view that advertising is a good thing – it is the means whereby new products enter the market thereby extending choice and ensuring effective competition. Advertising may also help consumers in an increasingly complicated market place by providing them with the information necessary for freedom of choice to be exercised between competing goods and services.

One of the clear objectives of the Office of Fair Trading is the promotion of competition in the provision of goods and services of all kinds: not only for the direct benefit of consumers, but as a means of promoting industrial and commercial efficiency. That necessarily involves our questioning any and every barrier to marketing and advertising. You will know that the initiatives taken by my Office have resulted in sweeping away the rigid restrictions on advertising that not long ago were the norm imposed by those professional bodies that govern accountants, lawyers, opticians, doctors and others.

But of course, while competition requires that people be free to advertise, misleading statements will distort competition. An efficient and truly competitive market depends upon the ready availability of truthful information and the suppression of misleading information and deception.

And the great paradox of competition is that those who are not succeeding in competition, those who are failing to compete on legitimate grounds may often resort to misleading the public. Obviously this is to the detriment of consumers but it is also to the disadvantage of their competitors. This is why certain rules and regulations are required. Regulation has often been regarded by the advertising industry as an unnecessary burden, a superfluous excrescence. It is no such thing – regulation is essential to give advertising the credibility and the reputation that are necessary for it to fulfil its marketing function. How can advertising effectively perform its task if lies are the norm or hyperbole is simply unrestrained?

The real problems for us all – those in the industry, consumer representatives, Parliament and Government – are where precisely are the lines to be drawn and who should exercise the restraints. In particular, is it to be done by self-regulation or by law and official Government appointed agencies? We can probably all agree that absolute freedom needs to be restrained where its value is outweighed by the harm it may do, but there is bound to be argument over where to draw the line and over time views will change.

And as to who should exercise the restraint, I think that question should be answered pragmatically. It is no good advocating self-regulation if there is no effective organisation within the industry to regulate it. Conversely, there is no point in imposing government regulation merely on the basis of some spurious generalisation that legislation is always more effective than self-regulation or that self-regulation seems to be less than effective elsewhere in the EC.

Where a self-regulatory system works; where there is a well-resourced piece of machinery provided by the industry to regulate it, with a proven track record, then let it continue to do so unimpeded. If it works, don't fix it.

I am an enthusiast for the work of the Advertising Standards Authority, and the way in which the British Code of Advertising Practice has worked and developed over the years. Both the ASA and the Code developed substantially in the 1970's in response to the prospect of Shirley Williams introducing statutory controls and the ASA has continued to respond since to changing needs. The phrase "legal, decent, honest and truthful" is well known but it is worth adding that the Code specifies two other essentials of good advertising: that all advertisements should be "prepared with a sense of responsibility both to the consumer and society" and that they should "conform to the principles of fair competition generally accepted in business".

In 1978, I published a report on this self-regulatory system of advertising control. The report was generally favourable, but it did highlight some deficiencies and made various recommendations which I'm glad to say the ASA "took on board". The report also identified the relatively few instances where the ASA was unable to provide an effective remedy and recommended that someone – and who better, I thought, than my Office – should be given a power to apply to the courts for an injunction to restrain an advertisement which was likely to deceive, mislead or confuse. In short, a sort of back-up for the ASA.

So when the EC proposed stronger legal controls in their 1984 Directive, the Government and the UK advertising industry were able to unite under a common banner of preserving our peculiarly British, but effective, system, adding only a regulatory back-up in the OFT to seek injunctions in court when sometimes the self-regulatory system failed. My proposals of 1978 therefore came to fruition in the 1988 Control of Misleading Advertisements Regulations.

My role under the Regulations is to support, not to replace the functions of such bodies as the ASA, the Direct Mail Services Standards Board, and the trading standards departments of local authorities.

In this way, the Regulations preserve all the benefits of long established means of advertising control, whilst providing a statutory back stop for use in exceptional circumstances.

The regulations are still in their infancy, but things appear to be working well. A new improved OFT/ASA relationship is developing (as indeed are relationships with other control bodies). The practicalities of "who does what and when" are sorting themselves out. Again, the ASA has responded to changing circumstances to establish and make viable the interplay between self-regulation and statutory control.

As can clearly be seen in the 1988 Regulations, statutory powers and self-regulation are compatible and mutually supportive. Legislative intervention of a particular kind is also needed for particular problem areas. There are many instances where there is an over-riding need for comprehensive and accurate consumer information which can only be achieved by legislating to ensure that specific information, uniformly presented, is available so that consumers can compare options and make the best choice to suit their particular needs.

I therefore have no doubt about the need for statutory intervention in the field of advertisements for credit. Credit facilities can be complex, the choice difficult for consumers to make, and the consequence especially with secured loans, disastrous if the consumer makes the wrong choice because he or she is misled or lacks the information needed for a sound decision.

That is why I felt it necessary firmly to remind credit advertisers, and their publishers, of their responsibilities to comply with the Consumer Credit Advertisements Regulations which came into operation on 1 February 1990, and of the consequences to them by way of enforcement, if they don't keep those responsibilities. The so-called health warning that must now accompany advertisements for secured credit – "Your home is at risk" – is essential to avoid people being misled.

There are certain circumstances where legislation is the only viable option. As I said earlier, it is no good advocating self-regulation if there is no trade association or other effective body within an industry to regulate it. That is what I found in the timeshare industry and hence my proposals for various legally enforced controls to deal with what has become a widespread scandal.

It may be that in the still continuing recent history of controls in this country over misleading advertising, we have stumbled upon a mix of self-regulation and legal regulation that may not satisfy any purist but may nonetheless be effective.

The precedent value of occasional judicial pronouncements combined with the continuous possibility of court action to combat deception seems to be a valuable supplement or complement to the well tried system of self-regulation.

So I would say to those in Brussels who are contemplating further legislation to control advertising, be pragmatic, do not deprecate a voluntary system merely as a matter of principle. Self-regulation may not work everywhere, but where it does, and it does in the UK, take care not to upset the effective status quo.

Sir Gordon Borrie

Appendix 2

This House Believes That the European Parliament Should Not Control Advertising

Roger Neill, IAA World President

Mr. Chairman, I must admit at the outset that this is a sad day for me. Sad, because, although I am personally a committed European, I must ask everyone here to support the motion that "this House believes that the European Parliament should not control advertising."

Sad, because on advertising issues the EC seems to be rushing helter skelter in exactly the opposite direction to the one which the Community was set up to create! But before I can do so, I must draw your attention to a point of detail that I am sure won't have escaped the notice of the many amongst you who are familiar with the workings of the Brussels, Strasbourg, Luxembourg triangle.

The European Parliament does not and cannot, by itself, control advertising! It does, however, deliver opinions on EC legislation proposed by the Commission, before decision by the Council of Ministers, and as such is in a position of considerable influence.

However, the thrust of the Motion is clear, and in the interest of being able realistically to continue, I shall propose that by the work "Parliament", we mean the whole lot of them, DG's, Commission, Council of Ministers and Parliament.

A Single Market

Let me begin by reminding you all that the establishment of an economy without barriers in the European Community by the end of 1992 will create a huge internal market of 340 million well-educated, affluent consumers. The purpose of "1992" is that marketers will compete freely and consumers will be able to exercise freedom of choice throughout this vast, new, single market.

Or will they?

In fact, reactionary forces have so infiltrated the issues involving advertising that the central 1992 goal of deregulation and freedom of choice is being severely compromised; reactionary forces which are determined to exploit use every opportunity to impose controls and limitations, particulary on advertising.

Let's pause for a moment to reflect on what advertising is, what it represents in society.

What Is Advertising?

Advertising is an essential part of any real democracy, which is always based on <u>freedom of choice</u>. Democracy recognizes and respects the ability of each individual person to assimilate information and to make well-informed choices. Advertising is also the voice of free enterprise. It is therefore anathema to zealous regulators everywhere, and to all who believe that society needs to be planned in a top-down way.

It is unfortunately the case that the EC seems to have more than its fair share of these people -- in all its institutions. Advertising is one of the most visible facets of the free market system, and, as such, it becomes an early target for "those who know best" to attack. They see advertising as a manipulative force in need of tight regulation or severe restriction -- preferably through legislation -- if the consumer is to be "protected." And so they frequently attack advertising by selecting the most restrictive regulation in force in one Member State and seeking to impose it, in the name of "harmonization", on all twelve.

But it is of the utmost importance that the 1992 programme really does create an open market, in which business is free to advocate legally-available products to people who are free to choose. Advertising will be a major driving force behind this new open market, yet without effective communication, genuine consumer choice will not exist. 1992 is all about operating a few market, and getting national products marketed across the whole of Europe. So it is surely nonsense to try to create an open market, while at the same time making effective advertising impossible.

The revival of Europe, indeed the <u>survival</u> of Europe, depends on the creation of a large, single market that, through economies of scale in production, in distribution and in research and development, allows business to develop and flourish on a larger scale.

The EC Commission, as such, is committed to the creation of a free market economy in a single market. But are they and the free market supporters in the Member States fully aware of the threats to the 1992 programme?

The purpose of the EC Commission's 1992 Directives is to liberalise. Unfortunately, many of the specific proposals are purely restrictive. It seems at this point that everywhere you look there are current or future threats to advertising: to the advertising of pharmaceuticals and motor cars; to the advertising of children's toys and alcohol; to the advertising of tobacco products and food products; to financial products; and to the whole of the direct marketing industry. What's more, there may be others in the regulatory pipeline we don't know about yet.

Mutual Recognition

One of the fundamental principles of the 1992 programme is the principle of "mutual recognition". Application of this agreed principle of mutual recognition to advertising services should mean that what is legally produced and then printed or broadcast in one Member State, should not be censored or restricted by others. It's an eminently sensible concept.

For example, the Directive on Transfrontier Broadcast (adopted last year) applies this principle of <u>mutual recognition</u>, by ensuring that broadcast transmitted from anywhere within the EC, that comply with the laws of their country of origin, must be freely accepted by receiving countries, without censorship of the incoming broadcast.

Principle of Subsidiarity

A second fundamental principle that has been adopted by the Commission is the principle of <u>subsidiarity</u>. The principle of subsidiarity means that what can be successfully and adequately achieved at one level of society, should not require interference from a higher level.

In the EC, the principle of subsidiarity means that the Community should not interfere in matters that can be competently handled by the Member States.

President Jacques Delors himself has said that subsidiarity is one of the "critical conditions which must be met if the Community is to be usefully governed."

One good example of the principle of subsidiarity is shown by the Directive on Misleading advertising (adopted in 1984). This Community Directive forbids Misleading advertising, but leaves the method of application open to national choice: by self-regulation, or by statutory law, or by a mixture of both. I believe that a well-managed system of self regulation is always preferable, always being faster in response than a protracted legal system of adjudication. But the point remains, that it's the national level which decides.

With such sensible principles to guide the development of Community legislation on the way forward to 1992 and beyond, why then are there so many threats to advertising?

The reason is because, despite the established principles of subsidiarity and mutual recognition, there is still no coherent policy on advertising at the European Institutions level. And very little real understanding of the value of advertising in all successful economies -- value to consumers, to manufacturers, to the media, to viewers and readers, in fact value to everyone.

On top of the lack of coherent policy, and the great chasm of lack of understanding, there is also the fact that the people dealing with advertising each have different sets of negative attitudes towards the subject.

First, there are those who believe that advertising is inherently bad and manipulative and therefore it has to be curtailed or banned.

Second, there are others who say that advertising is actually quite a good thing, but since it is fundamentally the purveyor of information to the consumer, it must not be too exciting or dramatic and must contain lots of factual information -- including (in some proposals) all the contents of the product label!

Third, there are those who say that there are differences in the way advertising is operated through the EC Member States, and if for no other reason than tidiness, those differences ought to be brought into line and harmonized.

At this point, I must admit very frankly that the "chasm of lack of understanding" which I described is partly the fault of the advertising industry -- ourselves. We have done an absolute inadequate job at explaining "how advertising works," and how it contributes to healthy economies. Across the entire political spectrum, there is ignorance about the function and benefits of advertising. But while the EC clears away obstacles to the free flow of products, some bureaucrats would like to replace them with obstacles designed to prevent people from knowing what the market has to offer. Why should we, the citizens of Europe, not be allowed to know the attributes, the qualities and the advantages of the products that are legally available to us?

At the same time, let's recognize that good advertising appeals both to the head and to the heart: to reason and emotion. We are not robots functioning on facts alone.

Single European Act

Why have all these threats become so much more dangerous in recent times? The answer lies partly in one specific measure. In 1987, the forward momentum to 1992 was given an extra boost by the Single European Act, which, in place of the customary unanimous voting, allowed qualified or weighted majority voting on all legislation which has as its object "the establishment and function of the internal market". Yet restriction of the rules and standards of advertising does absolutely nothing to contribute to "the establishment and functioning of the internal market." This Single Market machinery has been quite blatantly used for some quite specifically anti-1992 measures, without adequate justification, simply to satisfy the demands of vocal activists on particular issues and to make it easier to get new legislation on to the statute books.

It's quite clear that the liberalizing, deregulatory forces driving the EC forward have been greatly assisted, since the adoption of the Single European Act. However, we must be clear. Attempts are being made to introduce a series of Directives, based on the harmonization of the most restrictive practices, that suppress free commercial speech by curtailing the rights of advertisers to advocate their products and of consumers to receive market information.

We, Europe's citizens, have a right to hear about goods and services available to us. In order to communicate with consumers, advertisements must first capture their attention. In this swing toward harmonization, we are in practice being faced with "harmonization of the worst", the most restrictive.

Let's take some specifics:

- If Greece doesn't like advertisements for imported toys, should they be banned throughout the EC?

- If Ireland does not like ads for pregnancy-testing, should they be forbidden everywhere else?

- If Italy wishes to ban all advertising for medicinal products, should it be banned in 11 other countries?

Directives aimed at the <u>restriction of free commercial speech</u> are fundamentally opposed to what is intended to be a free and open market. These directives introduce new obstacles to trade just at the moment when the EC's internal barriers are being removed.

Some regulators pretend that showing the packaging and the name, is all that is needed in advertising. But lawyers could not possibly plead their Clients' cases in court simply on the basis of the Clients' names and the clothing they wear.

Advertising requires art and skill: knowledge and technique, to turn information into motivation: to move and convince either the jury in court -- or the jury in the market place.

It is surely nonsense to try to create an open market, while at the same time making effective advertising impossible.

Need for Self-Regulation

I think I should be very clear that I am not one of those who believe that there should be no regulation at all. People in a competitive market must accept the need for some degree of regulation. But the goal must be a regulatory framework in which <u>all</u> the participants can operate fairly -- free from <u>unwarranted</u> restrictions.

Advertising is <u>already</u> the subject of checks and balances in every one of the EC Member States -- by statute, by self-regulation or by a mixture of both. There is no reason why these checks and balances should not continue to co-exist, on the principle of subsidiarity and with mutual recognition body of the codes and of the systems of control.

We need the sort of regulation that enhances rather than hinders our ability to operate effectively.

But, put simply, restrictions on advertising in the Community will inevitably weaken the Internal Market, because advertising is so often the catalyst that makes the market itself grow. What's more, a weakened internal market will diminish European companies' competitive ability on the world scene. A company that is forbidden to make vigorous use of marketing communications in its home market will not be able to develop the necessary experience and expertise for successful marketing abroad.

If legislation stifles the ability of companies to market their wares freely, the EC Institutions could justifiably be accused of:

- erecting barriers to entry from newcomers;

- freezing monopoly positions where they already exist;

- discouraging product innovation;

- causing market shares to stagnate in their current positions.

It is indeed ironic that while the populations of Eastern Europe are escaping from the centrally controlled, dirigiste disaster called Communism, and clamouring to join our Community, it seems as though some people in the EC wish to impose on us many of the very restriction that Eastern Europe is seeking to reject.

A Free and Open Advertising Market

And so I call for a free and open advertising market, based on the principle of subsidiarity, of mutual recognition, and of self-regulation.

It must surely be obvious to all: that freedom of marketing communication is essential to all successful marketing; that it makes no sense to try to create an open, competitive market in the

EC unless the marketing communications that accompany brands are allowed to flow with equal freedom across European borders.

I welcome the progress of the EC. I wholeheartedly support the completion of the Single Market. But I equally wholeheartedly believe that to succeed, the Single Market must be as free and open for advertising services, as it is intended to be for all other good and services.

So I ought to be able to invite you to <u>oppose</u> this motion, but given the situation in practice, I must urge each and everyone of you, sadly, to <u>support</u> the motion.

With current attitudes within the Community, it could well be <u>disastrous</u> if the European Institutions control Advertising.

Thank you

Particular acknowledgement is made to the EAAA, Brussels, and the Advertising Association, London as important sources.

Appendix 3

International Code of Advertising Practice

International Chamber of Commerce

FOREWORD

The present edition of the **International Code of Advertising Practice** as adopted by the Executive Board of the ICC in its 47th session (Paris, 2 December 1986) has been updated in the light of developments since the previous edition of 1973 (ICC Publication n° 275).

As far as the Code itself is concerned most of the changes are of a relatively minor nature often aiming to clarify the text. The same applies to the Special Provisions which cover, in essence, the contents of what in the previous version was contained in Annex A relating to advertising for certain practices. Furthermore, the Guidelines for advertising addressed to children, adopted by the Executive Board of the ICC on 22 March 1982 are incorporated. On the other hand, most of Annex B of the previous version containing guidelines for advertising for particular products and services has not been incorporated in this new edition.

This was decided because it had become apparent that on this section a far more thorough revision was needed than could be carried out in the time set for the review of this Code. Since the last edition some international industry codes have emerged such as the IFPMA Code of pharmaceutical marketing practices. This raised the question whether detailed rules of interpretation on some or all of the areas covered were still needed and, if so, in what form. The Working Party on the Advertising Code has been given the task to study this matter.

INTRODUCTION

This edition of the ICC International Code of Advertising Practice follows the well-established policy of the ICC of promoting high standards of ethics in marketing by self-regulation against the background of national and international law.

The Code, which was first issued in 1937, later revised in 1949, 1955, 1966 and 1973, demonstrates that industry and commerce, including all parties involved in advertising, recognize their social responsibilities towards the consumer and the community, and the need to establish a fair balance between the interests of business and of consumers.

The edition combines past experience with current thinking based on the concept of advertising as a means of communication between sellers and customers. In this respect the ICC considers freedom of communication (as embodied in article 19 of the United Nations International Covenant of civil and political rights) as a fundamental principle.

The Code is designed primarily as an instrument for self-discipline but it is also intended for use by the Courts as a reference document within the framework of the appropriate laws.

The ICC believes that this new edition of the Code, like its predecessors, by promoting a further harmonization of advertising standards, will facilitate the circulation of goods and services across frontiers to the benefit of consumers and the community throughout the world.

SCOPE OF THE CODE

The Code applies to all advertisements for any goods, services and facilities, including corporate advertising. It should be read in conjunction with the other ICC Codes of Marketing Practice namely:
— Marketing Research Practice
— Sales Promotion Practice
— Direct Mail and Mail Order Sales Practice
— and Direct Sales Practice.

The Code sets standards of ethical conduct to be followed by all concerned with advertising, whether as advertisers, advertising practitioners or agencies, or media.

INTERPRETATION

The Code, including the Guidelines for advertising to Children (Sectorial Guidelines will be available separately), is to be applied in the spirit as well as in the letter.

Because of the different characteristics of the various media (press, television, radio and other electronic media, outdoor advertising, films, direct mail, etc.) an advertisement which is acceptable for one medium is not necessarily acceptable for another.

Advertisements should be judged by their likely impact on the consumer, bearing in mind the medium used.

The Code applies to the entire content of an advertisement, including all words and numbers (spoken and written), visual presentations, music and sound effects.

DEFINITIONS

For the purpose of this Code:

- the term "advertisement" is to be taken in its broadest sense to embrace any form of advertising for goods, services and facilities, irrespective of the medium used and including advertising claims on packs, labels and point of sale material.
- the term "product" includes services and facilities.
- the term "consumer" refers to any person to whom an advertisement is addressed or who is likely to be reached by it whether as a final consumer or as a trade customer or user.

BASIC PRINCIPLES

All advertising should be legal, decent, honest and truthful.

Every advertisement should be prepared with a due sense of social responsibility and should conform to the principles of fair competition, as generally accepted in business.

No advertisement should be such as to impair public confidence in advertising.

RULES

Decency

Article 1

Advertisements should not contain statements or visual presentations which offend against prevailing standards of decency.

Honesty

Article 2

Advertisements should be so framed as not to abuse the trust of the consumer or exploit his lack of experience or knowledge.

Article 3

1. Advertisements should not without justifiable reason play on fear.
2. Advertisements should not play on superstition.
3. Advertisements should not contain anything which might lead to or lend support to acts of violence.
4. Advertisements should avoid endorsing discrimination based upon race, religion or sex.

Truthful Presentation

Article 4

1. Advertisements should not contain any statement or visual presentation which directly or by implication, omission, ambiguity or exaggerated claim is likely to mislead the consumer, in particular with regard to

a) characteristics such as: nature, composition, method and date of manufacture, fitness for purpose, range of use, quantity, commercial or geographical origin;

b) the value of the product and the total price actually to be paid;

c) other terms of payment such as hire purchase, leasing, instalment sales and credit sale (see Special Provision b);

d) delivery, exchange, return, repair and maintenance;

e) terms of guarantee (see Special Provision a);

f) copyright and industrial property rights such as patents, trade marks, designs and models and trade names;

g) official recognition or approval, awards of medals, prizes and diplomas;

h) the extent of benefits for charitable causes.

2. Advertisements should not misuse research results or quotations from technical and scientific publications. Statistics should not be so presented as to imply a greater validity than they really have. Scientific terms should not be misused; scientific jargon and irrelevancies should not be used to make claims appear to have a scientific basis they do not possess.

Comparisons

Article 5

Advertisements containing comparisons should be so designed that the comparison itself is not likely to mislead, and should comply with the principles of fair competition. Points of comparison should be based on facts which can be substantiated and should not be unfairly selected.

Testimonials

Article 6

Advertisements should not contain or refer to any testimonial or endorsement unless it is genuine and related to the experience of the person giving it. Testimonials or endorsements which are obsolete or otherwise no longer applicable should not be used.

Denigration

Article 7

Advertisements should not denigrate any firm, industrial or commercial activity/profession or any product, directly or by implication, whether by bringing it into contempt or ridicule, or in any similar way.

Protection of privacy

Article 8

Advertisements should not portray or refer to any persons, whether in a private or a public capacity, unless prior permission has been obtained; nor should advertisements without prior permission depict or refer to any person's property in a way likely to convey the impression of a personal endorsement.

Exploitation of goodwill

Article 9

1. Advertisements should not make unjustifiable use of the name or initials of another firm, company or institution.

2. Advertisements should not take undue advantage of the goodwill attached to the name of a person, the trade name and symbol of another firm or product, or of the goodwill acquired by an advertising campaign.

Imitation

Article 10

1. Advertisements should not imitate the general layout, text, slogan, visual presentation, music and sound effects etc., of other advertisements in a way that is likely to mislead or confuse.

2. Where an international advertiser has established a distinctive advertising campaign in one or more countries, other advertisers should not unduly imitate this campaign in the other countries where he operates, thus preventing him from extending his campaign within a reasonable period of time to such countries.

Identification of advertisements

Article 11

Advertisements should be clearly distinguishable as such, whatever their form and whatever the medium used; when an advertisement appears in a medium which contains news or editorial matter, it should be so presented that it will be readily recognized as an advertisement.

Regard to safety

Article 12

Advertisements should not without reason, justifiable on educational or social grounds, contain any visual presentation or any description of dangerous practices or of situations which show a disregard for safety. Special care should be taken in advertisements directed towards or depicting children or young people.

Children and young people

Article 13

1. Advertisements should not exploit the natural credulity of children or the lack of experience of young people and should not strain their sense of loyalty.

2. Advertisements addressed to or likely to influence children or young people should not contain any statement or visual presentation which might result in harming them mentally, morally or physically.

Responsibility

Article 14

1. Responsibility for the observance of the rules of conduct laid down in the Code rests with the advertiser, the advertising practitioner or agency and the publisher, medium-owner or contractor.

   a) The advertiser should take the overall responsibility for his advertising.

   b) The advertising practitioner or agency should exercise every care in the preparation of the advertisement and should operate in such a way as to enable the advertiser to fulfil his responsibility.

   c) The publisher, medium-owner or contractor, who publishes, transmits or distributes the advertisement should exercise due care in the acceptance of advertisements and their presentation to the public.

2. Anyone employed within a firm, company or institution coming under the above three categories and who takes part in the planning, creation, publishing or transmitting of an advertisement, has a degree of responsibility commensurate with his position for ensuring that the rules of the Code are observed and should act accordingly.

Article 15

The responsibility for observance of the rules of the Code embraces the advertisement in its entire content and form, including testimonials and statements or visual presentations originating from other sources. The fact that the content or form originates wholly or in part from other sources is not an excuse for non-observance of the rules.

Article 16

An advertisement contravening the Code cannot be defended on the grounds that the advertiser or someone acting on his behalf has subsequently provided the consumer with accurate information.

Article 17

Descriptions, claims or illustrations relating to verifiable facts should be capable of substantiation. Advertisers should have such substantiation available so that they can produce evidence without delay to the self-regulatory bodies responsible for the operation of the Code.

Article 18

No advertiser, advertising practitioner or agency, publisher, medium-owner or contractor should be party to the publication of any advertisement which has been found unacceptable by the appropriate self-regulatory body.

Implementation

Article 19

This Code of self-discipline is to be applied nationally by bodies set up for the purpose and internationally by the ICC's International Council on Marketing Practice as and when the need arises.

SPECIAL PROVISIONS

The following provisions are intended to provide elaboration of relevant articles of the Code.

Guarantees

Provision a

Advertisements should not contain any reference to a guarantee which does not improve the legal position of the purchaser. Advertisements may contain the word "guarantee", "guaranteed", "warranty" or "warranted" or words having the same meaning only if the full terms of the guarantee as well as the remedial action open to the purchaser are clearly set out in the advertisements, or are available to the purchaser in writing at the point of sale, or with the goods.

Consumer credit, loans, savings and investments

Provision b

(1) Advertisements containing hire-purchase, credit sale or other consumer credit terms should be so presented that no misunderstanding could arise as to the cash price, deposit, schedule of payment, rate of interest and total cost of the goods as advertised or to the other conditions of sale.

(2) Advertisements offering loans should not contain any statement likely to mislead the public in respect of the type and duration of the loan, the securities required or other qualifications, the terms of repayment and the actual costs of interest and possible other charges.

(3) Advertisements relating to savings or investments should not contain any statement likely to mislead the public on the commitments undertaken, on the actual or estimated yield, stating the factors affecting this, and on possible tax benefits.

Unsolicited goods

Provision c

Advertisements should not be used in connection with the unfair sales method of supplying unsolicited products to a person who is required to pay for them unless he refuses or returns them, or who is given the impression that he is obliged to accept them (inertia selling).

Franchise schemes

Provision d

Advertisements by franchisors seeking franchisees should not mislead, directly or by implication, as to the support provided and likely reward, or the investment and work required. The full name and permanent address of the franchisor should be stated.

Parallel imports

Provision e

Advertisements for goods imported in parallel should avoid creating any misunderstanding in the minds of consumers concerning the characteristics of the goods offered or the ancillary services provided, particularly when these differ significantly from the goods otherwise distributed.

Poisonous and flammable products

Provision f

Advertisements for products which are potentially poisonous or flammable but which may not be readily recognized as such by consumers should indicate the potential danger of such products.

GUIDELINES FOR ADVERTISING ADDRESSED TO CHILDREN

The following guidelines are intended to provide interpretation of relevant articles of the Code.

The guidelines apply to advertisements for products whether paid for or given free

i) addressed to children under 14 years of age or whatever age is considered appropriate at the national level;

ii) in children's media (i.e. media specifically intended for children under 14 years of age or whatever age is considered appropriate at the national level).

Guidelines

Guideline 1 : Identification

Because of the particular vulnerability of children and in order to give special effect to Article 11 of the Code, if there is any likelihood of advertisements being confused with editorial or programme material, they should be clearly labelled "advertisement" or identified in an equally effective manner.

Guideline 2 : Violence

In giving effect to Article 13.2 of the Code it should be borne in mind that advertisements should not appear to condone violence in situations or actions which might contravene the law and/or generally accepted national standards of social behaviour.

Guideline 3 : Social Values

Advertisements should not undermine social values when suggesting that possession or use of a product alone will give the child a physical, social or psychological advantage over other children of the same age, or that non-possession of this product would have the opposite effect.

Advertisements should not undermine the authority, responsibility, judgment or tastes of parents, taking into account the current social values.

Guideline 4 : Security

To give effect to Articles 12 and 13.2 of the Code, advertisements should not contain any statement or visual presentation that could have the effect of bringing children into unsafe situations or of encouraging them to consort with strangers or to enter strange or hazardous places.

Guideline 5 : Persuasion

Advertisements should not include any direct appeal to children to persuade others to buy the advertised product for them.

Guideline 6 : Truthful presentation

To give effect to Article 4 of the Code, special care should be taken to ensure that advertisements do not mislead children as to the true size, value, nature, durability and performance of the advertised product. If extra items are needed to use it (e.g. batteries) or to produce the result shown or described (e.g. paint), this should be made clear. A product which is part of a series should be clearly indicated as should the method of acquiring the series.

Advertisements should not understate the degree of skill required to use the product. Where results of product use are shown or described, the advertisement should represent what is reasonably attainable by the average child in the age range for which the product is intended.

Guideline 7 : Price

Price indication should not be such as to lead children to an unreal perception of the true value of the product, for instance by using the word "only". No advertisement should imply that the advertised product is immediately within reach of every family budget.

Appendix 4

Canadian Code of Advertising Standards

Canadian Advertising Foundation

Advertising's Self-Regulatory Process

The <u>Canadian Code of Advertising Standards</u> has been developed to promote the professional practice of advertising. The Code's clauses set the criteria for acceptable advertising and form the basis upon which advertising is evaluated in response to consumer or trade complaints. The Code is generally endorsed by advertisers, advertising agencies, media which exhibit advertising, and suppliers to the advertising process. *(See appendix A)*

The Code is the principal instrument of self-regulation for the advertising industry in Canada, supplemented by the standards set by individual media and by other advertising-related associations. The Code does not supersede municipal, provincial or federal regulation affecting advertising. *(See appendix B)*

The Code is administered by the Advertising Standards Council, le Conseil des Normes de la Publicité, and by regional councils located in Vancouver, Edmonton, Calgary, Regina, Winnipeg and Halifax. The Council/Conseil and the regional bodies are supported and coordinated by the Standards Division of the Canadian Advertising Foundation. *(See appendix C)*

Definition of Advertising

For the purpose of this Code, *"advertising"* is defined as any paid message communicated by Canadian media with the intent to influence the choice, opinion or behaviour of those addressed by the commercial messages.

Application

The Code applies to advertisers promoting the use of goods and services, to corporations or institutions seeking to improve their public image, and to governments, government departments and crown corporations, provided such advertising meets the criteria set forth in the definition.

Exclusions

The Code does not govern or restrict the free expression of public opinion or ideas through advocacy advertising, or election advertising.

Scope of the Code

The Code deals with *how* products or services may be advertised, not with *which* products or services may be advertised. Thus, the authority of the Code applies only to the content of commercial messages and does not prohibit the promotion of legal products or services or their portrayal in circumstances of normal use. The content of the advertisement and audience reached or intended to be reached by the message are relevant factors in assessing its acceptability.

The Code

The Canadian Code of Advertising Standards has been approved and is supported by all participating organizations, and is designed to help set and maintain standards of honesty, truth, accuracy, fairness and taste in advertising. The principles underlying the Code and more detailed descriptions of its application are presented in the Manual of General Guidelines for Advertising.

No advertising shall be prepared or knowingly exhibited by the participating organizations which contravenes this Code of Standards.

The clauses should be adhered to both in letter and in spirit. Advertisers and advertising agencies must be prepared to substantiate their claims promptly to the Council upon request.

1.   Accuracy, Clarity

   (a)Advertisements must not contain inaccurate or deceptive claims, statements, illustrations, or representations, either direct or implied, with regard to price, availability or performance of a product or service. In assessing the truthfulness and accuracy of a message, the concern is not with the intent of the sender or precise legality of the presentation. Rather, the focus is on the message as received or perceived, that is, the general impression conveyed by the advertisement.

   (b)Advertisements must not omit relevant information in a manner which is deceptive.

   (c)All pertinent details of an advertised offer must be clearly stated.

(d)Disclaimers or asterisked information must not contradict more prominent aspects of the message and should be located and presented in such a manner as to be clearly visible.

2.   Disguised Advertising Techniques

No advertisement shall be presented in a format or style which conceals its commercial intent.

3.   Price Claims

(a)No advertisement shall include deceptive price claims or discounts, unrealistic price comparisons or exaggerated claims as to worth or value. "Regular Price", "Suggested Retail Price", "Manufacturer's List Price", and "Fair Market Value" are deceptive terms when used by an advertiser to indicate a savings, unless they represent prices at which a reasonable number of the item was actually sold within the preceding six months in the market place where the advertisement appears.

(b)Where price discounts are offered, qualifying statements such as "up to", "XX off", etc., must be in easily readable type, in close proximity to the prices quoted, and, where practical, legitimate regular prices must be included.

(c)Prices quoted in advertisements in Canadian media, other than in Canadian funds, must be so identified.

4.   Bait and Switch

Advertisements must not misrepresent the consumer's opportunity to purchase the goods and services at the terms presented. If supply of the sale item is limited, or the seller can fulfil only limited demand, this must be clearly stated in the advertisement.

5.   Guarantees

No advertisement shall offer a guarantee or warranty, unless the guarantee or warranty is fully explained as to conditions and limits and the name of the guarantor or warrantor is provided, or it is indicated where such information may be obtained.

6.   Comparative Advertising

Advertisements must not discredit, disparage or attack unfairly other products, services, advertisements, or companies or exaggerate the nature or importance of competitive differences.

7.   Testimonials

Testimonials, endorsations, or representations of opinion or preference must reflect the genuine, reasonably current opinion of the individual(s), group or organization making such representations, and must be based upon adequate information about or experience with the product or service being advertised, and must not otherwise be deceptive.

8.   Professional or Scientific Claims

Advertisements must not distort the true meaning of statements made by professionals or scientific authorities. Advertising claims must not imply they have a scientific basis which they do not truly possess. Any scientific, professional or authoritative claims or statements must be applicable to the Canadian context, unless otherwise clearly stated.

9.   Imitation

No advertiser shall imitate the copy, slogans, or illustrations of another advertiser in such a manner as to mislead the consumer.

10.   Safety

Advertisements must not display a disregard for public safety or depict situations which might encourage unsafe or dangerous practices, particularly when portraying products in normal use.

11.   Exploitation of Persons with Disabilities

Advertisements must not hold out false hope in the form of a cure or relief, either on a temporary or permanent basis, for persons who have disabilities.

12.   Superstition and Fears

Advertisements must not exploit superstitions or play upon fears to mislead the consumer.

13.   Advertising to Children

Advertising which is directed to children must not exploit their credulity, lack of experience, or their sense of loyalty, and must not present information or illustrations which might result in their physical, emotional or moral harm.

Child-directed advertising in the broadcast media is separately regulated by the Broadcast Code for Advertising to Children, also administered by the Canadian Advertising Foundation. Advertising to children in Quebec is prohibited by the Quebec Consumer Protection Act.

14.   Advertising to Minors

Products prohibited from sale to minors must not be advertised in such a way as to appeal particularly to persons under legal age and people featured in advertisements for such products must be, and clearly seen to be, adults under the law.

15.   Taste, Public Decency

It is recognized that standards of taste are subjective and vary widely from person to person and community to community, and are, indeed, subject to constant change. Advertising must not present demeaning or derogatory portrayals of individuals or groups; must not exploit violence, sexuality, children, the customs, convictions or characteristics of religious or ethno-cultural groups, persons with disabilities or any other person, group or institution in a manner which is offensive to generally prevailing standards.

Self-Regulation of Advertising in Canada

The Canadian Code of Advertising Standards was originally sponsored by the Canadian Advertising Advisory Board, the predecessor organization of the Canadian Advertising Foundation (CAF). First published in 1963, it has since been reviewed and revised periodically to keep it contemporary, and has been supplemented by other industry Codes. Change in the provisions of the Code is an ongoing process.

The CAF - Standards Division in Toronto handles all national advertising complaints and complaints from the Ontario region, when these concern English-language advertising; complaints from Quebec and all national French-language complaints, are handled by le Conseil des Normes de la Publicité in Montreal. The majority of these complaints are processed at the staff level and only unresolved complaints are referred to the Advertising Standards Council or le Conseil.

Across the country, regional councils - in the Atlantic provinces (Halifax), Manitoba (Winnipeg), Saskatchewan (Regina), Alberta (Calgary and Edmonton), and British Columbia (Vancouver) - handle local advertising complaints in their respective areas. Each council operates autonomously and, generally speaking, it is the full regional advertising council which reviews and rules on each complaint received.

Each council includes public representatives, nominated by consumer, academic or special interest groups, as well as representatives from advertisers, agencies and media.

Pre-Clearance Procedures

All English language broadcast commercials directed to children as well as English-language television commercials for feminine sanitary protection products, must be pre-cleared by special committees of the CAF prior to acceptance. Scripts and storyboards are checked by CAF staff but a final approval number is not given until the finished commercial has been viewed by the appropriate clearance committee.

Cosmetic advertising for broadcast must be pre-cleared by the appropriate government regulatory body. Broadcast scripts for cosmetic products may be submitted through the Toronto and Montreal offices of the Canadian Advertising Foundation. This service is offered in cooperation with the Health Protection Branch of the Department of Health and Welfare Canada.

A Pharmaceutical Advertising Advisory Board (PAAB) Code of Advertising Acceptance applies to advertisements for pharmaceutical products appearing in health-services magazines -- directed to doctors, dentists, hygienists, nurses and pharmacists. Such messages must also be pre-cleared. Because these messages are often highly technical, they are cleared by the Commissioner of the Pharmaceutical Advertising Advisory Board, of which the CAF is a member.

Role and Responsibilities of Council

The Advertising Standards Council, le Conseil and the regional councils are pledged to:

I   Review and, where appropriate, resolve public complaints regarding advertisements.

II   Work within the advertising industry and with consumer bodies in developing, updating, administering, and publicizing self-regulatory standards and codes.

III   Counsel individual advertisers and agencies on laws, regulations, standards and codes affecting advertising.

CAF staff in Toronto and Montreal maintain a tracking process to monitor trends in advertising, trends in advertising complaints, and to bring to the attention of the various advertising standards councils new developments so that the councils can review the information gathered and consider the appropriate action to be taken.

How to Complain

If you are exposed to advertising carried by Canadian media which you believe contravenes the Canadian Code of Advertising Standards, write to the Advertising Standards Council nearest you.

If it is a print advertisement, it helps if you can enclose a copy of the advertisement; with a broadcast message, identify the station, approximate time, the name of the product, etc. Give a brief written explanation as to why you think the message contravenes the Code.

The addresses of the various Councils are listed on page 14.

How Complaints are Received and Handled

All written complaints directed to the Toronto or Montreal office of the Canadian Advertising Foundation will be initially handled by Standards Division/le Conseil staff. Complaints to the Regional Councils are processed by the full council in that region. All written complaints will be acknowledged and reviewed and if there appears to be a Code violation, the advertiser will be notified of the nature of the complaint. The advertiser is required to respond to the enquiry and to provide the requested information so that a determination can be made as to whether the <u>Canadian Code of Advertising Standards</u> has been violated. If a violation has occurred, the advertiser is requested to amend the advertising in question or withdraw it. Once the advertiser has taken either of these two steps, the complaint will be closed and the complainant informed in writing of the corrective action taken by the advertiser.

If the complaint is not sustained, the complainant will be informed of the reasons why it has been determined that the advertising does not violate the Code.

If the advertiser or complainant disagrees with a staff or Council ruling, an appeal may be requested. The matter will be referred to, or back to, the Advertising Standards Council/le Conseil des Normes de la Publicité for a further review. If Council/Conseil sustains the complaint, the advertiser is notified, and asked to amend or withdraw the advertising. Generally, this closes the matter. Regardless of whether the complaint has been sustained or not, both the complainant and the advertiser will be notified of the outcome of an appeal. Occasionally an advertiser will be reluctant to take corrective action. When this occurs, the media involved will be notified indicating that this message has been judged to have contravened the Code. In general, this means that supporting media will not exhibit the advertising in that form.

Communications regarding the interpretation and application of the Code should be addressed to:

Canadian Advertising Foundation
Standards Division
350 Bloor Street East
Suite 402
Toronto, Ontario
M4W 1H5

or to:

le Conseil des Normes
de la Publicité
4823 ouest, rue Sherbrooke
suite 130
Montreal, Quebec
H3Z 1G7

Appendix A

Participants

The <u>Canadian Code of Advertising Standards</u> has been reviewed and approved by the following participating organizations:

Advertising and Sales Executive Club of Montreal
Association of Canadian Advertisers
Association of Medical Advertising Agencies
Association of Quebec Advertising Agencies
Better Business Bureau of Canada
Brewers Association of Canada
Canadian Association of Broadcasters
Canadian Broadcasting Corporation
Canadian Business Press
Canadian Cable Television Association
Canadian Community Newspapers Association
Canadian Cosmetic, Toiletry and Fragrance Association
Canadian Daily Newspaper Publishers Association
Canadian Direct Marketing Association* (See list of Other Industry Codes)
Canadian Magazine Publishers Association
Canadian National Yellow Pages Association
Direct Sellers Association
Grocery Products Manufacturers of Canada
Institute of Canadian Advertising
Le Publicité Club de Montréal
Magazines Canada
Non-Prescription Drug Manufacturers of Canada
Ontario Funeral Service Association
Outdoor Advertising Association of Canada
Pharmaceutical Advertising Advisory Board
Retail Council of Canada
Society of Ontario Advertising Agencies
Telecaster Committee of Canada
Trans Ad Limited
Trans-Canada Advertising Agency Network
Welcome Wagon Ltd.

The Canadian Advertising Foundation and the regional advertising standards councils also endorse in principle the <u>International Code of Advertising Practice</u>, developed by the International Chamber of Commerce and now adopted in some 30 countries.

Appendix B

Legislation Affecting Advertising

FEDERAL ACTS

Broadcasting Act (Sections 5(1),(2), 8(1),(2),(3),(4), 16)
Regulations: Advertising Generally
                Liquor, Beer, Wine and Cider Advertising Criteria
                Food and Drugs

Circulars

Pre-clearance of ads for food and drug commercials
Food advertising
Registration procedures for television commercials
Canadian Human Rights Act
Competition Act
Consumer Packaging and Labelling Act
Copyright Act
Criminal Code
Department of National Revenue - Customs and Excise Tariff
Items 99221-1, Schedule C, June 30, 1972
Food and Drugs Act
Canada Hazardous Products Act
Income Tax Act (Section 19)
National Trade Mark and True Labelling Act
Official Languages Act
Textile Labelling Act
Trade Marks Act

PROVINCIAL ACTS

British Columbia
Trade Practices Act
Consumer Protection Act and Regulations
Closing Out Sales Act
Human Rights Act
Motor Dealer Advertising Guidelines
Liquor, Beer and Wine Advertising Regulations

Alberta
The Unfair Trade Practices Act
Consumer Credit Transactions Act
Liquor, Beer and Wine Advertising Regulations

Saskatchewan
Consumer Products Warranties Act
Cost of Credit Disclosure Act
Liquor, Beer and Wine Advertising Regulations

Manitoba
Consumer Protection Act
Trade Practices Inquiry Act
Liquor, Beer and Wine Advertising Regulations

Ontario
Business Practices Act
Consumers Protection Act
Human Rights Code
Regulation 12B (credit advertising)
Liquor Control Act

Quebec
Charter of the French Language
(under above heading) Regulations - Language of Business and Commerce
Consumer Protection Act
(under above heading) Regulation - Children's Advertising
Lotteries Act - Publicity Contests and Lotteries
Broadcast Advertising Tax Act
Agricultural Products, Marine Products and Food Act
Liquor, Beer and Wine Advertising Regulations
Pharmacy, Professional Advertising Regulations
Roadside Advertising Act
Act Respecting Class Actions

New Brunswick
Consumer Product Warranty and Liability Act
Cost of Credit Disclosure Act

Nova Scotia
Consumer Protection Act
Liquor, Beer and Wine Advertising Regulations

Prince Edward Island
Business Practices Act
Consumer Protection Act
Highway Advertisements Act
Liquor, Beer and Wine Advertising Regulations

Newfoundland
Trade Practices Act
Consumer Protection Act
Exhibition of Advertisements (Billboards) Act
Liquor, Beer and Wine Advertising Regulations

Other Industry Codes

Advertising Code of Standards for Cosmetics, Toiletries and Fragrances
Broadcast Code for Advertising to Children
Cosmetic Code for Advertising Acceptance
CBC Advertising Standards
Code of Consumer Advertising Practices for Non-Prescription Medicines
Canadian Direct Marketing Association Code of Ethics and
        Standards of Practice
Guidelines for the Use of Comparative Advertising in Food Commercials
Guidelines for the Use of Research and Survey Data in
        Comparative Food Commercials
Pharmaceutical Advertising Advisory Board Code of
        Advertising Acceptance
Telecaster Committee of Canada Guidelines
Television Code of Standards for the Advertising of Feminine Sanitary
        Protection Products

Appendix C

You may obtain free copies (up to 5) of the <u>Canadian Code of Advertising Standards</u>, in French or English, by writing to:

CAF - Standards Council	*le Conseil des Normes de la Publicité*
350 Bloor Street East	*4823 ouest, rue Sherbrooke*
Suite 402	*suite 130*
Toronto, Ontario	*Montreal, Quebec*
Canada M4W 1H5	*Canada H3Z 1G7*

Regional Councils:

Advertising Standards Council - B.C.
P.O. Box 3005
Vancouver, B.C.
Canada V6B 3X5

Alberta Advertising Standards Council - Calgary
P.O. Box 2400, Station M
215 - 16 Street S.E.
Calgary, Alberta
Canada T2P 0W8

Alberta Advertising Standards Council - Edmonton
Box 5030, Postal Station E
Edmonton, Alberta
Canada T5P 4C2

Advertising Standards Council - Saskatchewan
P.O. Box 1322
Regina, Saskatchewan
Canada S4P 3B8

Advertising Standards Council - Manitoba
P.O. Box 848
1700 Church Avenue
Winnipeg, Manitoba
Canada R2X 3A2

Advertising Standards Council - Atlantic
P.O. Box 3112
Halifax, Nova Scotia
Canada B3J 3G6

Appendix 5

Le Code Canadien des Normes de la Publicité

Conseil des Normes de la Publicité

LE MÉCANISME

Le *Code canadien des normes de la publicité* fut rédigé dans le but de promouvoir la pratique professionnelle de la publicité.

Les articles du Code décrivent les critères qui rendent acceptable une publicité, et qui constituent le fondement de l'évaluation de toute publicité qui serait remise en question par des plaintes en provenance de consommateurs ou de l'industrie elle-même. Le Code est endossé de façon générale par les annonceurs, les agences de publicité, les médias qui diffusent de la publicité, ainsi que les fournisseurs qui interviennent dans le processus publicitaire. (Voir Annexe A).

Le Code est le principal outil utilisé en matière d'autoréglementation de l'industrie canadienne de la publicité ; viennent s'y ajouter, à titre de complément, les normes fixées par les médias pris individuellement et par les associations actives au sein de l'industrie. Les réglementations municipales, provinciales ou fédérales en matière de publicité ont préséance sur ce Code.

Le Code est administré par le Conseil des Normes de la Publicité, l'Advertising Standards Council et les conseils régionaux situés à Vancouver, Edmonton, Calgary, Regina, Winnipeg et Halifax. Le Conseil/Council et les conseils régionaux jouissent du soutien fourni par la Division des normes de la Fondation canadienne de la publicité qui en assure également la coordination.

LA DÉFINITION DE LA PUBLICITÉ

Dans le contexte de ce Code, la publicité se définit comme étant tout message payé, rendu public par les médias canadiens dans le but d'influencer le choix, l'opinion ou la conduite de ceux que vise ledit message commercial.

L'APPLICATION

Ce Code s'applique aux annonceurs qui promeuvent l'utilisation de biens et services, à des entreprises, compagnies ou institutions qui cherchent à parfaire leur image publique, ainsi qu'aux gouvernements, aux ministères et aux sociétés de la couronne, en autant que leurs publicités rencontrent les critères mentionnés dans la définition qui précède.

LES EXCLUSIONS

Ce Code ne régit, ni ne restreint la libre expression d'opinions publiques ou d'idées exprimées dans une publicité courante ou dans une publicité électorale.

L'AUTORITÉ DU CODE ET LA JURIDICTION DU CONSEIL

Le *Code canadien des normes de la publicité* se prononce sur la façon dont les produits ou les services peuvent être annoncés, et non pas sur quels produits et services peuvent être annoncés. Ainsi, l'autorité du Code porte uniquement sur le contenu des publicités, et n'interdit pas la promotion de produits ou de services légaux, ou leur illustration dans des circonstances d'usage normal.

Le contenu de la publicité et l'auditoire rejoint ou visé par la publicité constituent des facteurs d'évaluation pertinents lorsqu'il s'agit de déterminer si une publicité est acceptable ou non.

LE CODE

Le *Code canadien des normes de la publicité* a été approuvé et est endossé par tous les organismes participant au processus de la publicité, et il a pour but de contribuer à établir et maintenir des normes d'honnêteté, de véracité, d'exactitude, d'équité et de clarté dans la publicité. Les principes qui soustendent le Code et la description plus détaillée de ses applications font l'objet d'énoncés dans le *Manuel des lignes directrices en matière de publicité*.

Aucune publicité qui enfreint ce Code de normes ne doit être préparée, ni présentée en connaissance de cause par les organismes participants. (Voir Annexe A). On devra se conformer à l'esprit et à la lettre des articles qui suivent.

Advenant que le Conseil demande aux annonceurs et aux agences de publicité de prouver ce qu'ils énoncent dans leur publicité, ils doivent être prêts à lui répondre selon ses exigences.

1. Véracité, clarté, exactitude

(a) Les publicités ne doivent pas comporter d'allégations ou de déclarations inexactes ou mensongères énoncées directement ou implicitement quant au prix, à la disponibilité ou à l'efficacité d'un produit ou service. Lorsque le Conseil doit attester de la véracité d'un message, il ne s'intéressera pas à la légalité de sa formulation ou à l'intention de l'annonceur. Il considérera plutôt le message tel que reçu ou perçu, c'est-à-dire l'impression générale qui s'en dégage.

(b) Une publicité ne doit pas omettre une information pertinente de façon à être mensongère.

(c) Tous les détails pertinents se rapportant à une offre annoncée doivent être clairement énoncés.

(d) Toute exclusion de responsabilité ou toute information accompagnée d'un astérisque ne doit pas contredire les aspects importants du message, et doit être présentée et située dans le message de manière à être très visible.

2.   Techniques publicitaires déguisées

Aucune publicité ne doit être présentée dans un format ou un style qui masque son but commercial.

3.   Indications de prix

(a) Aucune publicité ne comportera d'indications de prix ou de rabais mensongères, ni de comparaisons irréalistes quant aux prix, ni de déclarations exagérées quant à la valeur ou aux avantages du produit ou du service en cause.

Les expressions « prix régulier », « prix de détail suggéré », « prix de liste du manufacturier » et « valeur marchande équitable » induisent en erreur lorsqu'elles sont utilisées par un annonceur individuel pour indiquer une économie, à moins qu'elles ne présentent des prix auxquels une quantité raisonnable d'articles ont réellement été vendus au cours des six mois précédents, dans le marché où la publicité est diffusée.

(b) Lorsque les rabais sont offerts, les énoncés les qualifiant, « jusqu'à », « xx de moins » et autres, doivent être présentés dans un caractère d'imprimerie facile à lire, se trouver à proximité des prix mentionnés et, en autant que cela est pratique, les prix réguliers doivent être cités.

(c) Les prix mentionnés dans les médias canadiens qui sont des montants autres que canadiens doivent être spécifiés.

4.   Appât et substitution

Les publicités ne doivent pas faussement donner à croire aux consommateurs qu'ils ont la possibilité de se procurer les marchandises ou services annoncés aux conditions indiquées, alors que tel n'est pas le cas.

Si la quantité de l'article offert est limitée, ou si le vendeur ne peut combler qu'une demande limitée, cela doit être clairement indiqué dans la publicité.

5.   Garanties

Aucune publicité ne doit offrir une garantie sans que ses conditions, ses limites et le nom du garant ne soient clairement indiqués, ou que l'on fasse mention de l'endroit où elle peut être obtenue.

6.   Publicité comparative

La publicité ne doit pas discréditer, attaquer ou dénigrer injustement les autres produits, services, publicités ou compagnies, ou exagérer la nature ou l'importance de différences entre produits concurrents.

7.   Témoignages

Les témoignages, endossements ou représentations d'opinion ou de préférence doivent refléter l'opinion véritable et raisonnablement actuelle de la personne ou des personnes, groupes ou organisations qui les donnent, se fonder sur des renseignements ou une expérience appropriée quant au produit ou service faisant l'objet de la publicité, et ne doivent pas être autrement trompeurs.

8. Déclarations de professionnels (les) ou de scientifiques

Les publicités ne doivent pas altérer la portée véritable des énoncés faits par des professionnels (les) ou des scientifiques reconnus. Les énoncés publicitaires ne doivent pas laisser entendre qu'ils sont prouvés scientifiquement quand ils ne le sont pas.

Tout énoncé ou déclaration scientifique, professionnel ou expert doit s'appliquer au contexte canadien, à moins qu'il n'en soit autrement mentionné de façon claire.

9. Imitation

Aucune publicité n'imitera les textes, slogans ou illustrations d'un concurrent de manière à induire le public en erreur.

10. Sécurité

Les publicités ne doivent pas témoigner d'indifférence à l'égard de la sécurité du public, ni présenter des situations de nature à encourager des pratiques inappropriées, imprudentes ou dangereuses, surtout lorsqu'elles illustrent des produits d'usage normal.

11. Exploitation des personnes handicapées

Les publicités ne doivent pas offrir de faux espoirs de guérison ou de soulagement, sur une base temporaire ou permanente pour les personnes handicapées.

12. Superstitions et frayeurs

Les publicités ne doivent pas exploiter les superstitions ou jouer sur les frayeurs pour tromper les consommateurs.

13. Publicité destinée aux enfants

La publicité qui est destinée aux enfants ne doit pas exploiter leur crédulité, leur inexpérience ou leur esprit d'acceptation, ni présenter des informations ou illustrations aptes à leur causer un tort physique, mental ou moral.

La publicité radiotélévisée destinée aux enfants est réglementée de façon distincte par le *Code de la publicité radiotélévisée destinée aux enfants*, administré par la Fondation canadienne de la publicité au Canada anglais.

La publicité destinée aux enfants est interdite au Québec par les articles 248 et 249 de la Loi de la protection du consommateur et le Règlement dont la loi est assortie.

14. Publicité destinée aux mineurs

Les produits dont la vente aux mineurs est défendue ne doivent pas être annoncés de manière à être particulièrement attrayants aux personnes qui n'ont pas encore atteint l'âge adulte légal.

Les personnes qui figurent dans des publicités portant sur ces produits doivent être, et paraître clairement des adultes tels que la loi les définit.

15. Matière de goût, d'opinion et de convenances
Il est acquis que les règles du bon goût sont subjectives, qu'elles varient considérablement selon les individus et les lieux, et qu'elles sont par conséquent en constante évolution.

La publicité ne doit pas dénigrer ou déprécier des individus ou des groupes d'individus ; elle ne doit pas exploiter la violence, la sexualité, les enfants, les coutumes, les croyances ou les traits caractéristiques des groupes religieux ou ethnoculturels, les personnes désavantagées ou quelque autre personne, groupe ou institution d'une manière offensante, compte tenu des normes de convenance généralement admises.

L'AUTORÉGLEMENTATION DE LA PUBLICITÉ AU CANADA

Le *Code canadien des normes de la publicité* fut, à l'origine, parrainé par le Bureau consultatif de la publicité au Canada, l'organisme qui précéda la Fondation canadienne de la publicité. Sa première édition remonte à 1963 et, depuis, il a fait l'objet de révisions et de refontes de façon suivie, de manière à ce qu'il réponde à l'évolution de la société. De plus, à ce Code s'en sont ajoutés d'autres. Les modifications apportées au Code depuis 1963 sont constantes.

La Division des normes de la Fondation canadienne de la publicité se trouve à Toronto et s'occupe de toutes les plaintes touchant la publicité nationale de langue anglaise, de même que celles qui portent sur la publicité ontarienne.

Les plaintes émanant du Québec, de même que les plaintes touchant la publicité nationale de langue française en provenance des communautés francophones hors Québec, relèvent du Conseil des Normes de la Publicité (CNP), dont le bureau se trouve à Montréal.

La majorité de ces plaintes sont traitées par le personnel du Conseil, et ce ne sont que les plaintes non réglées qui sont acheminées vers le Conseil des Normes de la Publicité qui regroupe 19 personnes bénévoles.

Des conseils régionaux, d'un bout à l'autre du pays - dans les Maritimes (Halifax), au Manitoba (Winnipeg), en Saskatchewan (Regina), en Alberta (Calgary et Edmonton) ainsi qu'en Colombie-Britannique (Vancouver) -, se chargent des plaintes au sujet de la publicité d'expression anglaise dans leur région respective.

Chaque conseil régional opère de façon autonome et, généralement parlant, c'est le conseil réuni au complet qui examine les plaintes reçues et se prononce à leur sujet. Chaque conseil régional regroupe des représentants du public désignés par des groupes de consommateurs ou d'intérêt public, ou des milieux de l'éducation.

LA PRÉAPPROBATION

Avant d'être acceptées, toutes les publicités anglophones radiotélévisées destinées aux enfants, de même que les publicités anglophones portant sur les produits d'hygiène féminine doivent être révisées par des comités spécialement mis sur pied à cette fin par la Fondation canadienne de la publicité. Les textes et les scénarios-maquettes font l'objet d'une vérification de la part du personnel de la Fondation, mais une approbation finale, sous forme de numéro, n'intervient qu'après le visionnement du message publicitaire final par le comité d'autorisation désigné.

Les publicités radiotélévisées portant sur les cosmétiques, produits de toilette et parfums, doivent être d'abord préapprouvées par le service gouvernemental approprié ou le Conseil. Les textes de publicité des produits cosmétiques, produits de toilette et parfums peuvent être approuvés par le Conseil. Ce service est offert en collaboration avec la Direction générale de la protection de la santé de Santé et Bien-être social Canada.

Le *Code d'acceptation de la publicité* du Conseil consultatif de la publicité pharmaceutique s'applique à toutes les publicités de produits pharmaceutiques publiées dans les magazines d'hygiène et services destinés aux médecins, dentistes, hygiénistes, infirmières et infirmiers. Ces publicités doivent, elles aussi, avoir été approuvées avant d'être acceptées par les médias. Du fait que ces publicités sont souvent éminemment techniques, leur approbation dépend du commissaire du Conseil consultatif sur la publicité pharmaceutique auquel siège la Fondation canadienne de la publicité.

LE RÔLE ET LES RESPONSABILITÉS DU CONSEIL

Le Conseil des Normes de la Publicité, l'Advertising Standards Council et les conseils régionaux s'engagent à :

1. Examiner et, selon le cas, régler les plaintes du public en matière de publicité.

2. Travailler de concert avec l'industrie de la publicité et les organismes de consommateurs afin de rédiger, mettre à jour, administrer et diffuser dans le grand public les normes d'autoréglementation et les codes d'éthique publicitaire.

3. Conseiller individuellement les annonceurs et les agences de publicité au sujet des lois, règlements, normes et codes qui touchent la publicité.

Le personnel à Montréal et à Toronto a développé un processus de repérage d'indices l'amenant à surveiller, (a) les tendances en matière de publicité, (b) les tendances révélées par les plaintes, et ce, afin d'attirer l'attention des divers conseils des normes quant aux nouveaux développements ; ainsi peuvent-ils, à l'examen de l'information recueillie, déterminer les actions appropriées à prendre.

COMMENT SE PLAINDRE

Si vous avez connaissance d'une publicité diffusée par les médias canadiens qui, à votre avis, contrevient au *Code canadien des normes de la publicité*, écrivez au Conseil des Normes de la Publicité. S'il s'agit d'un imprimé, il est bon de joindre un exemplaire ou une photocopie de la publicité ; s'il s'agit d'une publicité radio ou télédiffusée, indiquez la station, l'heure approximative, l'appellation du produit, etc.

Expliquez-nous simplement en quoi vous estimez que la publicité en question enfreint le Code.

L'adresse du Conseil de trouve à la page 9.

LE CHEMINEMENT DES PLAINTES

Toutes les plaintes écrites envoyées au Conseil des Normes de la Publicité sont d'abord examinées par son personnel. Elles font l'objet d'un accusé de réception : et si, à l'étude, il s'avère qu'elles semblent contrevenir, ou contreviennent à leur face même, à l'un des articles du Code, l'annonceur est prévenu de la nature de la plainte.

L'annonceur doit répondre à la communication du Conseil et fournir l'information requise, de manière à ce qu'il lui soit possible de déterminer si oui ou non il y a contravention au Code. Si oui, l'annonceur est prié de modifier sa publicité ou de la retirer. Dès que l'annonceur a posé un des deux gestes requis, la plainte est réglée, et le (la) plaignant (e) est informé (e) de la mesure adoptée par l'annonceur.

Si la plainte n'est pas retenue, le Conseil en informe le (la) plaignant (e) en motivant sa réponse à l'effet que la publicité ne contrevient pas au Code.

Si l'annonceur ou le (la) plaignant (e) n'est pas d'accord avec la décision du Conseil, il (elle) peut en appeler. Son appel sera transmis aux 19 membres du Conseil, afin qu'ils révisent le tout. Si les membres du Conseil retiennent la plainte, l'annonceur en est prévenu, et il est prié de modifier sa publicité ou de la retirer. Habituellement, cette intervention met un terme au processus.

Il est bien entendu que, quelle que soit la décision au sujet d'une plainte - retenue ou pas -, le plaignant et l'annonceur sont prévenus du résultat de leur appel. Il peut arriver, mais cela est exceptionnel, qu'un annonceur soit réticent à corriger sa publicité. Dans un tel cas, le média qui a diffusé sa publicité est prévenu par le Conseil que cette publicité a été jugée en contravention du Code. Cela signifie, règle générale, que le média ne diffusera plus la publicité dans sa forme originale.

Toute demande au sujet de l'interprétation et de l'administration du Code doit être dirigée au :

Conseil des Normes de la Publicité
4823, rue Sherbrooke Ouest
Bureau 130
Montréal (Québec)
H3Z 1G7

ANNEXE A

LES PARTICIPANTS

Cette dernière édition du *Code canadien des normes de la publicité* a été révisée et approuvée par les associations et groupes suivants :

• Advertising and Sales Executives Club of Montreal
• L'Association canadienne de la télévision par câble
• L'Association canadienne de la presse agricole
• L'Association canadienne des annonceurs
• L'Association canadienne des brasseurs
• L'Association canadienne des cosmétiques, produits de toilette et parfums
• L'Association canadienne des éditeurs de magazines
• L'Association canadienne des éditeurs de quotidiens
• L'Association canadienne des radiodiffuseurs
• L'Association canadienne des spécialités grand public
• L'Association canadienne du marketing direct (voir la liste des autres codes)
• L'Association de la publicité extérieure du Canada
• L'Association de la vente directe
• L'Association des agences de publicité du Québec
• L'Association des journaux communautaires canadiens
• L'Association nationale des Pages jaunes du Canada
• Association of Medical Advertising Agencie•s
• Bienvenue chez nous limitée
• Le Bureau d'éthique commerciale du Canada
• Le Comité des télédiffuseurs du Canada
• Le Conseil canadien du commerce de détail
• Le Conseil consultatif de la publicité pharmaceutique
• Les Fabricants canadiens de produits alimentaires
• L'Institut de la publicité canadienne
• Magazines Canada
• La Presse d'affaires canadienne
• Le Publicité-Club de Montréal
• Le Réseau transcanadien des agences de publicité
• La Société des agences de publicité de l'Ontario
• La Société Radio-Canada
• Trans-Ad Limited

Le Conseil des Normes de la Publicité appuie également, en principe, le *Code international de la publicité* de la Chambre de commerce internationale qui est en vigueur dans quelque 30 pays.

ANNEXE B

LES LOIS TOUCHANT LA PUBLICITÉ

Lois fédérales

•La Loi de la radiodiffusion : articles 5(1), (2), 8(1), (2), (3), (4) et 16

Règlements :
- portant sur la publicité en général
- portant sur les boissons alcooliques, la bière, le vin et le cidre
- aliments et drogues

Circulaires :
- autorisation des messages publicitaires d'aliments et de drogues
- publicité des aliments
- registre des méthodes touchant la réclame publicitaire télévisée

- La Loi sur les droits de la personne
- La Loi sur la concurrence
- La Loi sur l'emballage et l'étiquetage des produits de consommation
- La Loi sur le droit d'auteur
- Le Code criminel

Ministère du Revenu national :
- Item 99221-1 sur la taxe d'importation et d'accise, cédule tarifaire C, 30 juin 1972

- La Loi des aliments et drogues
- La Loi sur les produits dangereux
- La Loi de l'impôt sur le revenu : article 19
- La Loi sur la marque de commerce nationale et sur l'étiquetage exact
- La Loi sur les langues officielles
- La Loi sur l'étiquetage des textiles
- La Loi sur les marques de commerce

Lois provinciales

Alberta
- The Unfair Trade Practices Act
- Credit and Loan Agreements Act
- Liquor, Beer & Wine Advertising Regulations

Colombie-Britannique
- Trade Practices Act
- Consumer Protection Act and Regulations
- Closing Out Sales Act
- Motor Dealer Guidelines
- Liquor, Beer & Wine Advertising Regulations

Ontario
- Business Practices Act

- Consumer Protection Act
- Human Rights Code (voir les équivalents dans les autres provinces canadiennes)
- Regulation 12B (Credit Advertising)
- Liquor Control Act

Québec

- Charte de la langue française
- Règlements - La langue des affaires et du commerce
- Loi sur la protection du consommateur et son règlement de la publicité destinée aux enfants
- Loi sur les loteries, les courses, les concours publicitaires et les appareils d'amusement
- Loi relative à la taxe sur la publicité radio et télédiffusée
- Loi sur les produits agricoles et aliments
- Règlements sur la publicité des alcools, de la bière et des vins
- Règlements concernant la publicité professionnelle et pharmaceutique
- Loi sur la publicité extérieure
- Loi sur le recours collectif

Saskatchewan

- Consumer Products Warranties Act
- Cost of Credit Disclosure Act
- Liquor, Beer and Wine Advertising Regulations

Manitoba

- Consumer Protection Act
- Trade Pactices Inquiry Act
- Liquor, Beer and Wine Advertising Regulations

Nouveau-Brunswick

- Consumer Product Warranty & Liability Act
- Cost of Credit Disclosure Act

Nouvelle-Écosse

- Consumer Protection Act
- Liquor, Beer & Wine Advertising Regulations

Île du Prince-Édouard

- Business Practices Act
- Consumer Protection Act
- Highway Advertisements Act
- Liquor, Beer & Wine Advertising Regulations

Terre-Neuve

- Trade Practices Act
- Consumer Protection Act
- Exhibition of Advertisements (Billboards) Act
- Liquor, Beer & Wine Advertising Regulations

LES AUTRES CODES D'ÉTHIQUE PUBLICITAIRE

• Code d'acceptation de la publicité du Conseil consultatif de la publicité pharmaceutique

• Code d'acceptation de la publicité sur les cosmétiques

• Code d'éthique et de normes dans la pratique de l'Association canadienne de marketing direct

• Code de la publicité aux consommateurs des médicaments dispensés sans ordonnance médicale

• Code de la publicité destinée au grand public des cosmétiques, produits de toilette et parfums

• Code de la publicité radiotélévisée destinée aux enfants

• Code des normes concernant la publicité à la télévision des produits d'hygiène féminine

• Code du marketing direct touchant la publicité des produits horticoles

• Code publicitaire de Radio-Canada

• Directives du Comité des télédiffuseurs du Canada

• Lignes directrices de toute publicité comparative en matière d'alimentation

• Lignes directrices portant sur l'utilisation, dans les messages publicitaires, de données résultant d'enquêtes et de recherches en matière d'alimentation

• • Au nom de la Fondation canadienne de la publicité, administration par le Conseil des *Lignes directrices en matière de stéréotypes sexistes.*

ANNEXE C

On peut obtenir un exemplaire gratuit du *Code canadien des normes de la publicité*, en écrivant ou en téléphonant au :

Conseil des Normes de la Publicité
4823, rue Sherbrooke Ouest
Bureau 130
Montréal (Québec) , Canada H3Z 1G7
Téléphone: 514-931-8060   Télécopieur : 514-931-2797

Des exemplaires (un seul gratuit) du Canadian Code of Advertising Standards sont également disponibles au Conseil des Normes de la Publicité. On peut communiquer avec la Division des Normes de la Fondation Canadienne de la Publicité/CAF - Standards Division et l'Advertising Standards Council, en écrivant à :

CAF - Standards Division and Council
350 Bloor Street East
Suite 402
Toronto, Ontario, Canada M4W 1H5
Téléphone : 416-961-6311   Télécopieur : 416-961-7904

Les conseils régionaux sont les suivants :
Advertising Standards Council - B. C.
P. O. Box 3005
Vancouver, B. C., Canada V6B 3X5

Alberta Advertising Standards Council - Calgary
Box CH 3000
Calgary, Alberta, Canada T2P 0W8

Alberta Advertising Standards Council - Edmonton
Box 5030, Postal Station E
Edmonton, Alberta, Canada T5P 4C2

Advertising Standards Council - Saskatchewan
P. O. Box 1322
Regina, Saskatchewan, Canada S4P 3B8

Advertising Standards Council - Manitoba
P. O. Box 848
1760, Church Avenue
Winnipeg, Manitoba, Canada R2X 3A2

Advertising Standards Council - Atlantic
P. O. Box 3112
Halifax, Nova Scotia, Canada B3J 3G6

Appendix 6

National Advertising Division/ National Advertising Review Board Procedures

Council of Better Business Bureaus, Inc.

Council of Better Business Bureaus
National Advertising Division Resolution Process

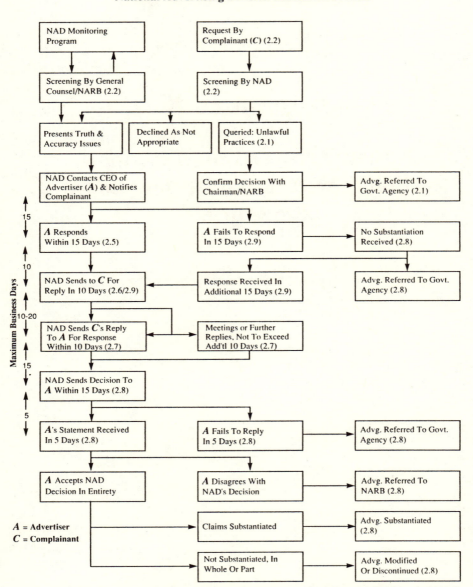

The numbers in parentheses refer to sections in NAD/NARB Procedures effective 4-1-90; amended 7-1-90; revised 11-1-91.

National Advertising Division
National Advertising Review Board
PROCEDURES
Voluntary Self-Regulation of National Advertising
Effective April 1, 1990
(As amended, July 1, 1990)

Since 1971, the Council of Better Business Bureaus' National Advertising Division (NAD) and the National Advertising Review Board (NARB) have served the public and the advertising industry. NAD investigates complaints about truth and accuracy in national commercial advertising. The NARB functions as a peer review group of NAD decisions should those cases be appealed. This voluntary self-regulatory process has handled more than 2800 cases. In the cases appealed to the NARB, it has experienced one hundred percent compliance by all parties.

A special NARB panel, after one year of study and input from hundreds of advertisers, advertising agencies, consumer advocates, Better Business Bureaus and government agencies, proposed new rules and procedures to resolve challenges to national advertising. The new rules were approved by the NARB and adopted by the National Advertising Review Council in December, 1989. They became effective April 1, 1990, and were amended July 1, 1990.

NAD/NARB is administered and solely funded by the Council of Better Business Bureaus, a not for profit organization supported by national advertisers, advertising agencies and the general business community.

November 1, 1991

ORGANIZATION

1.1   Purpose

The National Advertising Review Board (NARB) is a body of industry and public persons, as herein defined, sponsored by the National Advertising Review Council, Inc. (NARC) for the purpose of serving the public interest by sustaining high standards of truth and accuracy in national advertising. The NARC, a nonprofit corporation whose founding members are the American Advertising Federation, the American Association of Advertising Agencies, the Association of National Advertisers and the Council of Better Business Bureaus, shall be the governing body of the NARB for the election of the Chairman and members of the NARB, and adoption and implementation of rules for the organization and procedures of the NARB. **(See Section 1.3).**

1.2   Structure of the NARB

The National Advertising Review Board shall be composed of a Chairman, fifty members, and as many alternate members as the Chairman may specify, all elected by the NARC Board of Directors. Thirty members of the NARB shall be persons whose principal affiliation is with an advertiser; ten members shall be persons whose principal affiliation is with an advertising agency; and ten members shall be public members. If any member's principal affiliation changes, his eligibility to serve as a member will be reconsidered by NARC. The status and privileges of alternate members shall be the same as the status and privileges of regular members, except that alternate members are not qualified to vote upon any matter which comes before the full NARB. No member of the NARC Board of Directors, while so serving, shall be eligible to be a member or alternate member of the NARB.

1.3   Terms of Office

The term of office for NARB members shall be two years. A member is eligible for re-appointment for one additional term. An eligible member may be removed from office by a two-thirds majority of the total membership of the NARB and by no other means. A member elected to fill a vacancy on the National Advertising Review Board between annual meetings shall serve for the remainder of the vacated term and be eligible for reappointment to one additional two year term.

1.4   Compensation

Advertiser and advertising agency members and alternates of the NARB shall receive no compensation or reimbursement for expenses, except in exceptional circumstances authorized by the NARC Board of Directors. Nonindustry members shall receive per diem compensation in such amount as shall be determined by the NARC Board of Directors and shall be entitled to reimbursement for such out-of-pocket expenses as they shall incur in connection with the performance of their duties on the NARB.

1.5   The NARB Chairman

There shall be a Chairman of the NARB who shall be elected by the NARC Board of Directors for a term of one year and who shall be eligible for reelection. The Chairman shall receive such compensation for his services as shall be determined by the NARC Board of Directors.

1.6   Duties of the Chairman

The NARB Chairman shall be the overall coordinator of the activities of NARB and shall be its public spokesman. He shall appoint a panel composed of five NARB members to hear and decide each case which is brought before the NARB. In the event the Chairman is unable to appoint a qualified panel from among the regular membership of the NARB, he shall appoint the necessary

number of qualified alternate members to fill the panel. The Chairman shall also serve as liaison to the NARC Board of Directors and shall perform such other duties as may be directed by the NARB.

1.7   The NARB Executive Director

There shall be an Executive Director of the NARB who shall be appointed by the Chairman to serve as the Staff Executive.

1.8   Duties of the Executive Director

The Executive Director shall assist the Chairman in carrying out his duties. He shall also be responsible for managing the NARB office, preparing periodic reports of NARB activities, maintaining liaison with the NARC Board of Directors, the National Advertising Division (NAD) of the Council of Better Business Bureaus, Inc. (CBBB) and other organizations, and shall perform such other duties or projects as assigned by the Chairman.

1.9   The General Counsel

The CBBB shall provide an attorney who shall serve as General Counsel to the NARC, NAD and the NARB. The General Counsel shall provide legal advice to the NARC, NAD and/or the NARB at the request of any officer of NAD or the NARB, and to officers and Board members acting in their official capacities.

1.10   Meetings

There shall be at least one annual meeting of the NARB and such special meetings as the Chairman, in consultation with the NARC Board of Directors, deems necessary. NARB members shall be given at least fifteen days notice of annual and special meetings. At each annual meeting, the NARB shall conduct such organizational and other business as may come before it.

1.11   Standards

The NARB may promulgate, adopt, amend and publish, with the advice and counsel of the NARC Board of Directors, advertising standards to aid in its evaluation of the truth and accuracy of national advertising.

1.12   **Autonomy of the NARB**
In the review and disposition of all cases coming before it, the NARB shall be completely autonomous and independent of any and all other persons and organizations. It shall conduct its business and issue its reports and opinions with full regard for the public interest. The individual members of the NARB shall be answerable to no one for the decisions reached and actions taken by the NARB or any panel thereof.

1.13   **Definitions**
The term "national advertising" shall mean paid commercial advertising disseminated in all of the United States, or in a substantial section thereof, or test-market advertising prepared for national campaigns.

The term "advertiser" shall mean any person or other legal entity who uses "national advertising." **(See Section 2.2)**

The term "advertising agency" shall mean any organization engaged in the creation and placement of "national advertising."

The term "public or nonindustry member" shall mean any person who has a reputation for achievements in the public interest.

PROCEDURES

2.1   **A. Function of NAD**
The National Advertising Division of the Council of Better Business Bureaus (hereinafter NAD) shall be responsible for receiving or initiating, evaluating, investigating, analyzing, and holding initial negotiations with an advertiser on complaints or questions from any source involving the truth or accuracy of national advertising.

NAD shall publish the NAD Case Reports monthly, summarizing matters concluded during the previous month. These reports shall identify the advertiser, product, advertising agency, subject matter reviewed, NAD's decision and its rationale, or the fact the case is on appeal to the NARB. If the advertiser desires, a concise statement of his views shall be included. The complainant in each case shall be supplied with a copy of the report.

B. Referrals to Law Enforcement Agencies
When NAD's preliminary review indicates a probability that advertising promotes an unlawful product or service, or is false, deceptive or misleading and that the advertiser will not participate in the self-regulatory process, NAD shall prepare a review of the facts with relevant exhibits and, after consultation with the NARB Chairman, shall forward them to the appropriate federal or state law enforcement agency. Reports of such referrals may be included in the NAD Case Reports and/or other CBBB publications.

2.2   **Complaints**
A. Any person or legal entity, including NAD itself, may submit to NAD any complaint regarding national advertising, regardless of whether it is addressed to consumers, to professionals or to business entities.

B. Upon receipt of any complaint, NAD shall promptly acknowledge receipt of the complaint and, in addition, shall take the following actions:

(i) If NAD, in its judgement, concludes that the advertising complained of is: not national in character; the subject of litigation or an order by a court or government agency; permanently withdrawn from use prior to the date of the complaint; of such technical character that NAD could not conduct a meaningful analysis of the issues; or so trivial in nature as to merit no expenditure of NAD's resources, NAD shall advise the complainant that the complaint is not appropriate for formal investigation in this forum. When it can, NAD shall provide the complainant the name and address of any agency or group with jurisdiction over the complaint.
(ii) If the complaint relates to matters other than the truth or accuracy of the advertising, NAD shall so advise the complainant, as

provided above, and shall forward a copy of the complaint to the Chairman of the NARB who shall consider whether the complaint is appropriate for a consultive panel.

(iii) If the complaint relates to the truth or accuracy of a national advertisement, NAD shall promptly forward the complaint to the advertiser for its response.

(iv) Complaints regarding label directions or the basic performance of products and services, when not related to advertising claims; political and issue advertising; and questions of taste and morality are not within NAD's mandate. If the complaint, in part, relates to matters other than the truth and accuracy of the advertising, NAD shall so advise the complainant.

(v) NAD reserves the right to refuse to handle a case where the challenger publicizes, or otherwise announces, to third parties not directly related to the case the fact that specific advertising is being referred to NAD for resolution. The purpose of this right of refusal is to maintain a professional, unbiased atmosphere in which NAD can effect a timely and lasting resolution to a case in the spirit of furthering voluntary self-regulation of advertising and the voluntary cooperation of the parties involved.

C. Complaints originating with NAD shall be considered only after the General Counsel of the NARB has reviewed the proposed complaint and has determined that there is reason to believe that the complaint may be valid.

D. In all cases, NAD shall advise the advertiser of the identity of the complainant.

E. The Chairman and/or Executive Director of the NARB shall report to the NARB at its annual meeting on, among other things, the number, source and disposition of all appeals received by the NARB.

NAD shall report at least twice a year to a special panel of the NARB the number, source and disposition of all complaints received and cases published by the NAD, and such reports shall thereafter be published.

2.3   Parties to NAD/NARB Proceedings

The parties to the proceeding are NAD acting in the public interest, the advertiser acting in its own interest and the complainant, whose rights and obligations in an NAD/NARB proceeding are defined in sections 2.2, 2.4, 2.6, 2.7, 2.8, 2.9, 3.1, 3.2, 3.3, 3.5.

2.4   Information in NAD Proceedings

A. NAD shall not consider any data submitted by a complainant which has not been made available to the advertiser, and any materials submitted by a complainant on condition that they not be shown to the advertiser shall promptly be returned. In the case of studies, tests, polls and other forms of research, the data provided should be sufficiently complete to permit expert evaluation of such study, poll, test or other research. The complainant that provides incomplete records of its data not only weakens its argument, but may not thereafter change its mind and submit the missing components of the data once the investigation is in progress. NAD shall be the sole judge of whether the data are sufficiently complete to permit expert evaluation.

B. A challenged advertiser may submit data to NAD with the request that such data not be made available to the complainant. An advertiser seeking such treatment shall: (i) Identify in its submission which materials are confidential and which are not, and the basis of its request for confidentiality; and (ii) Affirm that the information for which confidentiality is claimed is not publicly available.

C. Where there is a request for confidentiality and the complainant has specialized knowledge of the subject matter as, for example, in a competitor challenge, the complainant is entitled to receive a comprehensive summary of the principal arguments submitted by the advertiser in its rebuttal of the challenge. Failure of the advertiser to provide this information will be considered significant grounds for appeal of a decision by a complainant. (See Section 3.1) In any event, NAD shall advise the complainant of the non-confidential parts of the advertiser's response.

D. Prior to the transfer of data to the advertiser or complainant, NAD shall obtain assurances that the recipients agree the materials are provided exclusively for the purpose of furthering NAD's inquiry; circulation should be restricted to persons directly involved in the inquiry, and recipients are required to honor a request at the completion of the inquiry that all copies be returned.

2.5   Response
The advertiser may, at any time prior to the fifteenth business day after it receives the complaint, submit a substantial written response in substantiation of the challenged advertisement.

2.6   Reply
If the advertiser submits a substantial written response, NAD shall promptly forward that response to the complainant, except for any material designated as confidential. Within 10 business days after it receives the advertiser's response, the complainant may submit a reply.

2.7   Additional Responses
A. If the complainant submits a reply, NAD shall promptly forward that reply to the advertiser. Within 10 business days after it receives the complainant's reply, the advertiser shall be entitled to submit a response. If the complainant does not submit a reply, NAD shall proceed to decide the challenge upon the expiration of the complainant's time to reply.

B. In the event that NAD requests further comments or data from an advertiser or complainant, the written response may be submitted within 10 business days of the request.

C. NAD, in its discretion, may accept a proposal by an advertiser or complainant for a meeting as substitute for, or in addition to, a written additional response. The proposal shall delineate the reasons for requesting a meeting, a date (to which the other parties have agreed), the identity of the company's representatives and the agenda.

D. The period of time available for all communications including meetings, governed by Rule 2.7 shall not exceed 20 business days.

2.8   Decision
A. Within 15 business days of its receipt of the last document authorized by Rules 2.5 to 2.7, above, NAD will formulate its decision on the truth and accuracy of the claims at issue, prepare the "final case decision," provide a copy to the advertiser and invite the advertiser to add an Advertiser's Statement within 5 business days of receipt. In the event that NAD decides some or all of the advertising claims at issue are not substantiated, the Advertiser's Statement shall state whether the advertiser agrees to modify or discontinue the advertising or chooses to take the issues to appeal, as specified in Section 3.1. NAD shall then immediately provide the advertiser and the complainant with copies of the "final case decision" and make copies available to the public.

B. NAD's decisions in the NAD Case Reports and any press release shall be published under the headings:

- Advertising Substantiated
- Advertising Referred to NARB
- Advertising Modified or Discontinued
- Advertising Referred to Government Agency
- No Substantiation Received

2.9   Failure to Respond
A. If an advertiser fails to file a substantial written response within the period provided in Rule 2.5, NAD shall release a "final case decision," summarizing the advertising claims challenged in the complaint, and noting the advertiser's default.

B. If the advertiser fails to file a substantial written response within an additional 15 business days, NAD may refer the file to the appropriate government agency and shall report that action in the next monthly NAD Case Reports.

C. If a complainant fails to file a reply within the time provided by Rule 2.6 or an advertiser fails to file a response within the time provided in Rule 2.7, the untimely document shall not be considered by NAD, or by any panel of the NARB.

3.1   Appeal

A. When an advertiser and NAD disagree on one or more issues involved in a case, either shall be entitled to panel review by the NARB. In such cases, NAD shall publish the referral among cases closed in the current period, specifying the issues to be decided by the panel. The advertiser shall be entitled to add an Advertiser's Statement.

B. Following publication of any decision under the headings "Advertising Substantiated," or "Advertising Modified or Discontinued," a complainant may request review by the NARB by filing a letter explaining its reasons within 10 business days of publication of the "final case decision" as described in Section 2.8. The letter should be addressed to the Chairman, NARB; Attention: Executive Director; 845 Third Avenue; New York, NY 10022. This letter, together with the relevant sections of the case record to be provided by NAD within 5 business days, will be reviewed by the Chairman, NARB, who within 10 business days after receipt of the record shall (1) determine if there is no substantial likelihood that a panel would reach a decision different from NAD's decision; or (2) proceed to appoint a review panel as outlined in Section 3.2. The Chairman, NARB, reserves the right to extend these time intervals for good cause, notifying all interested parties of such extension.

3.2   Appointment of Review Panel

The Chairman, upon receipt of an appeal, by an advertiser or NAD, or upon granting an appeal by a complainant, shall appoint a panel of qualified NARB members and designate the panel member who will serve as panel chairman.

3.3   Eligibility of Panelists

An "advertiser" NARB member will be considered as not qualified to sit on a particular panel if his/her employing company manufactures or sells a product or service which directly competes with a product or service sold by the advertiser involved in the proceeding. An "agency" NARB member will be considered as not qualified if his/her employing advertising agency represents a client which sells a product or service which directly competes with the product or service involved in the proceeding. A NARB member, including a nonindustry member, shall disqualify himself/herself if for any reason arising out of past or present employment or affiliation he/she believes that he/she cannot reach a completely unbiased decision. In addition, the Executive Director shall inform the advertiser and complainant of their right to object, for cause, to the inclusion of individual panel members, and to request that replacement members be appointed. Requests will be subject to approval by the Chairman, NARB. If the Chairman is unable to appoint a qualified panel, he shall complete the panel by appointing one or more alternate NARB member(s).

3.4   Composition of Review Panel

Each panel shall be composed of one "public" member, one "advertising agency" member, and three "advertiser" members. Alternates may be used where required. The panel will meet at the call of its chairman, who will preside over its meetings, hearings and deliberations. A majority of the panel will constitute a quorum, but the concurring vote of three members is required to decide any substantive question before the panel. Any panel member may write a separate concurring or dissenting opinion which will be published with the majority opinion.

3.5   Procedure of Review Panel

A. As soon as the panel has been selected, the Executive Director will inform all parties as to the identity of the panel members. At the same time, he will mail copies of the appeal to each of the panel members, and will, in like manner, send them any response or request submitted by any other party or parties. Within

10 days after receiving copies of the appeal, the panel members shall confer and fix the time schedule which they will follow in resolving the matter.

B. The panel, under the direction of its chairman, should proceed with informality and speed. If any person or organization involved in the dispute before NAD requests an opportunity to participate in the proceedings before the panel, he shall be accommodated. All parties to a matter before the panel shall be given 10 days notice of any meeting at which the matter is to be presented to the panel. Such notice shall set out the date and place of the meeting, and the procedure to be followed.

C. The case record in NAD/NARB proceedings shall be considered closed upon the publication of the "final case decision" as described in Section 2.8. No factual evidence, arguments or issues will be considered within the case record if they are introduced after that date.

D. The decision of the panel will be based upon the portion of the record before NAD which it has forwarded to the panel, the appeal, and any summaries of the record facts and arguments based thereon which are presented to the panel during its meeting with the parties. A party may present representatives to summarize facts and arguments which were presented to NAD, and these persons may be questioned by members of the panel. No facts or arguments will be considered by the panel if they are outside the facts or inconsistent with the arguments before NAD. If the advertiser has declined to share any of his substantiation with the complainant, the panel will honor his request for confidentiality, even though the complainant may have instituted the appeal. The complainant will therefore be excluded from the meeting during the time when such confidential substantiation is being discussed by the panel with NAD and the advertiser. In the event that newly discovered evidence germane to the issues to be decided by the panel becomes available, the panel may re-

mand the case back to NAD for its further consideration and decision.

3.6   Timing and Reporting of Panel Decisions
When the panel has reached a decision, it shall notify the NARB Chairman of its decision and the rationale behind it in writing and shall endeavor to do so within 15 business days. The Chairman, upon receipt of a panel's decision, shall transmit such decision and rationale to the advertiser who is party to the case, providing him with 5 business days to respond indicating his acceptance, rejection or any comments he may wish to make on the panel's decision.

Thereafter, the Chairman shall notify other parties to the case of the panel's decision, incorporating therein the response from the advertiser, and make such report public.

In the event that a panel has determined that an advertisement has not been substantiated or is misleading or deceptive, and the advertiser either fails to indicate that the specific advertisement(s) will be withdrawn or modified in accordance with the panel's findings within a time period appropriate to the circumstances of the case, the Chairman will issue a Notice of Intent to the advertiser that the full record on the case will be referred to the appropriate government agency. If the advertiser fails to respond or does not agree to comply with the decision of the panel within 10 days of the issuance of the Notice of Intent, the Chairman shall so inform the appropriate government agency by letter, shall offer the complete NARB file upon request to such government agency, and shall publicly release his letter.

3.7   Closing a Case
When a case has been concluded with the publication of a NAD decision or, when a panel has turned over a decision to the Chairman, and when the Chairman has executed the procedures in Section 3.6 of these "Procedures," the case will be closed and no further materially similar complaints on the claim(s) in question need be accepted by NAD or NARB.

3.8   Confidentiality of Panel Procedures

All panels, through the Executive Director, shall maintain a record of their proceedings, but a verbatim record is not required. All deliberations, meetings, proceedings and writings of a panel other than the written statement of its conclusions and the rationales behind them shall be confidential, with the sole exception of those which the Chairman of the NARB determines must be made available to an agency of the government. A NAD Case Reports and a NARB Panel Report, in those cases referred to a panel, are the only permanent records required to be kept as to the basis of an inquiry, the issues defined, the facts and data presented, and the conclusions reached by NAD and a NARB Panel, if one has been involved in the process.

GENERAL PROVISIONS

4.1   Amendment of Standards

Any proposals to amend any advertising standards which may be adopted by NARB may be acted on by a majority vote of the entire membership of the NARB at any special or regular meeting, or by written ballot distributed through the United States mails, provided that the text of the proposed amendment shall have been given to the members 30 days in advance of the voting date, and provided further that the Board of Directors of the National Advertising Review Council shall have been given notice of such proposed amendment at least 60 days in advance of the voting date, to afford said Board of Directors the opportunity to render advice and counsel to the NARB members on the proposal and to make such other proposals and recommendations as it deems necessary and appropriate.

4.2   Use of Consultive Panels for Matters Other Than Truth and Accuracy

From time to time, NARB will be asked to consider the content of advertising messages in controversy for reasons other than truth and accuracy, or the NARC or the NARB may conclude that a question as to social issues relative to advertising should be studied. In such cases the following procedures shall be employed to deal with such complaints:

4.3   Consultive Panels

The Chairman may consult periodically with the NARC Board of Directors or with the NARB to determine whether any complaints have been received, or any questions as to the social role and responsibility of advertising have been identified, which should be studied and possibly acted upon. If so, a consultive panel of five NARB members shall be appointed, in the same proportions as specified for adjudicatory panels in Section 3.4 above.

4.4   Panel Procedures

Consultive panels shall review all matters referred to them by the Chairman and may consult other sources to develop data to assist in the evaluation of the broad questions under consideration. No formal inquiry should be directed at individual advertisers.

4.5   Confidentiality

All panel investigations, consultations and inquiries shall be conducted in complete confidence.

4.6   Position Paper

If a consultive panel concludes that a position paper should be prepared to summarize its findings and conclusions for presentation to the full NARB, the paper shall be written by one or more members of the panel, or by someone else under its direction. The contents of the paper should reflect the thinking of the entire panel, if possible, but any panel member may write a separate concurring or dissenting opinion, which will be published with the panel report, if it is published.

4.7   Voting on Publication

Any such report prepared by a consultive panel will be submitted to the Chairman, who will distribute copies to the full NARB for its consideration and possible action. The members of the NARB will be given three weeks from the date of such distribution within which to vote whether to publish the report or not. Their votes will be returned to the Executive Director of the NARB. The report will be published only if a majority of the NARB members vote for its publication.

4.8   Publication

If a majority of the NARB votes for publication, the paper will be published promptly with appropriate publicity.

INTRODUCTION

In a presentation to FTC on October 24, 1989, Mary-Jane Raphael, Senior Vice President/NAD, explained the self-regulatory process. The following article excerpts large portions of this useful and highly informative presentation as a "refresher" course on the NAD/NARB self-regulatory process.

HOW THE PROCESS WORKS

"Acting as the investigatory arm, the NAD initiates inquiries, determines the issues, collects and evaluates the data, and makes the initial decision on whether or not claims are substantiated. Substantiated cases are reported in the next case report. But when the NAD finds that the claims in question are not adequately substantiated, we ask the advertiser to modify or withdraw the advertising. If discussion and negotiation with the advertiser fails to resolve the controversy, NAD appeals to the National Advertising Review Board--sometimes informally referred to as our 'Supreme Court'--which has a reservoir of 50 men and women representing advertisers, advertising agencies and the public. The NARB Chairman, Kenneth A. Cox, selects an impartial, representative panel of five members for each appeal and each panel publishes its decisions on an individual basis. Since our inception in 1971, NAD has published over 2400 cases. On only 46 occasions, representing only 2% of our caseload, has advertising been referred to the NARB. This proves to me--as I believe it should to you--that voluntary cooperation at the NAD level works--and works well."

WHERE CASES COME FROM

"NAD systematically monitors national consumer advertising on television, radio, cable and in print. Over the years, this has proved to be a major source of cases. However, most cases are initiated from external sources. NAD acts in the public interest when an individual consumer files a complaint about a national advertisement. Additionally, the 180 local Better Business Bureaus around the country refer consumer inquiries and their own questions on national advertising to NAD for action. An increasing proportion of cases have been based on competitor challenges, to the point that these now comprise the largest single external source of cases. In competitor challenges . . . NAD does not act as advocate for either competitor, but in the interest of the consumer."

COMPOSITION OF NAD STAFF

"In addition to myself, my staff at the NAD is composed of two vice presidents, an associate director and four advertising review specialists, plus a small support staff of secretaries and administrators. Dr. Ronald H. Smithies, Vice President and Director of NAD, joined us in 1980. A graduate of Fordham Law School, Dr. Smithies was admitted to the New York Bar in 1978. He has bachelor of science degrees in biochemistry and a doctorate in biochemistry and toxicology.

"Dr. Helen Boehm is the Vice President and Director of the Children's Advertising Review Unit (CARU). Dr. Boehm, an educational psychologist, joined us a year and a half ago, having previously directed a company specializing in the development, evaluation and marketing of products to children. A graduate of Boston University, she earned her masters and doctoral degrees at Columbia University."

CHILDREN'S ADVERTISING

"[NAD treats children's advertising] as a special category, requiring particular attention. Obviously, advertising that may be perfectly acceptable for adults could be misunderstood by children because of their still-developing perceptions. For that reason, [CARU] was established in 1974, and has a number of functions, both evaluative and advisory.

"CARU publishes *The Self-Regulatory Guidelines for Children's Advertising* to help advertisers and agencies deal sensitively and honestly with children. You have already heard about the networks' broadcast standards. Because of the special care and attention they give to their own children's broadcast standards, we tend to see very few cases involving network children's advertising. Independent stations and cable are another matter. However, we are very pleased that the Board of Directors of the independent stations' association (INTV) voted unanimously last year to endorse our CARU guidelines and encourage independent stations to use them.

"These guidelines are periodically reviewed by a distinguished group of child psychologists--The CARU Academic Advisory Panel--to ensure they reflect the latest findings from research into child behavior and attitudes. CARU also has a business advisory committee that helps us to stay on top of the latest trends in marketing to children.

"CARU monitors national broadcast, cable and print advertising directed to children under the age of 12, and like NAD, it responds to challenges from industry as well as consumer complaints. It conducts cases, effects changes through voluntary cooperation of advertisers and publishes these agreements in the NAD Case Report every month.

"For over a year now, CARU has been working with the industry--and its critics--in developing self-regulatory guidelines for 900/976 telemarketing commercials to children. Specifically, I am referring to the advertising of 900/976 telephone numbers whereby children are encouraged to call Santa Claus, The Easter Bunny or a favorite rock group. The networks, to date, do not accept this kind of advertising. However, independent and cable stations do. Again, we are very pleased that the INTV Board voted to endorse these guidelines-- even in draft form--and recommended them for consideration and use by independent stations. I am also very pleased to report that the Board of Directors of the Council of Better Business Bureaus formally approved these guidelines last month at our annual assembly. We plan to publish and distribute the guidelines in the very near future."

PRODUCT CATEGORIES--COMPARISON

[In her presentation, Raphael focused on three major product categories, comparing the activity in these categories between the late 1970s and late 1980s]:

1. Household Products

"In the mid-to late 70's, 11% of our published cases dealt with household products. However, in the late 80's this category has fallen to only 3% of our caseload. Why? Certainly not because competition has slackened. We believe there are fewer cases now because self-regulation--by virtue of the precedents NAD has published--demonstrated the way advertisers can sell these kinds of products, defining their competitive advantages while not compromising the principles of truth and accuracy."

2. Food and Beverages

"Throughout the late 70's, a principal theme was the development of taste preference claims, with Coca-Cola and Pepsi-Cola as the principal players. We're very proud to have been the forum where the Pepsi challenge was shaped, and to continue as experts in evaluation of taste preference claims. We have published approximately 120 cases to date on this theme; and not just for beverages, but for such food products as chicken, hot dogs, popcorn, breakfast cereals . . . to name but a few . . . and though the subjects may sound lightweight . . . the economic issues involved are of substantial importance.

"In recent years, three main themes have emerged to somewhat supplant taste preference claims--although we certainly still have our fair share of such claims. The newer themes are: 'Good Source' claims, 'Natural' Claims and Health claims, and serve to keep the category of foods and beverages in the forefront of our caseload today.

"Our investigation of 'Good Nutritional Source' claims has centered largely around the specific question of what amount of a vitamin or mineral is needed in a product for it to qualify as a 'good source.' The FDA provided a regulatory framework some years ago. But the inherent drawback is that their regulations applied to the nutrition panel on a food label. This is where the NAD has provided a valuable self-regulatory function. Through our series of cases with leading food companies like CPC International, Mrs. Paul's Kitchens, Prince Spaghetti, Campbell Soup, Stouffer Foods and Delmonte, we have helped to establish the principle that advertisers should not make claims for nutritional content in advertising that are inconsistent with the nutrition panel on the package label.

"We've developed the same self-regulatory approach to the area of fruits and vegetables--foods under the control of the USDA. Here's where we defined the importance of serving size disclosure. A good example is the advertising for avocados of a few years ago. The claims stated: 'Only 17 calories a slice' and that avocados were 'A Good Source of vitamins A, B1, C and E, Plus Potassium.' The problem was, the calorie claim was based on a slice equal to 1/16th of the fruit, while the vitamins and potassium claims were based on a portion of half the fruit! We've done a whole fruitbasket of cases, if you will, on grapes 'brimming with vitamins and minerals,' apples 'rich in niacin, calcium and iron' as well as cases on bananas, kiwi fruit, potatoes and grapefruit juice. In each case, NAD successfully negotiated a modification in the advertising to provide disclosure of serving size on which the 'good source' claims were based.

"A second theme of the 1980's in food and beverage advertising has been 'Natural' claims. 'Natural' is a difficult word to control because it's not a scientific term and, in fact, the meaning has changed over the years. In the early 80's NAD published more than 30 decisions involving 'Natural' claims and our effectiveness in this area, we believe, precluded the necessity for a regulatory agency to step in and formulate specific guidelines or regulations--something this Commission had considered doing a few years ago, I understand.

"The third theme on which we are seeing a heavy emphasis today--and where we feel we serve a pathfinder role--is the use of health claims in food advertising. This kind of nutrition advertising is not just a 'good source' claim as in 'high in calcium' but adds reference to a disease or health risk, as in 'high in calcium to help prevent osteoporosis.'. . ."

3. Retail Price Advertising

"The last category I'd like to briefly discuss with you is again one that positions us in the pathfinder role: The area of retail price advertising. I'm not going to draw a ten-year comparison as I did with the two previous categories. Instead, I have a specific example of the impact of one NAD case--which went all the way to the NARB--and the subsequent extensive publicity that followed the final decision.

"The case took place in 1988 and involved combined challenges of Montgomery Ward's advertising by a competitor and a Better Business Bureau, with particular emphasis on Ward's claim of 'Lowest Prices Guaranteed.' In NAD's opinion--which was supported by the NARB--this kind of superlative claim needs very specific substantiation. It should not be used merely to convey a price-matching policy, which was how Ward's was using it. Ward's agreed to modify its advertising--but at the same time formally requested that the use of 'lowest price' and similar claims by other advertisers be investigated.

"As a result of this recommendation--coupled with the urging by several other council members that the time was ripe, so-to-speak, for tackling this problem, the Council of Better Business Bureaus took the initiative in setting up an industry retail price advertising task force to examine current practices and make recommendations on updating the existing codes that apply to this category. . .

"This proposed new code that the task force has developed (now in draft form) has been deregulated to industry members, to your own Bureau of Consumer Protection, as well as state and local regulatory agencies for comments . . . Members of the task force include such heavyweights as Ward's, Sears, K-Mart, J.C. Penney, Federated Department Stores and Saks Fifth Avenue, to mention only a few.

"We are also working on the development of a monitoring program to be put into effect when the new code is approved, and we expect to make major inroads in policing (if you will) abuses in this advertising. As you well know, this kind of advertising has received a lot of attention at the state level. What the council is trying to do is achieve uniformity in this area. As I said earlier--this is another example of what we are doing--using the industry self-regulatory approach--so you won't have to."

LAWYER'S REFERENCE SERVICE

National Advertising Division Presentation to the Federal Trade Commission by Mary-Jane Raphael, Senior Vice President/NAD, October 24, 1989.

Appendix 8

The British Code of
Advertising Practice

Committee of Advertising Practice

INTRODUCTION

What is the Code?

1. The British Code of Advertising Practice – most often called simply 'the Code' or 'BCAP' – is the body of rules by which, the British advertising business has agreed, the overwhelming majority of the advertisements it produces should be regulated. The only substantial group of advertisements not covered by the Code are television and radio commercials, and these are subject to a very similar Code operated by the Independent Broadcasting Authority.*

2. The Code establishes a standard against which any advertisement may be assessed. It is a guide both to those concerned with commissioning, creating and publishing advertisements and to those who believe they may have reason to question what an advertisement says or shows.

3. The origin, aims and content of the Code are considered further in paragraphs 4 to 12 of this Introduction. The way in which effect is given to the Code, and the roles of the Committee of Advertising Practice (CAP) (formerly the Code of Advertising Practice Committee) and the Advertising Standards Authority Ltd (ASA), are described in paragraphs 13-35.

The origin and aims of the Code

4. The first edition of the Code was published in 1961. There had been a variety of voluntary advertising Codes before then; in particular, many publishing houses had – and still have – rules of their own about acceptability; but no earlier attempt had been made by the advertising business as a whole either to analyse the principles that underlay these various sets of rules or to bring them together into a coherent whole. The coming of independent television marked a watershed. When broadcast advertisements – commercials – began to be transmitted in 1955, they were required to conform to a single Code, administered by a new statutory authority. The need for a similarly unified system of control for non-broadcast advertising soon became clear.

5. The Advertising Association, which represents the interests of all sides of the British advertising business, responded by establishing the predecessor of the present Committee of Advertising Practice.

The new Committee was given the twin tasks of drawing up a Code and of devising a means of making sure that, so far as possible, what the Code required was done. The Committee's members were drawn from a wide range of advertising trade associations. The commercial interests of advertisers, advertising agencies and media can never be identical; but everybody in advertising shares an interest in seeing that advertisements are welcomed and trusted by the people to whom they are addressed. Unless advertisements are accepted and believed, they cannot do the job for which they are designed; and if they give offence, or appear untrue, they discredit those associated with them and the advertising business itself.

6.   But it is more than simple self-interest that underlies the Code. The great majority of people who work in advertising are committed to doing what each of them can to achieve the high standards inseparable from their status as professionals. They acknowledge obligations which go beyond those they have to clients or customers, employees or shareholders – obligations that they owe primarily to the public at large but also to their colleagues and competitors. As advertisers, they accept a duty to put their case honestly and fairly, and in a way that avoids gratuitous offence; as advertising agencies and publishers they recognise a responsibility not to create and not to disseminate advertisements which are misleading, dishonest, unfair or offensive.

7.   The model which CAP took for the first edition of BCAP was the International Code of Advertising Practice (ICAP), published for the first time in 1937 by the International Chamber of Commerce. Over twenty-five years, the International Code had won a wide measure of acceptance around the world, both from governments and from the advertising business. In its various versions, ICAP, now in its fifth edition, has underlain each of the eight successive editions of the Code.

The contents and scope of the Code

8.   It was clear from the outset that a British Advertising Code would have to go beyond a simple endorsement of ICAP's general principles. Advertisements should certainly be 'legal, decent, honest and truthful', as ICAP insists; what is also needed is guidance about how these principles can most effectively be put into practice, given the particular circumstances of advertising in Britain. BCAP seeks to provide this guidance through a combination of general rules, which apply to advertisements of all kinds, and specialised rules, which apply where particular groups of people are being addressed or particular kinds of product are being advertised.

9.   The central concern of the Code is with the *content* of
        advertisements. Except in a handful of cases, such as where the
        consumer's health or safety may be adversely affected, BCAP does not
        concern itself with matters other than the honesty, fairness and
        decency of the advertisement itself – it is not, for example, concerned
        with whether an advertisement is a 'good' advertisement in the sense
        of being effective, or beautiful. It does not presume to judge whether
        what is advertised is worth buying – or worth the price asked; nor, in
        general, does it attempt to regulate the terms on which people in
        advertising do business – with the public or with each other. The
        Code makes due allowance for public sensitivities but it does not
        seek the role of censor in matters of taste; nor does it offer itself as a
        basis for arbitration between conflicting ideologies. Lastly, the Code's
        rules are designed to provide guidelines for the content of
        advertisements; the same guidelines are not necessarily apt for the
        regulation of words and images in other contexts – in those parts of
        the media which are exclusively editorial, for example, or when
        commercial or persuasive material is incorporated in packaging,
        press releases or private communications. For these and other
        reasons, the self-regulatory system which is described in later
        paragraphs is not, in general, responsible for ensuring that such
        claims conform to the Code.

The publisher's prerogative

10.   The fact that an advertisement conforms to the Code is not a
        guarantee that it will be accepted for publication by every publisher
        to whom it is offered. Media owners refuse space to advertisements
        which break the Code, but they accept no obligation to publish every
        advertisement that is offered to them and which conforms to the
        Code.

Other codes

11.   Several member associations of CAP, such as the Proprietary
        Association of Great Britain (PAGB) and the Association of Mail Order
        Publishers (AMOP), maintain advertising codes of their own for their
        members (copies of these codes are available on request from the
        associations concerned). The provisions of BCAP, numerous as they
        are, cannot deal with every matter in the kind of detail which is often
        desirable in a particular area of business. Codes such as those of
        PAGB and AMOP do not cut across the provisions of BCAP; like many
        of the codes which have been promoted by the Office of Fair Trading
        under the Fair Trading Act 1973, they expressly make conformity with
        BCAP one of their own rules. The Mail Order Protection Schemes
        (MOPS), operated by the principal media associations, and the

Mailing Preference Scheme, supported by those involved in direct mail advertising, provide further examples of self-regulation in areas closely allied to advertising. The main aim of MOPS schemes is to provide reimbursement for consumers who have lost money as a result of the collapse of a mail order advertiser, while the Mailing Preference Scheme permits those who do not wish to receive direct mail advertising to have their names removed from many mailing lists.

The British Code of Sales Promotion Practice

12.   This, perhaps the most important of the codes which complement BCAP, was initiated in 1973 by CAP, a standing sub-committee of which is responsible for its administration. The Sales Promotion Code lays down rules on the content and conduct of such activities as premium offers and competitions. Importantly, it provides that all advertisements for such schemes should conform to BCAP. A fourth edition of the Sales Promotion Code was published in 1984.

THE ADMINISTRATION OF THE CODE

The self-regulatory system

13.   Restraints which are self-imposed are, for that very reason, more likely to be readily accepted than restraints imposed from outside; but, when the Code was launched, it was recognised that there would inevitably be occasions on which even such self-imposed rules were neglected. So ways were devised both of encouraging high levels of compliance and of co-ordinating the activities of those who would be concerned with seeing that the Code was observed. These arrangements, which have been refined and extended since 1961, are known collectively as the self-regulatory system. The system is not simply one of self-discipline and it does not depend upon the individual conscience as its only sanction. Self-regulation goes beyond the regulation of the individual by himself and connotes the regulation of a whole profession by its practitioners, acting together.

Self-regulation and the law

14.   Since the Code was first published, there has been an upsurge of legislation designed to protect the consumer, much of it with direct application to advertising. Self-regulation has developed so as to complement these legal controls. It provides an alternative – and sometimes the only – means of resolving disputes about advertisements. It encourages acceptance by advertisers of standards of practice which in a number of areas go beyond what is, or can sensibly be, required by law. On the other hand, it is not intended to

be used as a means of preventing the advertising of products which are legally sold but which some people find distasteful or believe to be harmful. What the flexibility and informality that are characteristic of self-regulation offer is the opportunity to avoid some practical and constitutional difficulties that limit the utility of controls imposed by law. The Code's rules can be easily and quickly adapted to changing circumstances – more easily and quickly than is usually possible with laws; and the way in which they are interpreted deliberately gives weight to the intentions of those who wrote the Code and not only – as would be the case in the courts – to the words in which those intentions happen to be expressed. Also, the self-regulatory nature of the system makes possible an investigatory process which encourages the advertiser to accept active responsibility for demonstrating that his advertisement conforms to the Code. It is for him to produce adequate justification both for what he says and for how he says it. If he cannot, or chooses not to, then his advertisement may be declared contrary to the Code.

15.   The self-regulatory system has been the subject of official scrutiny on two occasions: by the Office of Fair Trading in 1978 and by a Department of Trade working party in 1980. The investigations of both bodies concluded that, in general, the system worked well; both also suggested legislation to provide self-regulation with a more satisfactory framework within which to operate. This has been introduced following agreement, late in 1984, on the European Community's Directive on Misleading Advertising. The new powers given to the Director General of Fair Trading under the Control of Misleading Advertisements Regulations, passed by Parliament in 1988 to implement the Directive, will have the effect of providing self-regulation with a statutory back-up of a kind that has long been sought and will help it to work with even greater effectiveness.

16.   Neither the Code nor the self-regulatory system seeks to usurp the role of law or to hamper the enforcement of legal controls. The Code (B.2.1 and 2) emphasises that advertisements should satisfy all legal requirements and should avoid anything which might have the effect of bringing the law into disrepute. What self-regulation cannot offer is a means of law enforcement; and investigations are not pursued under the Code if they appear to ASA or CAP principally to concern matters which would be more appropriately resolved in a court of law. Complainants, however, are given every assistance in directing such matters to the quarter in which they are most likely to find qualified assistance.

Appendix 9

Looking Back—and Forward, Case Report 191

The Advertising Standards Authority (U.K.)

The Authority's 1989/90 Annual Report published this month is of particular interest because in the Chairman's Report Lord McGregor, at the conclusion of his term of office before handing over to Sir Timothy Raison on 1 January 1991, has taken the opportunity to review not merely 1989/90 but also the Authority's achievements during the past ten years. Lord McGregor writes:

"After a decade's experience as Chairman, I see the ASA not only as a buttress of the free press but also as promoting the administration of justice. The development of a variety of means which enable citizens to complain about the performance of concentrations of power has been a striking feature of the social history of the last forty years. There is now an elaborate network of complaints procedures, public and private, that has grown up unsystematically within a not very elaborate framework of statute law as a series of *ad hoc* responses to pressures from consumers in search of cures for grievances. Many of the bodies created to deal with complaints enforce their rules by hortatory procedures. Their aim is to set standards rather than to secure convictions, to persuade not to coerce. The ASA is part of this spectrum of quasi-judicial institutions which I regard in practice as being often of much greater significance in the daily lives of most people than are the civil courts. The special merits of the ASA are ease of access at no cost to complainants; a Code that is freely available to everyone; and effective sanctions against those in breach of it. The procedures of the Authority, like those of other bodies, are enlarging the content of democratic citizenship by conferring new rights to remedies for complaints which cannot easily or cheaply be pursued through the courts. During my term of office the public has used the system more and more extensively and has thus confirmed belief in the effectiveness of its remedies. The chorus which declaimed in the early 1980s that the

ASA was a toothless beast without legal sanctions has diminished to occasional voices, because people now know that if the Authority upholds a complaint the adjudication will be acted upon more swiftly and more effectively than by legal process."

Looking forward, the Report continues:

Direct Mail Standards

"This year Council has given much time to considering an extension of the Authority's remit to include direct mail and list and database management. Council has agreed to accept responsibility contingent upon an assurance that an approved Code of Practice will be drawn up and observed by CAP members and the industry, and administered by CAP under the supervision of the ASA."

European Commission

"In the course of the year there have been proposals from Brussels on tobacco, alcohol and pharmaceuticals which carry far-reaching implications for advertising in the United Kingdom. Vigilance is urgently required to protect both our own higher standards as well as the flexibility and effectiveness of our regime of self-regulation. All the industries and interests affected must play a part in ensuring that the Commission is well informed and accurately briefed about the United Kingdom's control system. For example, newspapers and periodicals have a vital interest because their revenues may be reduced significantly by actions in Brussels about which there have been no consultations."

In conclusion, the Report notes the modernisation of the Authority's Information Technology System and the restructuring of the joint ASA/CAP Secretariat to enable the Authority to deal effectively with its increased responsibilities in the '90s under its new Chairman, Sir Timothy Raison, MP and Director General, Mrs Matti Alderson.

The Authority's Annual Report published this month is prefaced as usual by the Chairman's personal review of the year. Lord McGregor this year pays particular tribute to George Bogle on his retirement as Chairman of the Advertising Standards Board of Finance. In a farewell address, Lord McGregor recalls George Bogle's achievements as the outstanding figure in the recent history of the ASA and self-regulation:

"First, you took the lead in persuading the whole industry to accept, finance and provide effective sanctions for an extended system of self-regulation through the enforcement of a code of rules for the content of print and some other forms of advertising. The reach of this system goes well beyond self-discipline because the rules apply to the whole advertising industry and are supported by a powerful sanction provided by newspapers and periodicals.

Second, you made the ASA as independent of the industry as constitutional ingenuity could ensure. At the beginning of my chairmanship, some people still said that the financial dependence of the Authority on the industry meant that it would adopt a deferential posture towards its paymaster. Nobody says this any longer. I have worked on several so-called independent bodies set up by governments and none of these escaped the pressures, rarely subtle, which were regularly applied by Ministers to secure decisions and recommendations that suited them. I can state that I have never at the ASA been subjected to illicit pressure from any advertiser, agency or part of the industry. Of course, the trouble with independent bodies is that they are likely to behave independently and advertisers and others have often made vigorous objections to decisions taken by the Authority; but pressure in this form is desirable and right. Without the independence upon which, George, you insisted and have promoted during your chairmanship of ASBOF, nobody in the industry or outside it would ever have taken the Authority seriously.

Third, I see the ASA which you shaped as one important bulwark of the free press which could not exist without advertising. If a statutory body with legally enforceable powers over advertising had been established in 1974, it could have provided a precedent for external control of the press itself. Indeed, one test of the success of your creation lies in the comparative effectiveness of the ASA and the Press Council.

Fourth, I think that we may see the ASA as promoting the administration of justice. An elaborate network of complaints procedures, public and private, has grown up unsystematically during the last thirty years or so as a series of 'ad hoc' responses to pressures from citizen consumers in search of both protection and cures for grievances. The ASA of your conception is part of this spectrum of quasi-judicial institutions. It is of value in enlarging the content of democratic citizenship by conferring what are in fact new rights to remedies which cannot easily or cheaply or effectively be pursued through the courts. In the course of enforcing rules and standards of conduct framed and imposed upon itself by the advertising industry, I believe that the ASA plays a part in demonstrating that the rule of law can be applied in everday commercial life and underlining the truth that observance of a voluntary code by an industry is morally superior to obedience to externally imposed statutory rules.

I feel that some sentences of the judgment in the first case arising last November from the enactment of the European Commission's directive on misleading advertising, may be read as a tribute to the success and likely permanence of what I think of as the Bogle system. In the course of laying down guidelines for the future exercise of discretion in such cases. Mr. Justice Hoffman said: "the British advertising industry has a system of self-regulation ... under the auspices of its voluntary regulatory body, the ASA". " ... the proper working of the self-regulated system is essential to the overall scheme of control ... " ... "It is in my judgment desirable and in accordance with the public interest to which I must have regard that the courts should support the principles of self-regulation". The guidelines emphasise one significant characteristic of the self-regulatory system of your parentage; namely, that it runs parallel with the work of statutory bodies and statutory provisions; it is not the ASA's function to attempt to usurp their powers."

The Chairman continues with a review of other events during the year.

The main body of the Annual Report summarises the work of the Authority's Monitoring and Complaints Departments and details the education programme of the External Relations Department.

The work of the Committee of Advertising Practice is also covered in the ASA Annual Report with the CAP Chairman's report. The Committee's detailed work is seen in action with reports from the Chairmen of the specialist sub-committees on Health and Nutrition, Finance, Mail Order and Direct Response and Sales Promotion.

Copies of the Annual Report can be obtained by writing to the Press Office, ASA Ltd., Brook House, 2–16 Torrington Place, London WC1E 7HN.

Appendix 11

L'Autodiscipline en Europe

Bureau de Vérification de la Publicité

L'AUTODISCIPLINE EN EUROPE

Nous présentons ci-dessous un panorama de l'autodiscipline dans la Communauté Européenne. De fortes disparités se dégagent que ce soit au niveau des structures ou au niveau de la pratique quotidienne. Certains pays n'apparaissent pas car ils ne possèdent pas d'organisme d'autodiscipline : ce sont le Danemark, la Grèce, le Luxembourg et le Portugal.

	BELGIQUE	ESPAGNE	GRANDE-BRETAGNE	IRLANDE
Organisme	Conseil de la Publicité/Jury d'Ethique Publicitaire Rue des Colonies 54, Boîte 13 1000 Bruxelles Tél. : 02/219 08 62	Autocontrol S.A. Avda Burgos, 16. Torre 111 28046 Madrid Tél. : 91/2 02 47 82	Advertising Standards Authority A.S.A. Limited Brook House - Torrigton Place London WC1E7HN Tél. : 01 - 828-2771	Advertising Standards Authority for Ireland IPC House 35-39 Stelbourne Road Dublin - 4 Tél. : 01/80 87 66
Création	1974	1977	1962	1967
Structure et représentation	7 syndicats représentant agences, annonceurs et médias. Environ 75 à 80 % de la publicité belge. 3 permanents.	Membres issus des agences, médias et annonceurs Comités ad hoc Pas de structure formelle. 3 permanents.	Financement assuré par prélèvement sur recettes publicitaires (hors audiovisuel). Le conseil de l'ASA est formé pour 2/3 de non-professionnels. 54 permanents.	Groupement d'associations et de groupes privés de médias. 3 permanents.
Relations avec les Pouvoirs Publics	Pure autodiscipline	Réglementation très lourde — Générale — Sur produits spécifiques (alimentation, cosmétiques, armes...)	Les T.V. et radios commerciales sont contrôlées par le IBA (Indépendant Broadcasting Authority). Relations suivies avec certains organismes gouvernementaux.	
Relations avec les consommateurs	Pure autodiscipline	Faible activité consumériste	Contacts suivis avec les organismes de consommation ou les organisations à vocation sociale.	
Existence de codes spécifiques (hors C.C.I.)	Oui — Médicaments — Cosmétiques — Crédit à la consommation — Amaigrissement, etc.		Oui	Adaptation du code britannique.
Fournit des conseils avant diffusion	Oui	Oui	Oui	Oui

	(suite)
Effectue des contrôles après diffusion	Oui
Traite les plaintes des consommateurs	Oui
Peut faire retirer une publicité	Oui

	ITALIE	PAYS-BAS	R.F.A.	FRANCE
Organisme	Istituto Dell'Autodisciplina Pubblicitaria Via Larga 15 20122 Milan Tel.: 02/872-869	Stichting Reclame Code Westermarkt 2. 1016 DK Amsterdam Tel.: 020/25.76.90 - 25.77.21	Zentral Ausschuß Der Werbewirtschaft (ZAW) Villichgasse 17. Postfach 20 14 14 5300 Bonn 2 (Bad Godesberg) Tel.: 82092-0	Bureau de Vérification de la Publicité 5, rue Jean Mermoz 75008 Paris Tel.: 43.59.89.45
Création	1977	1970	1949	1935/1953
Structure et représentation	L'Italie présente la particularité de faire financer par les professions une action où ils n'interviennent pas (juge, traitement des plaintes). Ce sont cependant les professionnels qui établissent les règles. 3 permanents.	Est composée des associations de publicitaires, d'éditeurs et de consommateurs. 4 permanents.	Association quadripartite : annonceurs, agences, supports et consultants ou techniciens. Fédération d'associations. Pas de monopole sur l'autodiscipline. Certaines branches ont leurs propres codes (tabac, médicaments). 3/2 permanents.	Regroupe annonceurs, agences et supports plus affiliation syndicats professionnels. 12 permanents.
Relations avec les Pouvoirs Publics		Ne participent pas à l'organisation. Cependant le gouvernement l'a reconnue d'utilité publique	Législation très forte. Peu de place pour l'autodiscipline. Actions de lobbying	Indépendance. Mais relations suivies.
Relations avec les consommateurs		Les organisations de consommateurs sont présentes dans l'organisme et participent à son financement.	Pure autodiscipline mais « volonté de dialogue » avec les consommateurs.	Les consommateurs sont représentés au Conseil d'Administration (INC).
Existence de codes spécifiques (hors C.C.I.)	Adaptation code CCI plus code concernant produits spécifiques (alcools, cosmétiques....)	Adaptation code CCI		Recueil de recommandations générales ou par secteur d'activité
Fournit des conseils avant diffusion	Oui	Non	Non	Oui
Effectue des contrôles après diffusion	Oui	Oui, mais rarement	Oui, mais rarement	Oui
Traite les plaintes des consommateurs	Oui	Oui	Oui	Oui
Peut faire retirer une publicité	Oui	Oui	Non	Oui

221

Appendix 12

Self-Regulation and Codes of Practice

European Advertising Standards Alliance

1. In recent years, the value of self-regulation by business has been increasingly recognised, not only in those countries with long traditions of this form of control, but also by transnational government agencies. The use of codes of practice to define and maintain common standards within a particular sector of business has also grown.

2. Self-regulation, sometimes also called self-discipline, is complementary to the framework of general company and consumer protection legislation within which it operates.
    It may be specifically supported by legislation. In the European Community (EC), for example, the Directive on Misleading Advertising (adopted 1984) provides a legislative framework, but expressly allows for self-regulatory controls to operate. This is entirely in line with the EC policies of proportionality (legislation should be in balance with the desired result, and not excessive), and subsidiarity (higher authorities should avoid imposing regulations which can be best drawn up and carried out by subordinate authorities).

3. The judiciary in a number of countries (eg France, Germany), recognise self-regulatory codes of practice, and often refer to these codes in their rulings. As an example, on several occasions the Dutch Code Committee has had to defend itself in a civil case where the advertiser argued that the Committee had acted illegally by:

    a.   deciding that a certain campaign was against the advertising code and,
    b.   publishing its "verdict"

    In all these cases the decision of the Code Committee was upheld by the judiciary, and in some cases the court expressed its appreciation of the work of the Committee as guardian of advertising ethics.

4. Many self-regulatory bodies advise advertisers and their agencies on existing legislation as well as their own codes.

5. Self-regulation has advantages in comparison with legislation. Self-regulatory codes require observance in the spirit as well as in the letter, the variety of sanctions is not limited. This

application is not bureaucratic and the procedures are easy to access and free of charge to the consumer; they can be readily reviewed and updated to take account of changing conditions and attitudes; and they command a high degree of commitment from business itself and its customers.

6.   Because of this commitment, codes can be phrased more broadly and less specifically than legislation. Indeed, they lose much of their effectiveness and their raison d'être if they become embodied in legislation. It should, however, be kept in mind that industry cannot be expected to enter into agreements against its own interests or better judgement.

7.   The existence of advertising self-regulatory bodies provide advertisers and their agencies with a point of reference in preparing advertising campaigns. In most countries they can seek advice on the interpretation of the codes (and often of relevant legislation) from the self-regulatory bodies before investing in the production of an advertisement. The Advertising Standards Authority in UK, for example, receives a great number of written submissions for pre-publication copy advice yearly, and many thousands of telephone enquiries. In Belgium, 25 to 30% of the activities of the Jury d'Ethique Publicitaire are devoted to giving advice before publication.

8.   It is, however, the very success of effective codes of practice which has led to some confusion between the different circumstances in which they may be used. These include true self-regulation, negotiated codes of practice, & agreements or statutory codes of practice. All three vary in fundamental respects and although distinctions may sometimes blur, it may be helpful to define them as follows.

A.   SELF-REGULATION

9.   A universal system might be : -

   i)   a universally applicable code of practice, drawn up on a cooperative and voluntary basis by the industry it is designed to control, and expressed in clear, unambiguous terms, which expand upon than legal requirements;

   ii)   free or very cheap access to the complaints-handling mechanism for consumers and other interested parties and to enforcement authorities and advice services, and encouragement for them to use it.

   iii)   an efficient and consistent monitoring, complaints handling and arbitration procedure to investigate and adjudicate apparent breaches of the code, which is provided by the industry concerned, sometimes with independent oversight;

iv)   effective sanctions should the code be infringed. including publication of the results of the monitoring and complaints investigation;

v)   wide publicity for the code to the business concerned, and to the public, and clear written information provided to all potential users.

10.   Not all self-regulatory codes include all these conditions, but, as examples, the self-regulation systems of the Irish, Italian, British, Dutch and French advertising business most closely meet these criteria. They apply to all creators, users and publishers of advertisements, whether in membership of a trade association or not, and the sanctions include refusing advertising from offenders (except where forbidden by anti-trust legislation), and adverse publicity for breaches of the code.

11.   National advertising self-regulation codes have a common base in the International Chamber of Commerce's Code of Advertising Practice, first published in 1937 and regularly updated since. They are, however, extended to deal with the particular circumstances, concerns and trading practices of individual countries, and to complement national law.

12.   Some self-regulatory codes in the marketing field may be more limited in their application, because they apply only to those companies in membership of the sponsoring trade association.

13.   Nevertheless, they usually enjoy wide support of the majority of traders in the sector and, when member companies' commitment to the code is publicised, there is an incentive for consumers to deal with such companies, knowing that defined standards will be met or, if not, they will have a quick and cheap means of taking action.

B.   FORMS OF SELF-REGULATION

14.   Self-regulation covers the bróad concept of control, usually by an independent, or semi-independent body comprising of the tripartite elements of advertising (advertisers, advertising agencies and the media, eg. Germany, Belgium), and in some cases (e.g. France, Ireland, Italy, the Netherlands, the UK) with non-advertising interests represented in the code body organizations.

15.   The bulk of the complaints filed with the Dutch Code Committee relates to simple cases of (often unintentional) deception, for example:

-     an article is wrongly depicted;
-     the price according to the advertisement is lower than it is in reality;
-     the promised article is not available or only in a negligible quantity.

In most cases the advertiser conceded that a mistake had been made and promised to pay more attention to the code in the future. To take an example, eggs produced by chickens that were fed exclusively with 4 types of high quality grain were said to be less detrimental to the cholesterol level than regular eggs. When the advertiser was unable to substantiate this claim both the TV commercial and the advertising campaign in print were stopped.

C.   SECTORAL CODES OF PRACTICE

16.   In addition to broad codes covering wide aspects of advertising, there are many sectoral codes developed by trade associations for product sectors, or for media. The International Chamber of Commerce, for example, has annexes on advertising to children and pharmaceutical advertising; as well as specific codes on direct marketing and sales promotions.

17.   Codes made by trade associations are either applied by the association, or by the general self-regulatory body. For example, for some 15 years the Dutch Direct Marketing organizations have (on a voluntary basis) provided a mail preference service (MPS). At present 63,712 persons are registered. Complaints about ineffectiveness of the system can be made to the Code Committee. In view of the fact that over the past years very few complaints about this matter have reached the Committee, we can conclude that the service works. In 1990 the MPS was extended with a mailbox sticker, for those who wished to keep out unaddressed mailbox advertising. The British Advertising Standards Authority now oversees a direct marketing, list and database management Code.

18.   In cases where the sectoral trade association applies its own code the rules are usually mandatory on all members and non-observance is sanctioned ultimately by the withdrawal of membership. A strict form of this system can be found among many professional associations which register their members as practitioners (eg. doctors, dentists, etc). A number of professions do not allow their members to advertise their services. Non-observance is dealt with by the offender being struck off the professional list.

D.   NEGOTIATED CODES OF PRACTICE

19.   Systems in which the ground rules are laid down by, or may only be changed at the instance of, an outside supervisory body are not self-regulatory. These are defined as Negotiated Codes.

20.   Negotiated codes of practice are drawn up between an industry and an official body and are not the sole initiative of the business sector concerned. They set out common standards for members of a particular trade or trade association, often in areas where legislation would be inappropriate

or too cumbersome, or where the authorities wish to introduce restrictions over a relatively long period.

21. Examples of such negotiated codes of practice are to be found in many European countries. They range from EC- generated codes to the sectoral codes negotiated by national government authorities with trade associations on such diverse subjects as environmental protection, shoe repairs and funerals.

22. Day-to-day implementation and the policing of the code is the responsibility of the trade association, but monitoring takes place from time to time by the official negotiating body. Such codes are clear, unambiguous and practicable to implement. The official body can be useful in publicising new provisions in the codes and ensuring their wide dissemination, and may subsidise or pay for appropriate educational literature.

23. Both the former types of codes of practice are limited to a specific product or business area, and have widespread support before publication. Both have adjudication procedures as an integral part of the code.

E.   **AGREEMENTS OR STATUTORY CODES OF CONDUCT**

24. Finally, there is a tendency by governments to impose "Codes" on sectors, or to cover specific media activities. The basis for control of advertising in the broadcast media, for example, is often primarily in the form of statutory codes based on legislation. These can be operated by government authorities, as France (the CSA), and the UK (the ITC).

25. In the case of media-specific statutory codes, it is normal to find that the provisions are based also on the current self-regulatory codes of practice. For example, in the UK the ITC Code augmented by the Independent Television Association (ITVA) guidelines, is similar to the Committee of Advertising Practice (CAP) code, but adds specific rules for television. Radio advertising is similarly regulated by the Radio Authority's code. Both codes are administered in the first instance by the ITVA; in the case of radio the ITVA acts on behalf of the Association of Independent Radio Contractors (AIRC). In France, the Conseil Supérieur de l'Audiovisuel (CSA) has asked the Bureau de Vérification de la Publicité to apply its code to French broadcasters.

26. It is clear that self-regulation has been accepted by the Dutch government from the fact that in 1988 the work of the Reclameraad, a government institution which handled complaints about radio and TV commercials, was handed over to the Code Committee. If the Committee finds a commercial is not in compliance with the Advertising Code it is taken off the air. In 1988 this happened 5 times; in 1989, 15 times, and in 1990, 17 times.

27. The statutory codes for broadcasting, therefore, can be seen as an extension of the self-regulatory codes applicable to all other media, but with specific rules as a response to concern that the broadcast media is special in its immediacy and penetration of households.

28. Other statutory codes exist for specific sectors. Because practitioners of advertising rarely have a hand in drafting these statutory codes or agreements, their rules can raise substantial problems of definition, ambiguity and difficulty of interpretation which generate dissatisfaction for business and consumers alike. Examples are the codes for financial sector advertising overseen by the British Securities and Investment Board.

29. The scope of an agreement may go beyond what is reasonable (or even desirable) for industry to control. Publication of such an agreement or statutory code may precede any consideration of the monitoring and adjudication procedures. For example, the scope of the World Health Organisation "Code" for the marketing of breast milk substitutes is ambiguously drafted. It covers the behaviour not only of manufacturers and of retailers, but of health professionals too, over whom business cannot and should not be expected to exercise control. The monitoring and adjudication procedures are not clearly defined, although the widely differing interpretations which can be placed on the text have caused disappointment and divisions, and made compliance, monitoring and adjudication extremely difficult.

30. Such agreements or statutory codes can be used by governments as a form of quasi-legislation, to tackle issues which would be difficult or costly to translate into legislation. Agreements or statutory codes of this kind should be clearly defined and expressed, in consultation with all interests, and the responsibilities of different sectors of the community separated and defined. Very clear monitoring and adjudication procedures should be an integral part of such agreements, so that business and consumers alike know where to take complaints and who will arbitrate on potential breaches, using what criteria.

31. The Dutch agreements between the Government Health departments and the tobacco manufacturers is a good example and contains all these elements including a code for advertising content administered through the College van Beroep. Such agreements should be called "agreements" or "statutory codes", to avoid confusion with sectoral codes of practice or with self-regulation.

F.   **SELF-REGULATION PROCEDURES**

32. Self-regulation allows the advertising business to respond effectively to social changes, and to act fast in an environment which is constantly changing. Advertising campaigns may last only a few days or weeks. They therefore require speedy monitoring procedures, and experienced

judgement to deal not only with factual inaccuracy but also matters of subjective interpretation, such as questions of taste and decency which are difficult to tackle in the law.

33.   As an example, in Holland in 1989 there was a sudden increase in the number of environmental claims in advertising. Different products, ranging from paint, automobiles and plastic shopping bags to entire sewage systems all claimed to be environmentally friendly. In a number of these cases the Dutch Code Committee found the "green" claims to be unacceptable. This led speedily to a combined effort by advertisers, consumers and environmental groups and within half a year a special code for Environmental claims was drawn up. The publicity caused by the introduction of this code made advertisers aware of the risks of exaggerating the environmental benefits of their products. The result has been that environmental claims have become more modest. "Less harmful to the environment" has replaced "good for the environment"; claims that plastic packaging may be recycled have been dropped in those cases where recycling facilities are not available; and claims which led the consumer to believe that the use of a product was beneficial to nature have decreased.

34.   The availability of self-regulatory bodies also provides the consumer with an address to write to express frustration or general dissatisfaction with an advertisement which cannot be quantified. This "safety valve" is useful for the consumer, and for the advertiser and his agency. Dissatisfaction may mean that the advertisement is pitched wrongly.

35.   In our view an effective enforcement system could cover several criteria :

i)   wide publicity of the code of practice to business and consumers, so that they understand the standards and condition imposed by the code, and can report apparent breaches;

ii)   a central secretariat to receive complaints from the public and from competitors, and also to look for breaches of the code instead of relying solely on complaints;

iii)   a clear explanation of the form in which a breach is to be reported, and the specific details needed to identify the cause of complaint accurately;

iv)   an efficient and speedy arbitration system to investigate apparent breaches, make a decision, and take relevant action, including the use of sanctions if necessary;

v)   a regular systematic and statistically sound system of search for breaches of the code, to supplement consumer and competitor complaints;

vi)   Publication of the findings

36. Effective complaint resolution is impossible where the code or agreement is capable of widely differing interpretations. It is made unnecessarily difficult when there is no central national secretariat to which the public has cheap and easy access, and which can either itself respond rapidly to complaints or can redirect them rapidly to the appropriate body. (In the UK, for example, complaints about broadcast advertising, whether domestic or from abroad, which are addressed to the Advertising Standards Authority are immediately forwarded to the broadcasting authorities which have competence for television and radio commercials).

37. Codes of practice are ineffective when there is no national arbitration body (perhaps with a proportion of disinterested members) to adjudicate fairly and consistently on whether or not a breach has taken place.

38. Unless such a system is agreed, there will be no common ground on which to build a stable and effective base for higher standards. A variety of interests will place their own interpretation upon the requirements of the code or agreement, and reach their own conclusions about breaches, and either be disappointed when action is not taken upon their findings or risk abusing the sanction of adverse publicity. The result is not higher standards, but unproductive conflict.

39. Where a code of practice is universally understood and there is a national body to deal with complaints, the public becomes an integral and useful part of the monitoring operation. Their complaints may not always be upheld, but they are given reasons for the decision and make a useful contribution to the continuous effort to maintain the most effective standards.

40. Monitoring processes can be conducted along the following lines:

   i)   a wide statistical sample drawn from press and magazines weighted according to readership and frequency of publication;

   ii) sampling of special categories of products - slimming, hair restorers, alcohol, etc: or of particular topical issues, such as environmental claims, home protection and personal safety.

G. CONCLUSIONS

41. With the advent of the European Communities' Single Market, the benefit to consumers of the established and experienced national self-regulatory organizations will be enhanced. Consumers can continue to use their national contact point knowing that their comments will be dealt with or redirected promptly.

42. Self-regulation has much to offer both consumers and governments. These include : -

- The promulgation of standards to deal with areas of conduct difficult to define and enforce by legal regulation;

- The ability to act immediately to stop contravening advertisements without legal/bureaucratic proceedings.   Legislative/regulatory codes are mainly enforced by court/regulatory proceedings which can be cumbersome, time consuming and almost always costly. A self-regulatory procedure is more beneficial to the public than a prosecution under a legislative/regulatory code against an advertiser, which, in many cases, could be long after the advertisement has been published or broadcast, and may impose inadequate penalties;

- The application of a common standard by all media proprietors to a particular advertisement. Under legislative/regulatory codes different interpretations may result in media proprietors applying the codes differently to a particular advertisement;

- The ability to maintain and improve standards of advertising. Under legislative/regulatory codes experience shows standards tend to drop to the minimum permissible under the law;

- The ability to change codes or their interpretation swiftly to cover new developments or changing circumstances faster than legislation or regulation;

- The ability to apply special safeguards, such as pre-publication approval, for certain products or in certain media (where this is allowed by law);

- The availability in many countries of a body of experienced staff who can advise advertisers on advertising copy if doubts arise before the advertisement is produced;

- The availability of organizations to which consumers, who are reluctant to use statutory enforcement mechanisms, are much readier to complain;

- The cost savings to government and the consumer in policing a complex system adequately;

- The commitment of business to its responsibilities toward the consumer, and to making the self-regulatory system effective.

Index

Each of the thirty-eight country profiles is organized along similar lines: organizing for self-regulation, functioning of self-regulation, the consumer movement, government involvement, and trend. Therefore, this index does not list these subtopics under each country entry. Page numbers in **bold** indicate country entry.

About the Author

JEAN J. BODDEWYN is Professor of Marketing and International Business as well as Coordinator of the International Business Program at Baruch College of the City University of New York. He is the editor of *International Studies of Management and Organization* and also serves on the editorial review board of many leading journals. Among his books are *Comparison Advertising: A Worldwide Study* and *Advertising Self-Regulation and Outside Participation: A Multinational Comparison* (Quorum, 1988).